SpringerBriefs in Education

We are delighted to announce SpringerBriefs in Education, an innovative product type that combines elements of both journals and books. Briefs present concise summaries of cutting-edge research and practical applications in education. Featuring compact volumes of 50 to 125 pages, the SpringerBriefs in Education allow authors to present their ideas and readers to absorb them with a minimal time investment. Briefs are published as part of Springer's eBook Collection. In addition, Briefs are available for individual print and electronic purchase.

SpringerBriefs in Education cover a broad range of educational fields such as: Science Education, Higher Education, Educational Psychology, Assessment & Evaluation, Language Education, Mathematics Education, Educational Technology, Medical Education and Educational Policy.

SpringerBriefs typically offer an outlet for:

- An introduction to a (sub)field in education summarizing and giving an overview of theories, issues, core concepts and/or key literature in a particular field
- A timely report of state-of-the art analytical techniques and instruments in the field of educational research
- A presentation of core educational concepts
- An overview of a testing and evaluation method
- A snapshot of a hot or emerging topic or policy change
- An in-depth case study
- A literature review
- A report/review study of a survey
- An elaborated thesis

Both solicited and unsolicited manuscripts are considered for publication in the SpringerBriefs in Education series. Potential authors are warmly invited to complete and submit the Briefs Author Proposal form. All projects will be submitted to editorial review by editorial advisors.

SpringerBriefs are characterized by expedited production schedules with the aim for publication 8 to 12 weeks after acceptance and fast, global electronic dissemination through our online platform SpringerLink. The standard concise author contracts guarantee that:

- an individual ISBN is assigned to each manuscript
- each manuscript is copyrighted in the name of the author
- the author retains the right to post the pre-publication version on his/her website or that of his/her institution

Soila Lemmetty

Learning-Based Innovation

Lessons Learned from Finnish Police and Technology Organizations

Springer

Soila Lemmetty
School of Educational Sciences
and Psychology
University of Eastern Finland
Joensuu, Finland

ISSN 2211-1921 ISSN 2211-193X (electronic)
SpringerBriefs in Education
ISBN 978-3-032-26910-2 ISBN 978-3-032-26911-9 (eBook)
https://doi.org/10.1007/978-3-032-26911-9

This work was supported by University of Eastern Finland and Research Council of Finland [349117].

This Springer imprint is published by the registered company Springer Nature Switzerland AG
The registered company address is: Gewerbestrasse 11, 6330 Cham, Switzerland

For Eemil, who shows me the future, and for mummu (in memoriam), who taught me about the past.

Acknowledgements and Declarations

This book brings together the lessons learned from Research Council of Finland [349117]–funded postdoctoral research project (2022–2025), in which I explored innovation through the lens of learning theories. The project was an unforgettable journey for me as a researcher—not only because it generated new understanding and culminated in this book, but also because it brought into my life a professional community I had only dreamed of.

I am grateful to the Research Council of Finland for funding the project, and to the Faculty of Philosophy at the University of Eastern Finland, especially the School of Educational Sciences and Psychology as well as the colleagues in education and adult education, for their exceptional support, encouragement, flexibility, and help throughout the project years.

My warmest thanks go to the police officers and other experts of policing who contributed to the study, for your time and for helping me learn about a work context still unfamiliar to me. I am equally grateful to the production, administration, and product development staff, as well as the managers of the participating technology organization for the long-standing collaboration and for patiently explaining your work and products despite my limited technological background. Thank you to my research collaborators for welcoming me into your groups, writing with me, and teaching me so much about both the craft and the content of research: Vlad, Alex, Biggi, Stephen, Ingunn, and Stephanie, to name just a few.

One of the most meaningful outcomes of these years was the formation of the Continuous Learning in Working Life (JATKOT) research group. Sara, Marianne, Oana, Katja, Jasmiina, Teemu, Maria, Maija, Tuomo, Mia, Emilia, Antti, Sari, Meiju and Anne. Your expertise is invaluable, and it is a privilege to continue working with you also in the forthcoming years. I especially want to thank Oana for serving as a pre-reader of this book and for offering such insightful comments.

Research demands moments of detachment. Huge thanks to Eme for ensuring that I do not overwork myself by giving me a life to care for and share. Thank you also to you who make my life rich beyond work and parenthood.

Declaration of Interest The author declare that she has no known competing financial interests or personal relationships that could have appeared to influence the work reported in this paper.

Declaration of generative AI and AI-assisted technologies in the writing process During the preparation of this work the author used Copilot and ChatGPT to English language proofreading. After using these tools, the author reviewed and edited the content and text as needed and takes full responsibility for the content of the published work.

Contents

About the Author

Dr. Soila Lemmetty is an associate professor of adult education at the School of Educational Sciences and Psychology at the University of Eastern Finland, where she leads the Continuous Learning in Working Life (JATKOT) research group. Her research focuses on adult learning in working life contexts, as well as on innovation and wellbeing at work. She also holds a research fellow position at the University of Stuttgart, Institute of Entrepreneurship and Innovation Science, and the title of docent at the University of Jyväskylä. Further information about her work and previous publications can be found here: https://uefconnect.uef.fi/en/soila.lemmetty/

Chapter 1
Building Innovation Through Learning: An Introductory Perspective

Abstract This chapter presents the core concepts of learning-based innovation (LBI), focusing on workplace learning, innovation, and the book's overarching theoretical framework, which draws on employee-driven innovation. The chapter identifies the research gaps that motivated the book and establishes the conceptual foundations for the studies presented. In addition, it outlines the prework, objectives, and methodological choices of the EDLI project, which forms the basis of this volume, and introduces the organizations that took part in the research.

Keywords Learning-based innovation · Employee-driven innovation · Workplace learning · Innovation · Ethnography · Police organization · Technology organization

Continuous adult learning and innovation are central to developing modern work practices and renewing society. In the 2020s, these processes are being reshaped by rapid technological advances, including artificial intelligence, digitalization, and automation, as well as by societal disruptions, ranging from wars, pandemics, and environmental challenges to polarization and democratic erosion. Such turbulence calls for flexible innovation activities and multifaceted perspectives on work-life development, highlighting the value of the learning, competence, and participation of all those engaged in working life. How, in practice, are learning and innovation intertwined and supported in daily workplace activities? What kinds of competence form the building blocks of value-creating innovation processes? Who has visible (or hidden) access to participation in innovation? What kinds of challenges are associated with innovation in different types of organizations?

S. Lemmetty, *Learning-Based Innovation*,
SpringerBriefs in Education, https://doi.org/10.1007/978-3-032-26911-9_1

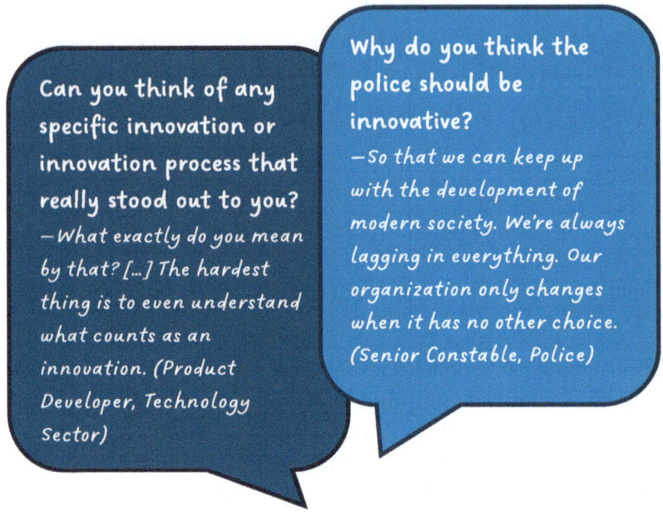

The quotations above come from individuals working in expert roles in working life. In the first quotation, a product developer in the technology sector struggles with the concept of innovation, highlighting the difficulty of understanding what "innovation" even means. *Why is the very concept of innovation challenging for a top expert whose job is to develop innovations?* How can anyone be expected to understand what innovation means in their own work if even someone working at the forefront of technological development finds it difficult to grasp? In the second quotation, an experienced senior constable engaged in preventive, proactive, and developmental police work reflects on why the police should be innovative. Why does he think that the police are always one step behind or only change when forced to? *Is it true that police is as un-innovative as the quotation might at first suggest?*

1.1 Background and Premises for Researching Innovation and Learning

This book explores learning-based innovation (LBI) as a central phenomenon of working life, one that affects everyone at work. The concept of LBI may sound tautological if understood as a specific type of innovation, as innovation is, by definition, always 'learning-based': Its very foundation lies in novelty, which presupposes learning. Thus, the following question arises: *What would a non-LBI even be?* In this book, LBI does not refer to a particular *form* of innovation; rather, it is viewed as a perspective and approach through which innovation and innovative activity are examined. Here, this concept refers, first, to the idea that innovation is viewed through learning-based theoretical frameworks, particularly theories and concepts developed in the workplace learning literature, and second, to the focus on the proximal phenomena of learning and their relationship to innovation, including learning practices, forms of competence, and pedagogy.

LBI is not presented as an entirely new lens for innovation research. It is acknowledged in this book that leading scholars in the fields of learning and innovation (e.g., Billett et al., 2023a; Derrick, 2020; Ellström, 2010; Høyrup, 2010; Lundvall, 1992; Smith, 2017) have already engaged in critical and constructive debates on how innovation should be understood from a learning perspective. Lundvall's (1992) long-standing description of innovation as "a phenomenon that involves a continuous process of learning—searching and exploring—which leads to new products, technologies, organizational forms, and market innovations" recognizes learning as a central component of innovation. Building on these researchers' pioneering work, this book approaches *workplace learning* as a key mechanism underpinning innovation.

Especially within the tradition of employee-driven innovation (EDI), on which this book also builds, researchers' interest in examining innovation from a workplace learning perspective emerged in the 2010s (e.g., Høyrup, 2010; Ellström, 2010), and has expanded steadily, particularly in the 2020s (e.g., Lemmetty & Billett, 2023; Lidman et al., 2023; Derrick, 2020; Smith, 2017). The reason for this focus lies in the profound transformation of working life, the growing importance of expertise, and the recognition of employees' participation and potential as drivers of innovation. In a stable world, learning could be ensured primarily through training, and innovation through structured top-down development programs. However, in today's rapidly changing and unpredictable world shaped by technological, demographic, and ecological shifts (Beier et al., 2025), innovation demands arise on a daily basis, requiring continuous, forward-looking learning in which people must acquire knowledge that does not yet even exist. This also makes daily support for learning and innovation in organizations essential.

Innovation is a development process and outcome that creates novelty and value for different actors or for an organization, whether in the form of a structure, model, product, concept, or process (Høyrup, 2010). Learning forms the foundation of innovation, as the competence (skills, knowledge, and attitudes) built through learning enables the development of new solutions and the renewal of work practices (Lemmetty & Billett, 2023). The cycle between learning and competence development thus forms the basis for innovation. The following section outlines the key concepts of *innovation* and *workplace learning* that ground this volume, including their historical development and main approaches. The chapter then considers the research gaps identified in the field, which this book aims to address.

1.1.1 Innovation

In innovation research, the concept of innovation has traditionally been defined as either an outcome or a process with *novelty* and *value* (Høyrup, 2010). Early scholarship, most notably Schumpeter (1934), emphasized innovation as something that is realized in practice, often as a concrete outcome, such as a new product or technology. Thus, early innovation research assessed the value and novelty of innovations by focusing mostly on outcomes. However, this outcomes-oriented perspective provides only a limited snapshot of innovation and has thus been seen as insufficient (Smith, 2017; Haapasaari et al., 2018). From the 1980s onward, research shifted toward understanding innovation as a linear or nonlinear interactive process (Kline & Rosenberg, 1986). The innovation process—the steps or sets of steps through which innovations evolve—became a central focus of interest in innovation research, leading to the development of numerous innovation process models (cf. Meissner & Kotsemir, 2016; Scott & Bruce, 1994; Sossa et al., 2019). Some studies have focused primarily on the individual and group-level idea-forming phases (e.g., Ness & Søreide, 2014), while others have outlined system-level processes (e.g., Allen & Stephen, 2013; Ramstad, 2009). From a process perspective, innovation has often been compared and linked to creativity. However, to distinguish between innovation and creativity, creativity has been related to the ideation phase, while innovation has been connected to the promotion and implementation of ideas (Amabile, 1996). However, the innovation process as a whole is seen to include all these phases: the generation, promotion, and implementation of a (creative) idea (Scott & Bruce, 1994).

Contemporary perspectives on innovation typically integrate both views, recognizing *innovation as a process that simultaneously produces tangible outcomes* (Anderson et al., 2014; Damanpour & Aravind, 2012). Based on the modern understanding, innovation is a continuous process of *change*, in which novelty and value take on different forms and meanings over time and across cultural–historical contexts (Kerosuo et al., 2010; Lemmetty & Billett, 2023; Martins & Terblanche, 2003; Rehn & Vachhani, 2006), and the adoption of valuable new ideas or practices within this process, shaped by social and economic contexts (Crossan & Apaydin, 2010). Taking contextuality and temporality into account has changed the definition of innovation's novelty and value and raised the question: What is perceived as new and valuable within that specific context in comparison to the present or the past? Organizational scholars are often in agreement that defining the value and novelty of innovation should consider the organization's cultural and historical context (Brandi & Hasse, 2012; Lemmetty & Billett, 2023; Martins & Terblanche, 2003). Innovation therefore does not refer only to an outcome or process that, as such, revolutionizes the entire world, but in organizational context, it is something valuable and novel for the organization in which it is created. Thus, novelty does not necessarily imply something entirely unprecedented; it may involve a new combination of existing elements or an update of prior practices (Høyrup, 2010). Consequently, innovation's value is not set in stone; rather, it is constructed and interpreted through the lens of culture and depends on how people see and use it.

1.1.2 Workplace Learning

Workplace learning, which refers to the practices through which individuals and groups *learn at work, for work, and through work*, encompasses processes that shape and transform both thinking and action, building new knowledge, competence, skills, understanding, and attitudes (Billett, 2014; Billett, 2026; Ellström, 2010). Since the 1990s, workplace learning has traditionally been studied from perspectives such as formal or informal learning (e.g., Lave & Wenger, 1991; Marsick & Watkins, 1990), learning as acquisition or as participation (Sfard, 1998), and individual, social, team, and organizational learning (Sessa & London, 2006). The traditional distinction between formal learning (training conducted for work purposes) and informal learning (learning occurring during work) has gradually shifted toward understanding learning as a continuous process that spans these different contexts (Manuti et al., 2015; Svensson et al., 2004). In this volume, workplace learning is seen not only as episodic but also as occurring naturally and continually through tasks and practices (Billett, 2014; Prugsamatz, 2010; Sessa & London, 2006). In daily work, it arises as individuals encounter challenges, interpreting situations, and constructing knowledge through reflection on experiences. Such reflection is most effective when individuals possess sufficient conceptual and explicit tools and frameworks, which are typically acquired through formal education, to analyze, structure, and evaluate their daily experiences (Svensson et al., 2004). Continuity and constructivist learning of adults thus occur between education, in which conceptual and theoretical knowledge is developed, and work, in which this knowledge is applied to understand experiences gained from participation in social and cultural practices during which individuals both shape and are shaped by communal activity (Billett, 2004; Gherardi, 2009; Rogoff, 1995).

From a practice-based perspective, workplaces are seen as historically and culturally constructed and continuously evolving systems in which learning is embedded in ongoing participation and the development of practices (Billett, 2002, 2014; Gherardi, 2009). Learning thus involves not merely socialization into existing norms and routines (Billett, 2014; Bourdieu, 1977), but also the active reconstruction and transformation of those guided by individual agency and the opportunities provided by the environment (Billett, 2001, 2004; Lemmetty, 2020). Here, workplace learning is particularly examined through a sociocultural lens, as this perspective accounts not only for individual cognitive development but also for the significance of work environments and communities. Sociocultural theory posits that learning occurs through human interaction in all contexts and activities (John-Steiner & Mahn, 1996; Vygotsky, 1978; Wenger, 1998), emphasizing the reciprocal shaping of individual thinking and action by cultural, social, and institutional environments. Because learners operate within organizational contexts, attention should be given to the goals, processes, and support mechanisms enabling employees to develop their expertise and work practices while meeting organizational and societal needs. Workplace learning thus serves a dual purpose: Individuals advance their skills to achieve personal goals, such as employability and career development, while simultaneously fulfilling expectations and goals set by employers, work communities and other stakeholders.

1.1.3 Research Gaps and Goals of the Book

This book brings together the examination of innovation and workplace learning. The choice to focus on these two aspects is based on observations from the field of innovation research that an approach emphasizing individual and group roles in innovation, as well as the importance of their learning, has not yet become part of the mainstream in this field, even though learning is widely acknowledged as a central element of innovation (e.g., Lundvall, 1992). Significant gaps remain in this research area, four of which are particularly evident in the background of this work.

1.1.3.1 The Multiple Contexts and Roles of Employees in Innovation

First, innovation research has traditionally emphasized large-scale, top-down processes within business- and technology-oriented domains, often assuming that innovation is specific to certain industries or organizational forms with product development functions and relatively flat hierarchies (Holmquist & Johansson, 2019; Høyrup, 2010). This has led to the widespread view that innovation occurs primarily in private-sector organizations with high autonomy and flexibility, while being less relevant in contexts bound by regulations and formal constraints. Yet empirical evidence shows that innovation is not restricted to these settings: It can emerge in any form of work (Amabile, 1996), including public-sector organizations in which innovation processes may take different forms (Hasu et al., 2014; Renkema et al., 2021; Wihlman et al., 2014). Many innovations develop incrementally within everyday work, driven by employees across organizational levels (Brem & Puente-Díaz, 2020; Høyrup, 2010). These bottom-up processes underscore the role of individuals and groups as active participants whose learning, expertise, and creative potential shape innovation. Together, these perspectives suggest that innovation should be understood as a multifaceted phenomenon rooted in employees' daily activities and learning rather than confined to specific sectors or specialized units. This highlights the importance of supporting individuals' and groups' participation in innovation processes and calls for more empirical research across diverse contexts to build a comprehensive and inclusive understanding of innovation.

1.1.3.2 A Learning-Based Theoretical Perspective on Innovation and Empirical Research on Learning Practices

Second, although the significance of learning for innovation has been acknowledged in principle (Darsø & Høyrup, 2012), empirical research explicitly addressing the relationship between learning and innovation remains scarce (Battistelli et al., 2019). This is particularly the case from the perspectives of learning theories (Darsø & Høyrup, 2012) and learning practices embedded in work (Derrick, 2020; Lemmetty & Billett, 2023). As a result, the practices and micro-level processes through which innovations emerge in workplaces are still insufficiently understood (Darsø & Høyrup, 2012). At the same time, workplace learning research has partly neglected the fact that beyond subjective experiences, learning produces objective outcomes. Learning not only enriches individual competence but also results in tangible and documentable outputs, such as new ideas, models, and practices—that is, innovations (Ellström, 2010). Research (e.g., Ramstad, 2009; Wang et al., 2020) has shown that the diversity of competences within a work community is a key resource for innovation, but how exactly does this diversity become transformed into actual innovations? Empirically examining workplace learning and competence as well as the practices associated with them offers deeper and more comprehensive insight into how innovation process develops across different organizational levels.

1.1.3.3 Different Types of Innovation and Diverse Perspectives on Value

Third, innovation research has traditionally emphasized the economic value of innovations, which are often framed as breakthroughs or products assessed primarily through business-related measures (Høyrup, 2010). However, from a contemporary perspective, such a narrow focus is increasingly viewed as insufficient, as it overlooks the many other benefits that innovations may bring, including social, environmental, and cultural value (Edwards-Schachter, 2018), as well as the value of different learning experiences, wellbeing, or employment for individuals (Høyrup, 2010. From this perspective, it has become essential to examine not only what kinds of value and novelty innovations create but also for whom (Høyrup, 2010). A dominant view is that innovations are radical changes capable of transforming entire industries, although research has shown that innovations may emerge as incremental improvements or small-scale initiatives that initially benefit individuals or work groups but, over time, acquire broader importance (Voxted, 2018). Despite these advances, innovation studies have paid less attention to everyday innovations and the multiple forms of value that they may embody (e.g., through the learning experiences of individuals and groups). Addressing these gaps requires mapping different types of innovation across organizational contexts and examining their impacts for various actors, enabling a more nuanced understanding of the diverse values that innovations can produce.

1.1.3.4 The Absence of Innovation Challenges and the Role of Pedagogy for Innovation

Fourth, organizations often struggle to engage employees in innovation activities, even when staff possess ideas and their potential to contribute is recognized in research (Bäckström & Lindberg, 2018; Holmquist & Johansson, 2019; Moosa & Panurach, 2008). Without opportunities to participate, these ideas cannot be developed or materialized, indicating a need for greater understanding of how participation in innovation can be strengthened and supported in everyday work practices. Studies have shown that innovation may fail to materialize if the organization's decision-making structure is too hierarchical, if innovation is left solely to employees without managerial support (Studemund & Wallington, 2016), or if the organization lacks cross-organizational learning opportunities (Al-Saleem & Aldakheel, 2024). Instead, we know that innovation tends to thrive in workplaces where people are trusted, empowered, and genuinely involved in decision-making (Renkema & Bos-Nehles, 2024). In today's increasingly efficiency-driven working life, where learning demands are rising, work is becoming fragmented, cognitive load is increasing, responsibility for both work and learning has shifted more onto individuals, and technological environments challenge collaboration and interaction (e.g., Korunka & Kubicek, 2017; Lemmetty, 2020, 2024a), it is even more crucial to adopt pedagogical approaches that actively support learning and participation for innovation. In addition, guiding all employees in ways that promote sustainable and positive outcomes—such as improved wellbeing, strengthened competence, and enhanced collaboration—and that help prevent risks associated with learning and cognitive load, including burnout and reduced willingness to engage in development, is an important pedagogical direction for workplaces. In short, supporting innovation in practice requires both attention to participation and careful consideration of how learning is understood, enabled, resourced, and experienced in organizations.

1.1.3.5 Purpose of the Book

This book presents a deep and multifaceted understanding of innovation as an everyday, learning-based phenomenon, aiming to address the research gaps outlined above. The purpose of the book is to provide a comprehensive account of LBI from the following perspectives:

- the roles and agency of different actors and how these are constructed within the context of innovation activities;
- the significance and forms of workplace learning and competence within innovation processes;
- the innovation projects emerging from everyday work, including their outcomes and value creation;
- the pedagogical support required to foster purposeful innovation activities and to enhance employee participation in innovation within organizations.

In this work, the examination begin, in the second chapter, by considering participation as an activity shaped by an individual's agency and the opportunities afforded by the environment, an activity that is also reflected in the formation of innovation roles. Within agency, the expertise of individuals and communities, as well as its further development through learning, becomes central. Consequently, the third chapter examines in more detail the kinds of competence required in innovation activities and the ways in which learning within the innovation process is conveyed, both in the creation of innovation and in the development of competence as it becomes embodied in artefacts, tools, and practices. The fourth chapter approaches innovations as projects that can be structured according to their nature, type, and the value they generate. Viewing innovations through the lens of projects made visible the evolutionary character of innovation highlighted the significance of learning in different types of innovation projects and in their evolution and brought forward initial observations about the challenges that may accompany innovation activities. These challenges are addressed particularly in the fifth chapter, where the key problems identified in innovation activities are presented alongside an innovation pedagogy perspective that offers ways to address them, as well as the central pedagogical methods to support innovation work. Together, the chapters construct a comprehensive picture of LBI, which is presented in the sixth chapter.

A holistic picture of LBI is built in this book through the theoretical openings and empirical insights provided by the Employee-Driven Learning and Innovation (EDLI) project, the starting points of which are described next. EDLI project provides empirical investigations of LBI in two different contexts: a police organization and a technology company.

1.2 Employee-Driven Learning and Innovation: The EDLI Project

This book is grounded in the EDLI—Employee-Driven Learning and Innovation as Multi-Perspectival Phenomenon: Longitudinal Ethnographic Research from Police and Technology Work Contexts—research project, funded by the Research Council of Finland from 2022 to 2025. The project's purpose was to increase multi-perspectival and sociocultural understanding of employee-driven learning and innovation. The project's qualitative and empirical focus was on Finnish working life and directed toward two distinct organizational contexts: a Finnish police organization and a medium-sized Finnish high-tech company also operating in international business environments. By examining both public- and private-sector settings and encompassing both operational and expert work, the project offered a unique lens into learning and innovation across diverse work environments.

The following section provides a brief overview of employee-driven learning and innovation based on previous research, serving as a starting point for the book's aim of building an empirically and theoretically grounded understanding of LBI. It then introduces the contexts examined in the project, and thus in this volume. Finally, the project's methodology, data, and analyses are described.

1.2.1 Toward a Definition of Learning-Based Innovation

The EDLI project was grounded in the framework of employee-driven innovation (EDI) (for a comprehensive account of the theory and its developmental stages, see Lemmetty et al., Forthcoming). EDI refers to creative activities in the workplace in which employees play a central role (Høyrup, 2012; Kesting & Ulhøi, 2010; Renkema et al., 2021). It involves ordinary employees' active and systematic participation in the ideation, innovation, and renewal of products, practices, and services and the ways of producing them, with a view to creating new solutions that add value to organizations and stakeholders (cf. Høyrup, 2012). In research, the term *ordinary employee* has been used to denote any member of an organization's staff—workers, managers, or professionals (Smith, 2017). Typically, it refers to individuals whose main responsibilities do not necessarily involve generating new ideas or developing and producing innovations (Kesting & Ulhøi, 2010). EDI has been described as encompassing both idea generation and implementation, meaning that it is not only about isolated moments of individual inspiration but also about advancing, further developing, and realizing ideas (Flocco et al., 2022; Smith, 2017). Within the broader field of innovation studies, research on EDI has so far remained relatively marginal, although in recent years, it has gained increasing recognition (e.g., Bäckström & Lindberg, 2018; Bäckström & Mosleh, 2021; Billett et al., 2023a, 2023b; Høyrup et al., 2018; Mosleh et al., 2024).

In this book—and in the EDLI project on which it is based—the notion of employee-drivenness is extended and deepened by emphasizing employees' competence, everyday learning and participation as central foundations of innovation. Before the empirical phase of the study began, the project carried out a conceptual review of research on EDI and workplace learning (for more details, see Lemmetty & Billett, 2023). The purpose was to examine how EDI relates to learning and to clarify the nature of the processes by drawing on earlier theories and perspectives, as well as to elaborate on EDI and learning as intertwined and ongoing processes in and through work.

The conceptual review (Lemmetty & Billett, 2023, p. 170; see also Fig. 1.1) concluded that the employees' learning process associated with EDI involves both *adaptive learning* and *innovative learning* (see Ellström, 2001, 2010). Adaptive learning occurs when individuals and groups develop an understanding of something that has already been invented and is known. Concretely, this may mean that new employees learn to understand existing—previously developed—practices or products by participating in workplace activities and engaging in social interaction with more experienced colleagues. This adaptive learning then serves as a resource and building block for further innovative learning, which takes place when individuals or groups learn—individually or socially—something genuinely new that

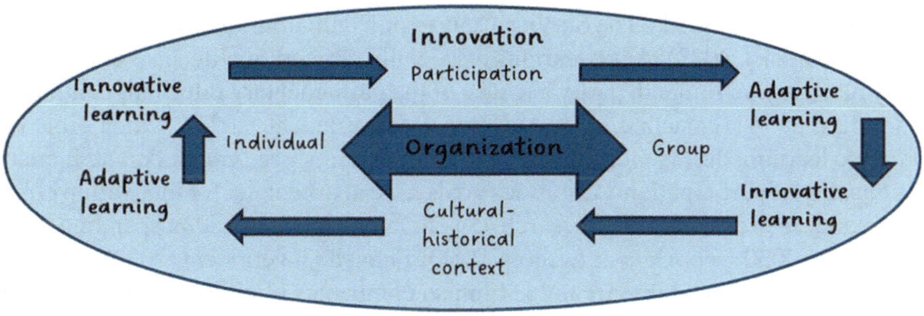

Fig. 1.1 Employee-driven learning and innovation (EDLI) as a process of continuous learning (Figure adapted from Lemmetty & Billett, 2023, p. 171)

does not yet exist. This, in turn, is a prerequisite for the emergence of new innovations. For innovations to be realized and actualized within an organization, they must be situated in their cultural–historical and social contexts through the participation of individuals and communities. Through employees' actions, innovation becomes embedded in the foundation of the organization, serving as an object of learning for future adaptive learning processes. In this sense, innovation as a process is a continuous, individual- and group-level phenomenon in the context of EDI.

Drawing on these insights, four key characteristics of EDI and learning as a phenomenon internal to the organization were formulated (Lemmetty & Billett, 2023, pp. 171–172). These serve as starting points and guiding principles for the empirical research underlying this book:

- EDI and workplace learning are closely intertwined phenomena that emerge in and through work.
- Learning in the EDI process occurs simultaneously at the intra-personal and interpersonal levels as a reciprocal process of adaptive and innovative learning.
- EDIs are only realized and become meaningful within the cultural–historical and social contexts of particular enterprises.
- The continuity of innovations and learning processes is enabled by participation.

1.2.2 *Finnish Working Life as a Context of the Study*

In this book, the LBI analysis is contextualized within Finnish working life. Finland is known as a 'model country' for education and skills in the twenty-first century. From the 1990s to the 2010s, Finland invested heavily in the reform of working life and the promotion of workplace innovations (Alasoini, 2015). Like other Nordic countries, Finland has been at the forefront of technological and organizational changes in Europe (Anttila et al., 2019; Beblavý et al., 2012; Eurofound, 2017). In addition, Finnish adults have top-level basic skills internationally (Organisation for Economic Co-operation and Development [OECD], 2025), and they feel that they regularly learn new things at work (The Service Centre for Continuous Learning and Employment's [SECLE], 2023). Adult learning, especially for working life, has been increasingly discussed in Finland, partly because of the parliamentary reform of continuous learning that was launched in 2019 (Finnish Government, 2023), which aimed to promote learning during working careers, meet learning needs at work, and increase the equality of participation. Ambitious goals have also been set for innovation policy in Finland, such as increasing research, development, and innovation spending to 4% of GDP by 2030 (see Alaja & Lemola, 2023; Finnish Government, 2023).

Despite all of Finland's strengths, Finnish companies often focus on cost cutting and extending the lifecycle of existing products rather than creating new innovations, and only about a quarter of Finnish companies are considered 'truly innovative', according to Mattila et al. (2015). Within companies and organizations, innovation and development activities are still often isolated *islands* rather than processes spanning the entire organization. In addition, employee participation in development and support for learning in supervisory work is uneven: Nearly 40% of Finnish employees feel that their competence has hardly been influenced by the workplace (Finnish Work Environment Barometer, 2023). Time spent on training and employer-provided training has decreased significantly in recent years (Hörkkö et al., 2022; Lyly-Yrjänäinen, 2022), and recent political decisions have cut or removed support measures aimed at adult education and organizational innovation. Societally, adult lifelong learning policy and innovation policy have traditionally been separate in Finland, with development work in lifelong learning focused mainly on adult education, while innovation support has targeted companies and business sector. However, there are signs in the 2020s that combining and harmonizing these policies is increasingly becoming a target (Alasoini et al., 2023; Finnish Government, 2023; Gronchi et al., 2023).

Finnish working life is culturally built on the Nordic model, in which democracy, low hierarchies, a culture of trust, and participatory, human-centered approaches to innovation have traditionally been seen as key values (Shapiro, 2022). Yet, according to Anttila et al. (2019), both public and private sector organizations in the Nordic countries are shifting away from work arrangements that support high levels of learning and autonomy toward more restricted and formalized structures. In these environments, employees' opportunities to explore new knowledge and use it as a basis for innovative problem-solving in everyday work become limited. At the same time, working life is marked by wellbeing challenges, data intensification, and growing inequalities, to name just a few of the key issues. Addressing these challenges requires humanly and socially responsible solutions, which in turn necessitate multi-perspectivity and diversity through the strong involvement of different actors and experts (see also Köykkä et al., Forthcoming). Global threats further amplify these demands. Accelerating digitalisation, the green transition, geopolitical uncertainty, and broader concerns about democratic decline and the erosion of social cohesion affect not only the Nordic countries. Nevertheless, Nordic research on innovation, learning, trust, and participatory structures can offer valuable insights for global innovation and learning policy (Suominen et al., 2024; Sotarauta, 2023).

1.2.3 *Innovation Research in the Private and Public Sectors*

Innovation has traditionally been associated primarily with pioneering technological advances in the private sector, especially in the R&D departments of industrial firms (Alves et al., 2018; Crossan & Apaydin, 2010). However, this perception has changed over the years (Høyrup, 2012). In addition to product innovation, innovation can be classified as process, market, organizational, and service innovation (Sundbo, 2003) as well as strategic, work practice, and procedural innovation (Billett et al., 2023a). When the definition of innovation includes not only the product but also many other types of innovation processes, the need for innovation research becomes more evident also in public organizations (Fligstein, 2021; Høyrup, 2010). However, public- and private-sector organizations have been seen as very different environments for innovation (Sørensen et al., 2018). In the public sector, there has been an emphasis on excessive hierarchy, strictness of job roles, and avoidance of mistakes (Renkema et al., 2021), hindering the possibilities for innovation, while in the private sector, agile and autonomy-generating practices have been seen as opportunities for innovation (e.g., Sørensen et al., 2018). The environment provided by organizations, which enables new ideas and initiatives, is in any case important. In the EDLI project, innovation and learning were studied in two distinct contexts: in the Finnish police, especially in preventive policing, and in a private top-level high-technology company.

1.2.3.1 The Police Organization and Preventive Policing

Police work is a multifaceted responsibility including law enforcement, public safety, and community engagement. Moreover, the police play a central role in strengthening social inclusion, equality, and societal well-being (Ellefsen et al., 2023). The police have a legitimate authority both to exercise control and supervision and to protect individual freedom in an open society (Björk, 2012). This dual role requires the use of discretion, which officers often exercise alone, in real time, and under pressure, without immediate external oversight (Cohen, 2022). Consequently, police work contains a degree of autonomy that, in the context of innovative research, offers an interesting counterpoint to the prevailing view of the police as an authoritarian, hierarchical, and restrictive organization. In Finland, the Police Act (Ministry of the Interior, 2011) defines the police's core tasks as safeguarding the rule of law, maintaining public order, preventing crime, and ensuring cooperation with other authorities and communities. These duties demand situational judgment, professional expertise, and strict adherence to laws and regulations, which guide the police's dual role of protecting and regulating society (Björk, 2012). As societal dynamics evolve, the police's role is also shifting. Policymakers are increasingly emphasizing transparency in policing, creating pressure for innovations that can address the growing complexity of modern police work (Huotari, 2021; Vanhanen, 2020). This reflects a broader shift in the public sector, in which innovation is no longer limited to technological advances but also includes organizational and procedural approaches tailored to society's changing needs (Høyrup, 2010). However, many studies on *police-related innovations* have still focused mainly on technological advancements and efficiency-driven goals (see e.g. Ernst et al., 2021; Huotari, 2021), neglecting innovations based on social value and the development of organizations. This reflects a broader and persistent view of police organisations and policing as largely reactive in nature and strongly guided by hierarchy, command, and risk avoidance (Huotari, 2021). This structure has made police organizations less conducive to employee-driven cultures or innovations in which workers are actively involved in shaping practices and developing new solutions. For these reasons, research on innovation and workplace learning in policing has been limited overall, although it has grown in recent years. Scholars such as Engelmann and Tatnell (2025), Filstad and Gottschalk (2011)), Lemmetty and Collin (2022) and Bjørgo and Damen (2020) have offered new perspectives on police work as a developing, expertise-based practice and have examined police organizations as learning organizations with both constraints and opportunities. A key finding in this body of research is that, in the Nordic context, policing is not as authoritarian, rigid, or restrictive of development and learning as the general discourse and traditional perspectives have often suggested. However, perceptions of police work vary across countries (Bayerl et al., 2014), and it is still often assumed that innovativeness does not always align well with a police work culture that can be relatively conservative (Karp & Stenmark, 2011).

Police work in specialized operations, however, may offer a different story. Special operations can include investigative work, alert and control work, and management and development work. *Specialized* may mean that the work is focused on specific target groups or organized differently from traditional policing. The key to the specialized functions is the specific expertise of the employees in the practices and processes related to their functions or target groups. Preventive policing (PP), which is the main policing context in this research, is an example of specialized police work that emphasizes proactive efforts to prevent problems and crimes before they occur.

Taponen (2023) approached PP as a form of proactive police work (Weisburd & Majmundar, 2018). Proactive police work refers to any policing strategy or practice aimed at reducing or preventing crime and disorder rather than reacting to crimes in progress or prosecuting those already committed. Taponen defined PP through four policing models emphasizing prevention. First, general surveillance refers to the police's visible presence in public spaces, and it is based on undetermined observation (now including online observation). It represents the most common and traditional form of PP. Second, targeted surveillance refers to planned and analysis-based monitoring focused on specific locations, times, or individuals, with the aim of preventing crimes before they occur. Third, problem-oriented policing is based on identifying the root causes of crimes and disturbances and finding context-appropriate solutions in collaboration with stakeholders (e.g., other authorities and communities). Fourth, community-oriented policing promotes safety by enhancing resident and community participation, ensuring social cohesion, and strengthening individuals' sense of responsibility, while also increasing interaction between the police and local communities.

PP represents a noteworthy shift in traditional policing: It introduces proactive and developmental approaches that challenge the traditional reactive paradigm and highlight how innovation can take root in policing (Ellefsen et al., 2023). By nature, PP requires collaboration with multiple stakeholders, including public authorities, NGOs, and local communities. Officers working in PP navigate unpredictable, context-dependent challenges that demand expertise, independent decision-making, and quick situational responses (Vanhanen, 2020). Their work emphasizes both professional knowledge and self-direction, in which collective learning often takes place through discussions, knowledge sharing, and joint reflection (Lemmetty & Collin, 2022). These processes contribute not only to the refinement of expertise but also to the development of evaluative skills and practices that sustain continuous learning (Vanhanen, 2020).

PP has proven effective in reducing crime-related costs and strengthening social security, both by directly preventing crime and by creating conditions that discourage it (Muir, 2021). The transition from reactive policing to more proactive, preventive models requires a willingness to innovate across organizational levels and to align practices with broader societal prevention strategies (Morabito, 2010). Given the police's societal role as a cornerstone institution and guarantor of security, police innovation research is especially compelling: It offers insights into how socially and sustainably oriented innovations emerge, what organizational opportunities and tensions shape their realization, and how these processes connect to adult workplace learning and innovation in working life more broadly. Thus, from the perspective of innovation, special operations, especially PP, are an appropriate research target, as the work done in them cannot always be directed, anticipated, or organized in a systematic and controlled way; instead, this work is flexible and variable. In addition, community policing itself has been seen as an innovation, the practices of which, however, have not been widely adopted or studied in policing (Morabito, 2010).

1.2.3.2 The Top-Level High-Technology Company

The technology organization that participated in the study is an SME (a small and medium-sized enterprise) which employs experts in product development, communications, management, sales, and human resources as well as production personnel who assemble, package, and manufacture products. Studying learning and innovation in technology sector SMEs is essential because SMEs make up around 99% of businesses globally and generate a substantial share of employment and economic activity, meaning that their learning capacity has significant societal impact (Short, 2019). Moreover, as SMEs rely heavily on experiential, network-based and informal learning, understanding these processes is key to supporting their innovation potential and long-term competitiveness (Short, 2019).

In the technology sector, competence development, on-the-job learning, and innovation are emphasized in the daily work of those working in specialist positions. Designers, engineers, developers, and other employees working in specialist positions develop new technological applications, environments, and solutions for the needs of different industries and customers. Therefore, digitalization and technological development have a particularly strong impact on the work of these experts. The requirements for on-the-job learning reflect how technology development requires a deep understanding of processes, continuous problem-solving (Collin et al., 2017a, 2017b), and innovation (Ulrich & Mengiste, 2014) to create new, valuable, and usable products and services (Anderson et al., 2014). In the technology sector, continuous learning is an essential part of organizations' operations (Scheeres et al., 2010). Because of the rapid changes driven by digitalization, maintaining competence and keeping up with developments require the examination of learning opportunities from new perspectives: As formal education is not always able to support the learning of individual technologies with sufficient agility, daily learning in the workplace and in work processes has become an essential part of expert work in the technology sector (Lemmetty, 2020). In technology-oriented work, learning is particularly supported by challenging and meaningful tasks as well as collaboration with others. In contrast, learning and creativity are hindered by, for example, routine tasks, a constant sense of hurry, outdated technologies, boundaries between professional groups, and short-term efficiency demands (Vähäsantanen & Eteläpelto, 2018). The importance of learning is central to such creative, problem-based, and development-oriented expert work, whose goal is continuous innovation.

The technology sector is, however, highly heterogeneous, which makes it difficult to draw general conclusions about organizations or their practices. Nevertheless, alongside creativity and learning, and partly as a prerequisite for them, the field is often characterized by expectations of strong self-direction (Lemmetty, 2020). Many technology companies therefore seek to support experts' creativity and innovativeness through, for example, low hierarchies and agile ways of working (Holbeche, 2015). This is essential, as rapidly developed new products, services, and solutions cannot be efficiently created in traditional, hierarchical, top-down organizations (Lee & Edmondson, 2017).

Not all members of the target organization work at the same location or even in the same city; instead, some of the staff and departments are spread out regionally. In this case, particularly expert work within the organization is also carried out remotely and in a decentralized manner. Remote work both challenges and enables the innovation work of experts, and digitalization shapes the ways in which organizations strategically organize their innovation activities, changing perceptions of what innovation means in general (Hund et al., 2021). Digital transformation can support organizations' innovation capacity, including through resource management, the blurring of boundaries, and cost reductions (Kim et al., 2024). Purposefully designed digital environments can offer opportunities for change at both the individual and organizational levels (Barabaschi et al., 2022). In here, informal interaction is important not only for achieving formal goals but also for the professional learning of personnel, as learning and innovation in organizations are largely based on collaboration, a sense of belonging, and interaction (Brown & Duguid, 2001). Online learning situations can be equivalent to effective face-to-face encounters, physically distant colleagues can also experience a sense of community and collaboration, and, with the right support, digital technology can strengthen this collaboration (Wilson et al., 2008).

While these tools have many positive effects, they also have negative aspects. Remote and online work reduces spontaneous interaction and informal encounters, which can reduce knowledge sharing and thus weaken innovation (Bellis et al., 2022).

In addition to experts, the technology organization that participated in the study also employs personnel in production tasks. These so-called *blue-collar* employees work physically in the organization's factory in work that is basically performed. Although blue-collar employees' work tasks are often described as relatively simple and repeatable, Decius et al. (2021), referring to Hirsch-Kreinsen and Ten Hompel (2014), argued that the efficient and effective performance of blue-collar work relies heavily on experience-based knowledge. Accordingly, learning and competence development are considered essential in blue-collar work (see Decius et al., 2021). However, in Finland, it has been observed that blue-collar employees experience fewer learning opportunities for, and less support in, learning from their superiors than experts and those in management positions (SECLE, 2023). This can be explained not only by the organizational operating methods but also by the lower level of education of blue-collar personnel and their previous negative learning experiences (for more details, see Decius et al., 2021). Although production work is more predetermined and guided by production lines, learning on the job is also central to blue-collar work, especially for the transfer of tacit knowledge, the development of work methods, and the high-quality performance of work (Decius et al., 2021; Saari & Koivunen, 2022). Blue-collar workers utilize their accumulated tacit knowledge not only for work performance but also for the development of their work, making it important for organizations to also understand the value of blue-collar workers' practical skills and to develop activities that support the sharing of this knowledge and the participation of these workers (Saari & Koivunen, 2022).

1.2.4 Methods, Participants, Data, and Analysis

The EDLI project underlying this work was based entirely on the premises of mobile and participatory ethnography (Lindhult & Axelsson, 2021; Muskat et al., 2018; Porter, 1994). The implementation of the project, the methods, and the related phases and practices are described in full in Lemmetty and Vanhanen (2025). The overall project data consisted of interviews ($N = 53$) collected in the target organizations as well as mobile ethnographic diaries, transcribed discussions, and observation materials. The methodological choices were based on the idea that understanding innovation from a learning perspective requires the researcher to have a strong interaction with participants, a contextual understanding of the organizations under study, and a multidimensional depiction of sociocultural perspectives through qualitative research.

Although the entire project and its data can be seen as forming the background of this work, the citations and analyses of the material presented in this book are mainly based on the interview data from the project (see Table 1.1). The book also presents narrative type stories (Lemmetty, 2024a) and vignettes (Lemmetty &

Glaveanu, Forthcoming) that were developed in earlier publications from the project, in addition to authentic interview quotes and data examples. The research interviews were conducted as individual thematic interviews. A total of 23 police officers working as senior constables (15), police sergeants (5), and chief inspectors (3) in three different police departments in Finland participated in the interviews. All were involved in a specific function, mainly PP. In addition, 30 people from the technology organization participated in the interviews, of whom eight were in management or head-of-department positions, eight were team leaders or leading specialists, and 14 were specialists or (blue-collar) workers. To ensure anonymity, the organizations are referred to in this volume as the "technology organization" and "police organization".

For the police study, research permission was granted by the Finnish National Police Board in 2022. After this, the researcher contacted senior leaders in three police departments located in different parts of Finland, who helped distribute the invitation to personnel working in preventive policing. In the technology-sector organization, research and development collaboration had already been established prior to this project, and the organization informed its personnel about the project at the outset Participation was voluntary. All participants received an information sheet and a privacy notice before taking part in the study. Written informed consent was obtained from each participant. Participants were free to withdraw from the study for as long as their data could still be identified and removed from the dataset. A data management plan was prepared before the data collection began, guiding the secure handling of the data by the responsible researcher only. Authentic raw data (e.g., audio recordings) were destroyed after transcription, and pseudonyms were assigned during the transcription process.

Thematic interview data from the technology organization and the police organization were collected in the fall of 2022 and the spring of 2023, respectively. The interviews were conducted face to face at participants' workplaces (i.e., in the premises of the organizations studied). In the interviews, participants were first asked to describe their work in general terms as well as their work and education histories. The innovation theme was introduced by explaining to participants how innovation is understood broadly in this project: "Innovation in this study means any new idea, perspective, practice, product, or approach that has novelty value at work—for oneself, for one's team or organization, and perhaps even for society. Innovation can come in many forms: small and large". This preliminary definition was presented because it was assumed that it might be problematic for the employees, especially but not only the police employees, to perceive their own work from the perspective of innovation, which, in typical discussions, is associated with patents, products, and technologies.

The interview framework included the following themes: work and work history, innovation and development, competence, learning at work, participation, and organizational support and constraints. Each theme was accompanied by supporting questions, including the following: What do you think innovation means in your own work context? What kind of innovation processes do you recognize in your work? How have you participated in innovation activities, and how have the processes progressed? What kind of competence has the work, particularly participation in

Table 1.1 Participants and interview data

Code	Organization	Position group	Duration[a]	Experience[a] (years)
PP1	Police	Chief inspectors	45 min	20+
PP2	Police	Chief inspectors	1.5 h	20+
PP3	Police	Chief inspectors	1 h	20+
PP4	Police	Police sergeants	2 h	10–20
PP5	Police	Police sergeants	1 h	10–20
PP6	Police	Police sergeants	1.5 h	20+
PP7	Police	Police sergeants	1 h	20+
PP8	Police	Police sergeants	1 h	10–20
PP9	Police	Police sergeants	1 h	20+
PP10	Police	Police sergeants	1 h	20+
PP11	Police	Police sergeants	1 h	10
PP12	Police	Senior constables	1 h	10–20
PP13	Police	Senior constables	1 h	<5
PP14	Police	Senior constables	1 h	<5
PP15	Police	Senior constables	1 h	10–20
PP16	Police	Senior constables	1 h	<5
PP17	Police	Senior constables	1 h	10–20
PP18	Police	Senior constables	1 h	20+
PP19	Police	Senior constables	1 h	10–20
PP20	Police	Senior constables	1 h	10–20
PP21	Police	Senior constables	30 min	<5
PP22	Police	Senior constables	1 h	10–20
PP23	Police	Senior constables	1.5 h	20+
TP1	Technology	Managers and department heads	1.5 h	20+
TP2	Technology	Managers and department heads	50 min	10–20
TP3	Technology	Managers and department heads	50 min	10–20
TP4	Technology	Managers and department heads	50 min	<5
TP5	Technology	Managers and department heads	50 min	20+
TP6	Technology	Managers and department heads	50 min	10–20
TP7	Technology	Managers and department heads	1 h	20+
TP8	Technology	Managers and department heads	1 h	10–20
TP9	Technology	Leading specialists and team leaders	1 h	20+
TP10	Technology	Leading specialists and team leaders	50 min	10–20
TP11	Technology	Leading specialists and team leaders	40 min	<5
TP12	Technology	Leading specialists and team leaders	1 h	10
TP13	Technology	Leading specialists and team leaders	30 min	10–20

(continued)

Table 1.1 (continued)

Code	Organization	Position group	Duration[a]	Experience[a] (years)
TP14	Technology	Leading specialists and team leaders	40 min	10–20
TP15	Technology	Leading specialists and team leaders	2 h	20+
TP16	Technology	Leading specialists and team leaders	1 h 10 min	20+
TP17	Technology	Specialists and employees	50 min	10–20
TP18	Technology	Specialists and employees	50 min	10–20
TP19	Technology	Specialists and employees	1 h	10–20
TP20	Technology	Specialists and employees	50 min	10–20
TP21	Technology	Specialists and employees	50 min	10–20
TP22	Technology	Specialists and employees	1.5 h	20+
TP23	Technology	Specialists and employees	35 min	<5
TP24	Technology	Specialists and employees	1 h 15 min	20+
TP25	Technology	Specialists and employees	30 min	<5
TP26	Technology	Specialists and employees	30 min	<5
TP27	Technology	Specialists and employees	30 min	<5
TP28	Technology	Specialists and employees	1 h	10–20
TP29	Technology	Specialists and employees	40 min	<5
TP30	Technology	Specialists and employees	1 h	20+

[a]Duration refers to the length of the interview. Experience refers to the total number of years of work experience of each participant in the police or the technology organization

innovation activities, required? What kind of learning has been associated with work and innovation activities? What kind of support have you received from the organization for innovation and development work? What kind of challenges and constraints do you see for innovation? The interviews aimed to get the interviewees to give concrete examples based on their own experiences. The interviews were different in their thematic progression, as the interviewees wanted to be given as much freedom as possible to describe things authentically from their own perspectives. Clarifying questions were asked for each interview, depending on the interviewee's stories and the interesting perspectives spontaneously observed in them. Thus, the interview material became rich and diverse in content. The duration of the interviews varied from 30 min to 2 h. The interview materials were transcribed, and respondents' direct personal data were anonymized.

The research project involved several sub-studies to achieve the research goal of increasing multi-perspectival and sociocultural understanding of employee-driven learning and innovation. Some of these sub-studies have been published as independent research publications (Lemmetty, 2024a, 2024b, 2025; Lemmetty & Vanhanen, 2025; Lemmetty & Billett, 2023; Lemmetty & Glaveanu, forthcoming), some are under review in scientific journals, and some are published for the first time in this book. Before the actual sub-study-specific systematic analyses were carried out, the entire material was read through several times, and notes and key observations were recorded in a research diary. Notes taken during interviews, field notes from the technology organization, and notes written at different stages of the research played essential roles in the construction of the major themes and perspectives. Because the project was ethnographic in its origins, the production of the overall analysis was ongoing throughout the project, and the overarching conclusions and insights drawn in this work cannot be located in a specific individual research phase, analysis, or piece of data as such.

However, the sub-studies of the project were guided by different qualitative methods, including content analysis (Bengtsson, 2016; Hsieh & Shannon, 2005; see Lemmetty, 2025), thematic analysis and typifying (e.g., Braun & Clarke, 2006; Clarke & Braun, 2013; see Lemmetty, 2024a), and narrative research methods (e.g., Polkinghorne, 1995; see Lemmetty, 2024b). A diverse analytical examination resulted in cross-sectional and multi-perspectival observations of the phenomena targeted by the project: employee participation and roles, the significance of competence and learning, and the value of and support for development work. The purpose of this book is to present and examine the project's results at a level that goes beyond the individual sub-studies, while briefly highlighting the key findings of some specific sub-studies, and thus to refine their interpretation in line with the perspectives chosen in the work (roles and agency, processes and competence, values and projects, and pedagogy).

References

Alaja, A., & Lemola, T. (2023). *Minne menet tutkimus- ja innovaatiopolitiikka*? [Where are you going, research and innovation policy?] Teollisuuden palkansaajat Ry.

Alasoini, T. (2015). Two decades of programme-based promotion of workplace innovation in Finland: Past experiences and future challenges. *European Journal of Workplace Innovation, 1*(1), 35–54. https://doi.org/10.46364/ejwi.v1i1.160

Alasoini, T., Selander, K., Antila, J., Hakonen, N., Lyly-Yrjänäinen, M., & Näätänen, A.-M. (2023). *Osaaminen, yhteistyö ja osallistuminen: Innovaatioihin perustuvan tuottavuuskasvun tekijät suomalaisilla työpaikoilla* [Competence, collaboration, and participation: Factors of innovation-based productivity growth in Finnish workplace]. Työterveyslaitos. Retrieved from https://julkari.fi/handle/10024/146376

Allen, T., & Stephen, J. (2013). Innovation: A knowledge transfer perspective. *Production Planning & Control, 24*(2–3), 208–225. https://doi.org/10.1080/09537287.2011.647875

Al-Saleem, A. I., & Aldakheel, M. K. (2024). Barriers to workforce-driven innovation in healthcare. *Cureus, 16*(10), Article 72316. https://doi.org/10.7759/cureus.72316

Alves, M. F. R., Galina, S. V. R., & Dobelin, S. (2018). Literature on organizational innovation: Past and future. *Innovation & Management Review, 15*(1), 2–19. https://doi.org/10.1108/INMR-01-2018-001

Amabile, T. M. (1996). *Creativity and innovation in organizations*. Harvard Business School Background Note. Retrieved from https://www.hbs.edu/faculty/Pages/item.aspx?num=13672

Anderson, N., Potočnik, K., & Zhou, J. (2014). Innovation and creativity in organizations: A state-of-the-science review, prospective commentary, and guiding framework. *Journal of Management, 40*(5), 1297–1333. https://doi.org/10.1177/0149206314527128

Anttila, T., Oinas, T. S., & Mustosmäki, A. (2019). Towards formalisation: The organisation of work in the public and private sectors in Nordic countries. *Acta Sociologica, 62*(3), 315–333. Retrieved from https://www.jstor.org/stable/48595526

Bäckström, I., & Lindberg, M. (2018). Behavioural implications of employee-driven innovation: A critical discourse analysis. *International Journal of Innovation Management, 22*(7). https://doi.org/10.1142/S1363919618500585

Bäckström, I., & Mosleh, W. S. (2021). The inclusive organisation: Management practices of employee-driven innovation (EDI). *International Journal of Innovation Management, 25*(6), 1–19. https://doi.org/10.1142/S1363919621500687

Barabaschi, B., Barbieri, L., Cantoni, F., Platoni, S., & Virtuani, R. (2022). Remote working in Italian SMEs during COVID-19: Learning challenges of a new work organization. *Journal of Workplace Learning, 34*(6), 497–512. https://doi.org/10.1108/JWL-10-2021-0132

Battistelli, A., Odoardi, C., Vandenberghe, C., Di Napoli, G., & Piccione, L. (2019). Information sharing and innovative work behavior: The role of work-based learning, challenging tasks, and organizational commitment. *Human Resource Development Quarterly, 30*, 361–381. https://doi.org/10.1002/hrdq.21344

Bayerl, P. S., Horton, K. E., Jacobs, G., Rogiest, S., Reguli, Z., Gruschinske, M., Costanzo, P., Stojanovski, T., Vonas, G., Gascó, M., & Elliott, K. (2014). Perspectives on the police profession: An international investigation. *Policing: An International Journal of Police Strategies & Management, 37*(4), 728–745. https://doi.org/10.1108/PIJPSM-11-2013-0112

Beblavý, M., Maselli, I., & Martellucci, E. (2012). *Workplace innovation and technological change.* CEPS Special Reports. Retrieved from https://ssrn.com/abstract=2147619

Beier, M. E., Saxena, M., Kraiger, K., Costanza, D. P., Rudolph, C. W., Cadiz, D. M., Petery, G. A., & Fisher, G. G. (2025). Workplace learning and the future of work. *Industrial and Organizational Psychology, 18*, 84–109.

Bellis, P., Trabucchi, D., & Buganza, T. (2022). How do human relationships change in the digital environment after COVID-19 pandemic? The road towards agility. *European Journal of Innovation, 25*(6), 821–849. https://doi.org/10.1108/EJIM-02-2022-0093

Bengtsson, M. (2016). How to plan and perform a qualitative study using content analysis. *Nursing Plus Open, 2*, 8–14. https://doi.org/10.1016/j.npls.2016.01.001

Billett, S. (2001). Learning through work: Workplace affordances and individual engagement. *Journal of Workplace Learning, 13*(5), 209–214. https://doi.org/10.1108/EUM0000000005548

Billett, S. (2002). Toward a workplace pedagogy: Guidance, participation, and engagement. *Adult Education Quarterly, 53*(1), 27–43. https://doi.org/10.1177/074171302237202

Billett, S. (2004). Workplace participatory practices: Conceptualising workplaces as learning environments. *The Journal of Workplace Learning, 16*(6), 312–324. https://doi.org/10.1108/13665620410550295

Billett, S. (2014). Mimesis: Learning through everyday activities and interactions at work. *Human Resource Development Review, 3*(4), 462–482. https://doi.org/10.1177/1534484314548275

Billett, S. (2026). *Learning through work: Practices, purposes and outcomes.* Routledge.

Billett, S., Tan, J., Chan, C., Chong, W. H., & Keat, J. S. C. (2023a). Employee-driven innovations: Zones of initiation, enactment and learning. In W. O. Lee, P. Brown, A. L. Goodwin, & A. Green (Eds.), *International handbook on education development in Asia-Pacific*. Springer. https://doi.org/10.1007/978-981-16-2327-1_67-1

Billett, S., Yang, S., & Chia, A. (2023b). Innovations and learning at work. Local factors and contributions. In H. Bound, A. Edwards, K. Evans, & A. Chia (Eds.), *Workplace learning for changing social and economic circumstances.* Routledge.

Bjørgo, T., & Damen, M.-L. (Eds.). (2020). *The making of a police officer: Comparative perspectives on police education and recruitment* (1st ed.). Routledge. https://doi.org/10.4324/9780429277221

Björk, M. (2012). Five points about the police and the fleeting nature of trust. In C. Björngren Cuadra & O. Fransson (Eds.), *Trust and confidence: Ongoing challenges for professionals* (pp. 109–130). Gleerups.

Bourdieu, P. (1977). *Outline of a theory of practice*. Cambridge University Press.

Brandi, U., & Hasse, C. (2012). Employee-driven innovation and practice-based learning in organizational cultures. In S. Høyrup, M. Bonnafous-Boucher, C. Hasse, M. Lotz, & K. Møller (Eds.), *Employee-driven innovation: A new approach* (pp. 127–148). Palgrave Macmillan.

Braun, V., & Clarke, V. (2006). Using thematic analysis in psychology. *Qualitative Research in Psychology, 3*(2), 77–101. https://doi.org/10.1191/1478088706qp063oa

Brem, A., & Puente-Díaz, R. (2020). Are you acting sustainably in your daily practice? Introduction of the Four-S model of sustainability. *Journal of Cleaner Production, 267*. https://doi.org/10.1016/j.jclepro.2020.122074

Brown, J. S., & Duguid, P. (2001). Knowledge and organization: A social–practice perspective. *Organization Science, 12*(2), 198–213. https://doi.org/10.1287/orsc.12.2.198.10116

Clarke, V., & Braun, V. (2013). *Successful qualitative research: A practical guide for beginners*. SAGE Publications.

Cohen, G. (2022). In pursuit of police ethics: An analysis of ethics content in state-mandated basic police training curricula. *Public Integrity, 24*(3), 292–305. https://doi.org/10.1080/10999922.2021.1933340

Collin, K., Herranen, S., & Riivari, E. (2017a). What kinds of aspects frame professional agency and creativity in information technology work*? Business Creativity & the Creative Economy, 3*(1), 88–98. https://doi.org/10.18536/bcce.2017.10.3.1.08

Collin, K., Lemmetty, S., Herranen, S., Paloniemi, S., Auvinen, T., & Riivari, E. (2017b). Professional agency and creativity in information technology work. In M. Goller & S. Paloniemi (Eds.), *Agency at work: Professional and practice-based learning* (pp. 263–282). Springer. https://doi.org/10.1007/978-3-319-60943-0_13

Crossan, M. M., & Apaydin, M. (2010). A multi-dimensional framework of organizational innovation: A systematic review of the literature. *Journal of Management Studies, 47*(6), 1154–1191. https://doi.org/10.1111/j.1467-6486.2009.00880.x

Damanpour, F., & Aravind, D. (2012). Managerial innovation: Conceptions, processes, and antecedents. *Management and Organization Review, 8*(2), 423–454. https://doi.org/10.1111/j.1740-8784.2011.00233.x

Darsø, L., & Høyrup, S. (2012). Developing a framework for innovation and learning in the workplace. In H. Melkas & V. Harmaakorpi (Eds.), *Practice-based innovation: Insights, applications and policy implications* (pp. 135–254). Springer. https://doi.org/10.1007/978-3-642-21723-4_8

Decius, J., Knappstein, M., Schaper, N., & Seifert, A. (2021). Investigating the multidimensionality of informal learning: Validation of a short measure for white-collar workers. *Human Resource Development Quarterly, 34*(1), 45–74. https://doi.org/10.1002/hrdq.21461

Derrick, J. (2020). "Tacit pedagogy" and "entanglement": Practice-based learning and innovation. *Journal of Workplace Learning, 32*(4), 273–284. https://doi.org/10.1108/JWL-07-2019-0094

Edwards-Schachter, M. (2018). The nature and variety of innovation. *International Journal of Innovation Studies, 2*(2), 1–15. https://doi.org/10.1016/j.ijis.2018.08.004

Ellefsen, H. B., Bjørkelo, B., Sunde, I. M., & Fyfe, N. R. (2023). Unpacking preventive policing: Towards a holistic framework. *International Journal of Police Science & Management, 25*(2), 196–207. https://doi.org/10.1177/14613557231163403

Ellström, P.-E. (2001). Integrating learning and work. Problems and prospects. *Human Resource Development Quarterly, 12*(4), 421–435. https://doi.org/10.1002/hrdq.1006

Ellström, P.-E. (2010). Practice-based innovation: A learning perspective. *Journal of Workplace Learning, 22*(1/2), 27–40. https://doi.org/10.1108/13665621011012834

Engelmann, L., & Tatnell, A. A. T. (2025). Blending the 'craft' and 'science' of policing: Challenges and opportunities for police as professional learning organizations. *Policing: A Journal of Policy and Practice, 19*. https://doi.org/10.1093/police/paaf036

Ernst, S., ter Veen, H., & Kop, N. (2021). Technological innovation in a police organization: Lessons learned from the National Police of The Netherlands. *Policing: A Journal of Policy and Practice, 15*(3), 1818–1831. https://doi.org/10.1093/police/paab003

Eurofound. (2017). *Sixth European conditions survey: Overview report.* Office for Official Publications of the European Communities.

Filstad, C., & Gottschalk, P. (2011). Becoming a learning organization: The espoused values of police managers from two Norwegian districts. *The Learning Organization, 18*, 486–500. https://doi.org/10.1108/09696471111171321

Finnish Government. (2023). *Yhdessä jatkuvaa oppimista uudistamassa: Jatkuvan oppimisen uudistus -hankkeen loppuraportti* [Renewing continuous learning together: Final report of the continuous learning reform project]. Retrieved from https://julkaisut.valtioneuvosto.fi/items/2dfeabf9-1167-4a93-a261-11798a553671

Finnish Work Environment Barometer. (2023). *Työolobarometri 2023.* [Work environment barometer 2023]. Retrieved from https://julkaisut.valtioneuvosto.fi/handle/10024/165554

Fligstein, N. (2021). Innovation and the theory of fields. *AMS Review, 11*, 272–289. https://doi.org/10.1007/s13162-021-00202-2

Flocco, N., Canterino, F., & Cagliano, R. (2022). To control or not to control: How to organize employee-driven innovation. *Creativity and Innovation Management, 31*(3), 396–409. https://doi.org/10.1111/caim.12500

Gherardi, S. (2009). Practice? It's a matter of taste! *Management Learning, 40*(5), 535–550. https://doi.org/10.1177/1350507609340812

Gronchi, I., Leppänen, J., Sarkia, K., Ahokas, J., Järvensivu, P., Salminen, V., & Uitto, H. (2023). *An operative model for implementing missions* (Policy Brief 2023:20). Prime Minister's Office. Retrieved from https://julkaisut.valtioneuvosto.fi/server/api/core/bitstreams/20c77a25-a7b4-44ba-9c48-cf9ceac28869/content.

Haapasaari, A., Engestrom, Y., & Kerosuo, H. (2018). From initiatives to employee-driven innovations. *European Journal of Innovation Management, 21*(2), 206–226. https://doi.org/10.1108/EJIM-09-2016-0085

Hasu, M., Honkaniemi, L., Saari, E., Mattelmäki, T., & Koponen, L. (2014). Learning employee-driven innovating: Towards sustained practice through multi-method evaluation. *Journal of Workplace Learning, 26*(5), 310–330. https://doi.org/10.1108/JWL-10-2013-0079

Hirsch-Kreinsen & Ten Hompel: Hirsch-Kreinsen, H., & Weyer, J. (2014). Wandel von Produktionsarbeit–Industrie 4.0. Soziologisches Arbeitspapier 38. *Technische Universität Dortmund.*

Holbeche, L. (2015). *The agile organization: How to build an innovative, sustainable and resilient business.* Kogan Page.

Holmquist, M., & Johansson, A. (2019). Employee-driven innovation: An intervention using action research. *Technology Innovation Management Review, 9*(5), 44–53.

Hörkkö, E., Silvennoinen, H., & Järvinen, T. (2022). Työssä oppimisen mahdollisuudet ja työelämän luottamus palkansaajien kokemina Suomessa vuosina 2004–2016. [Opportunities for workplace learning and working life trust as experienced by employees in Finland, 2004–2016]. *Työelämän tutkimus, 20*(3), 305–332.

Høyrup, S. (2010). Employee-driven innovation and workplace learning: Basic concepts, approaches and themes. *Transfer: European Review of Labour and Research, 16*(2), 143–154. https://doi.org/10.1177/1024258910364102

Høyrup, S. (2012). Employee-driven innovation: A new phenomenon, concept and mode of innovation. In S. Høyrup, M. Bonnafous-Boucher, C. Hasse, M. Lotz, & K. Møller (Eds.), *Employee-driven innovation* (pp. 3–33). Palgrave Macmillan.

Høyrup, S., Redien-Collot, R., & Teglborg, A.-C. (2018). Introduction. *International Journal of Entrepreneurship and Innovation Management, 22*, 317–322.

Hsieh, H. F., & Shannon, S. E. (2005). Three approaches to qualitative content analysis. *Qualitative Health Research, 15*(9), 1277–1288. https://doi.org/10.1177/1049732305276687

Hund, A., Heinz-Theo, W., Beimborn, D., & Weitzel, T. (2021). Digital innovation: Review and novel perspective. *Journal of Strategic Information Systems, 30*(4). https://doi.org/10.1016/j.jsis.2021.101695

Huotari, T. (2021). *Innovaatio ja innovatiivisuus poliisitoimessa: esseitä historiasta, teoriasta ja filosofiasta* [Innovations and innovativeness in the police and policing: Essays on history, theory, and philosophy]. Police University College.

John-Steiner, V., & Mahn, H. (1996). Sociocultural approaches to learning and development: A Vygotskian framework. *Educational Psychologist, 31*(3–4), 191–206.

Karp, S., & Stenmark, H. (2011). Learning to be a police officer: Tradition and change in the training and professional lives of police officers. *Police Practice & Research, 12*(1), 4–15. https://doi.org/10.1080/15614263.2010.497653

Kerosuo, H., Kajamaa, A., & Engeström, Y. (2010). Promoting innovation and learning through change laboratory: An example from Finnish health care. *Central European Journal of Public Policy, 4*(1), 110–131. Retrieved from https://doaj.org/article/9ea8e1c1aee64b6dbe573ec4a6bee528

Kesting, P., & Ulhøi, J. P. (2010). Employee driven innovation: Extending the license to foster innovation. *Management Decision, 48*, 65–84. https://doi.org/10.1108/00251741011014463

Kim, J. M., & Park, J. H. (2024). When is digital transformation beneficial for coupled open innovation? The contingent role of the adoption of Industry 4.0 technologies. *Technovation, 136*, 103087. https://doi.org/10.1016/j.technovation.2024.103087

Kline, S. J., & Rosenberg, N. (1986). An overview of innovation. In R. Landau & N. Rosenberg (Eds.), *The positive sum strategy: Harnessing technology for economic growth* (pp. 275–307). National Academy Press.

Korunka, C., & Kubicek, B. (2017). *Job demands in a changing world of work: Impact on workers' health and performance and implications for research and practice.* Springer. https://doi.org/10.1007/978-3-319-54678-0

Köykkä, K., Lemmetty, S., & Schönberger, B. (In Press). Leadership practices leveraging cultural diversity for responsible innovation. Accepted for publication in *IEEE Engineering Management Journal.* (Forthcoming, 2026)

Lave, J., & Wenger, E. (1991). *Situated learning: Legitimate peripheral participation.* Cambridge University Press.

Lee, M. Y., & Edmondson, A. C. (2017). Self-managing organizations: Exploring the limits of less-hierarchical organizing. *Research in Organizational Behavior, 37*, 35–58. https://doi.org/10.1016/j.riob.2017.10.002

Lemmetty, S. (2020). *"Self-learning is present every day—In fact, it's my job": Self-directed workplace learning in technology-based work.* Doctoral dissertation. University of Jyväskylä.

Lemmetty, S. (2024a). Real-time and long-term challenges of remote learning and innovation: Cases from police and technology organisations. *Vocations and Learning, 17*, 565–587. https://doi.org/10.1007/s12186-024-09354-1

Lemmetty, S. (2024b). Explaining the innovation dichotomy: The contexts, contents, conflicts, and compromises of innovation stories. *Frontiers of Narrative Studies, 10*(1), 126–149. https://doi.org/10.1515/fns-2024-2007

Lemmetty, S. (2025). "Failure is future success": Expanding knowledge through learning practices in a continuous innovation process. *Innovation.* https://doi.org/10.1080/14479338.2025.2573102.

Lemmetty, S., Bäckström, I., & Pajuoja, M. (Forthcoming). *Employee-driven innovation: How people shape change at work.* Palgrave Macmillan.

Lemmetty, S., & Billett, S. (2023). Employee-driven learning and innovation (EDLI) as a phenomenon of continuous learning at work. *Journal of Workplace Learning, 35*(9), 162–176. https://doi.org/10.1108/JWL-12-2022-0175

Lemmetty, S., & Collin, K. (2022). Co-occurrence of sociocultural elements and self-direction in learning situations: A police organization case study. *Adult Learning, 34*(4), 220–229. https://doi.org/10.1177/10451595221094072

Lemmetty, S., & Glaveanu, V. (Forthcoming). From possibility thinking to employee-driven innovation. Accepted for publication in S. Lemmetty, I. Bäckström & M. Pajuoja (Eds.), *Employee-driven innovation in public and private organizations: How people shape change at work.* Palgrave Macmillan.

Lemmetty, S., & Vanhanen, S. (2025). Methodological dilemmas of participatory and mobile ethnography in researching learning in organizational context. *Learning in Context, 2*(1–2). https://doi.org/10.1016/j.lecon.2025.100012

Lidman, L., Gustavsson, M., & Fogelberg Eriksson, A. (2023). Learning and employee-driven innovation in the public sector: The interplay between employee engagement and organisational conditions. *Journal of Workplace Learning, 35*(9), 86–100. https://doi.org/10.1108/JWL-05-2022-0055

Lindhult, E., & Axelsson, K. (2021). The logic and integration of coproductive research approaches. *International Journal of Managing Projects in Business, 14*(1), 13–35. https://doi.org/10.1108/IJMPB-07-2020-0215

Lundvall, B. A. (1992). *National systems of innovation: Towards a theory of innovation and interactive learning*. Pinter Publishers.

Lyly-Yrjänäinen, M. (2022). *Työolobarometri 2021* [Workplace barometer 2021]. Retrieved from https://urn.fi/URN:ISBN:978-952-327-610-9

Manuti, A., Pastore, S., Scardigno, A. F., & Morciano, D. (2015). Formal and informal learning in the workplace: A research review. *International Journal of Training and Development, 19*(1), 1–17. https://doi.org/10.1111/ijtd.12044

Marsick, V. J., & Watkins, K. E. (1990). *Informal and incidental learning in the workplace*. Routledge.

Martins, E. C., & Terblanche, F. (2003). Building organisational culture that stimulates creativity and innovation. *European Journal of Innovation Management, 6*(1), 64–74. https://doi.org/10.1108/14601060310456337

Mattila, P., Alasoini, T., & Klemetti, M. (2015). *Vain joka neljäs suomalaisorganisaatio on oikeasti innovatiivinen.* [Only one in four Finnish organizations is truly innovative]. Press release Retrieved from https://mb.cision.com/Main/68/9717192/339145.pdf

Meissner, D., & Kotsemir, M. (2016). Conceptualizing the innovation process towards the "active innovation paradigm": Trends and outlook. *Journal of Innovation Entrepreneurship, 5*(14). https://doi.org/10.1186/s13731-016-0042-z

Ministry of the Interior. (2011). *Police act*. Retrieved from https://www.finlex.fi/en/laki/kaannokset/2011/en20110872_20131168.pdf.

Moosa, N., & Panurach, P. (2008). Encouraging front-line employees to rise to the innovation challenge. *Strategy & Leadership, 36*(4), 4–9. https://doi.org/10.1108/10878570810888704

Morabito, M. (2010). Understanding community policing as an innovation: Patterns of adoption. *Crime & Delinquency, 56*(4), 564–587. https://doi.org/10.1177/0011128707311643

Mosleh, W. S., Bäckström, I., Manfrini, C., & Leue-Bensch, C. (2024). Organizing employee-driven innovation (EDI) through game-based formats: Understanding participation. *Creativity and Innovation Management, 34*(1), 47–60. https://doi.org/10.1111/caim.12625

Muir, R. (2021). *Taking prevention seriously: The case for a crime and harm prevention system.* The Police Foundation. Retrieved from https://www.cgi.com/sites/default/files/2021-05/the-police-foundation-taking-prevention-seriously-may-21.pdf.

Muskat, B., Muskat, M., & Zehrer, A. (2018). Qualitative interpretive mobile ethnography. *Anatolia: An International Journal of Tourism and Hospitality Research, 29*(1), 98–107. https://doi.org/10.1080/13032917.2017.1396482

Ness, I. J., & Søreide, G. E. (2014). The room of opportunity: Understanding phases of creative knowledge processes in innovation. *Journal of Workplace Learning, 26*, 545–560.

Organisation for Economic Co-operation and Development (OECD). (2025). *Survey of adult skills (PIAAC)*. Retrieved from https://www.oecd.org/en/about/programmes/piaac.html

Polkinghorne, D. E. (1995). Narrative configuration in qualitative analysis. In J. A. Hatch & R. Wisniewski (Eds.), *Life history and narrative* (pp. 5–23). Falmer Press.

Porter, M. (1994). "Second-hand" ethnography: Some problems in analysing a feminist project. In A. Bryman & R. G. Burgess (Eds.), *Analysing qualitative data* (pp. 67–88). Routledge.

Prugsamatz, R. (2010). Factors that influence organization learning sustainability in non-profit organizations. *The Learning Organization: An International Journal, 17*(3), 243–267. https://doi.org/10.1108/09696471011034937

Ramstad, E. (2009). Developmental evaluation framework for innovation and learning networks: Integration of the structure, process and outcomes. *Journal of Workplace Learning, 21*(3), 181–197. https://doi.org/10.1108/13665620910943924

Rehn, A., & Vachhani, S. (2006). Innovation and the post-original: On moral stances and reproduction. *Creativity and Innovation Management, 15*(3), 310–322. https://doi.org/10.1111/j.1467-8691.2006.00390

Renkema, M., & Bos-Nehles, A. (2024). The implementation of bottom-up innovation in a formalized context: A resource-mobilization perspective. *Creativity and Innovation Management, 33*(4), 639–653. https://doi.org/10.1111/caim.12607

Renkema, M., Meijerink, J., & Bondarouk, T. (2021). Routes for employee-driven innovation: How HRM supports the emergence of innovation in a formalized context. *The International Journal of Human Resource Management, 33*(17), 3526–3559. https://doi.org/10.1080/09585192.2021.1913625

Rogoff, B. (1995). Observing sociocultural activity on three planes: Participatory appropriation, guided participation, and apprenticeship. In J. V. Wertsch, P. del Rio, & A. Alvarez (Eds.), *Sociocultural studies of mind* (pp. 139–164). Cambridge University Press.

Saari, T., & Koivunen, T. (2022). Tacit knowledge in blue-collar work: How workers use it to fulfil their side of the psychological contract. *International Journal of Organizational Analysis, 30*(7), 173–183. https://doi.org/10.1108/IJOA-09-2021-2972

Scheeres, H., Solomon, N., Boud, D., & Rooney, D. (2010). When is it OK to learn at work? The learning work of organizational practices. *Journal of Workplace Learning, 22*(1/2), 13–26. https://doi.org/10.1108/13665621011012825

Schumpeter, J. A. (1934). *The theory of economic development*. Harvard University Press.

Scott, S. G., & Bruce, R. A. (1994). Determinants of innovative behavior: A path model of individual innovation in the workplace. *Academy of Management Journal, 37*(3), 580–607. https://doi.org/10.2307/256701

SECLE. (2023). *Haastattelututkimus: Mitä työikäiset ajattelevat jatkuvasta oppimisesta.* [Interview study: What working-age adults think about continuous learning]. Retrieved from https://www.jotpa.fi/fi/julkaisut/tutkimukset/haastattelututkimus-mita-tyoikaiset-ihmiset-ajattelevat-jatkuvasta

Sessa, V. I., & London, M. (2006). *Continuous learning in organizations: Individual, group, and organizational perspectives*. Taylor & Francis.

Sfard, A. (1998). On two metaphors for learning and the dangers of choosing just one. *Educational Researcher, 27*(2), 4–13. https://doi.org/10.3102/0013189X027002004

Short, H. (2019). Learning in SMEs. *Human Resource Development International, 22*(5), 413–419. https://doi.org/10.1080/13678868.2019.1658368

Smith, R. (2017). Work(er)-driven innovation. *Journal of Workplace Learning, 29*(2), 110–123.

Sørensen, H., Ussing, L., Wandahl, S., & Christensen, R. (2018). Key mechanisms for employee-driven innovation in governmental client organizations. *International Journal of Entrepreneurship and Innovation Management, 22*(4–5), 427–450. https://doi.org/10.1504/IJEIM.2018.100 13629

Sossa, J., Rebolledob, J., Manuel, J., Hincapiéc, M., & Zartad, R. (2019). Innovation management models: A literature review. *International Journal of Innovation, Creativity, and Change, 10*(6), 175–194.

Sotarauta, M. (2023). *A plethora of transformative innovation policy tensions: Lessons for regional restructuring* (Sente Working Paper 51/2023). Tampere University.

Studemund, A., & Wallington, J. (2016). *The challenges of employee-driven innovation and its relation to decision structures* [Summary]. ENTN39 Master's Corporate Entrepreneurship and Innovation Internship and Degree Project. Lund University. https://www.lu.se/lup/publication/8876172/

Sundbo, J. (2003). Innovation and strategic reflexivity: An evolutionary approach applied to services. In L. V. Shavinina (Ed.), *The international handbook on innovation* (pp. 97–114). Pergamon. https://doi.org/10.1016/B978-008044198-6/50008-5

Suominen, A., Pihlajamaa, M., Deschryvere, M., Nieminen, M., Lehenkari, J., Bhatia, R., Lähteenmäki-Smith, K., Martins, J. T., Rilla, N., Hyytinen, K., Merisalo, M., Valkokari, K., & Hajikhani, A. (2024). *Shaping the future of Finnish innovation: The evolution of Finnish innovation policy and the path ahead*. VTT Technical Research Centre of Finland.

Svensson, L., Ellström, P.-E., & Åberg, C. (2004). Integrating formal and informal learning at work. *Journal of Workplace Learning, 16*(8), 479–491. https://doi.org/10.1108/13665620410566441

Taponen, J. (2023). *Poliisin vaikuttavuus: Suoritteiden laskennasta vaikuttavuuden tutkimukseen* [Police effectiveness: From performance calculations to impact research]. Doctoral dissertation, University of Helsinki.

Ulrich, F., & Mengiste, S. A. (2014). The challenges of creativity in software organizations. In B. Bergvall-Kåreborn & P. A. Nielsen (Eds.), *Creating value for all through ITB* (pp. 16–34). Springer.

Vähäsantanen, K., & Eteläpelto, A. (2018). Professional agency and learning in the work of software professionals. In C. Harteis (Ed.), *Machines – change – work: An educational view on the digitalization of work* (pp. 161–179). Springer.

Vanhanen, S. (2020). *Monialainen yhteistyö kotouttamisessa: Näkökulmana poliisin työ* [Multidisciplinary collaboration in integration: The perspective of police work]. University of Jyväskylä.

Voxted, S. (2018). Conditions of implementation of employee-driven innovation. *International Journal of Entrepreneurship and Innovation Management, 22*(4–5), 471–488. https://doi.org/10.1504/IJEIM.2018.092974

Vygotsky, L. S. (1978). Mind in society: The development of higher psychological processes. In M. Cole, V. John-Steiner, S. Scribner, & E. Souberman (Eds.), *Mind in society* (pp. 19–58). Harvard University Press.

Wang, L., Li, S., & You, Z. (2020). The effects of knowledge transfer on innovation capability: A moderated mediation model of absorptive capability and network reliance. *Journal of High Technology Management Research, 31*(1), Article 100372. https://doi.org/10.1016/j.hitech.2020.100372

Weisburd, D., & Majmundar, M. K. (Eds.). (2018). *Proactive policing: Effects on crime and communities*. National Academies Press. https://doi.org/10.17226/24928

Wenger, E. (1998). *Communities of practice: Learning, meaning, and identity*. Cambridge University Press. https://doi.org/10.1017/CBO978051180393

Wihlman, T., Hoppe, M., Sandström, U., & Sandmark, H. (2014). Employee-driven innovation in welfare services. *Nordic Journal of Working Life Studies, 4*(2), 159–180. https://doi.org/10.19154/njwls.v4i2.3869

Wilson, J. M., Boyer O'Leary, M., Metiu, A., & Jett, Q. R. (2008). Perceived proximity in virtual work: Explaining the paradox of far-but-close. *Organization Studies, 29*(7), 979–1002.

Chapter 2
Roles in LBI: Employees as Innovation Agents

Abstract This chapter examines, drawing on prior research and findings from the EDLI project, the significance and roles of employees in organizations' innovation activities. It provides a concise overview of the history of innovation research from the perspective of innovation roles, outlining the contemporary understanding of innovation as a human-centered phenomenon grounded in people's developmental actions and the construction of roles. The chapter also introduces the concept of innovation agency, a lens through which the roles and participation of different employees in innovation processes can be analyzed, understood, and developed. Furthermore, the chapter explores how innovation agency and innovation roles are constructed and manifested by analyzing qualitative interview data collected from both a police organization and a technology organization.

Keywords Innovation roles · Innovation agency · Participation · Role theories · Police organization · Technology organization · Interview data

To develop innovations that help organizations cope with the fast pace and new demands of work in a sustainable way, workplaces should make versatile use of the skills, experience, and ideas of the entire staff (Ellström, 2010). All employees, regardless of their job description and industry, have a huge amount of understanding and expertise related to everyday work, organizational operations, and work content, as they concretely apply work practices, observe the challenges and gaps, and continuously gather new information from clients, colleagues, and other networks (Kesting & Ulhøi, 2010). However, this potential will not be realized unless personnel have real opportunities to participate in innovation activities in the organization's everyday life and development projects. Participation in this context refers not only to a person's physical presence (representation) in a certain situation but also to their real involvement. Based on Billett's (2004) description, participation is understood as a multi-stage process of acquiring, gathering, combining, applying, reflecting on, and sharing information in the community and work environment. It is a central starting point for agency and the definition of roles at work. This chapter starts from the foundation of employee-driven innovation (EDI) (Høyrup, 2010), based on the

S. Lemmetty, *Learning-Based Innovation*,
SpringerBriefs in Education, https://doi.org/10.1007/978-3-032-26911-9_2

idea that every employee, regardless of their formal position or task, develops or has the potential to develop different innovation roles in working life and workplaces. These roles describe and guide participation in innovation activities, but they also limit and enable it. In this book, a role is seen as a construct, the development of which is a complex sociocultural process. The purpose is to explore the following question: How can the innovation role, which determines participation in learning-based innovation (LBI) activities in working life, be constructed and implemented from the perspective of agency?

2.1 Innovation Roles and Agency

If a new person asks you what role you play in your job, what do you answer? Most often, the answer is based on a formal job title or job description. But what kind of image does this answer give the questioner about the innovativeness of your work? For example, if your title is inventor or product developer, the questioner may see you as a busy ideator with a floppy hat on your head. If you are a financial coordinator or production worker, you may be perceived as a precise Excel operator or an implementer of production line routines. This way of perceiving work roles through titles and organizational structures reflects, on the one hand, classical sociology (M. Weber, 1904–1905/1980, 1917/1946), in which roles are seen as positions of status and power, and, on the other hand, the early tradition of social psychology, in which roles are seen as being built on expected actions (Mead, 1934). The research literature has produced a wealth of understanding regarding what roles are in working life, or in life in general, and how they develop, and these traditional role concepts are still very much alive in our everyday lives. To date, roles have been studied to a fairly limited extent in the context of innovation activities, with innovation research typically focusing on processes, outcomes, and strategies. However, role perspectives are touched upon in several theoretical frameworks for innovation research. The employee-driven innovation (EDI) framework is an excellent example of this, as its underlying idea is that the employee plays a central role in the development of innovations. This chapter examines innovation roles as constructs in which structures related to the environment, social expectations and conditions, and the agency of the individual (activity, influence, and thinking) are central.

2.1.1 Theoretical Foundations of Roles

When examining working-life roles, one could focus on theories developed within the frameworks of numerous diverse scientific disciplines, but it would not be meaningful to present all of them here. However, in the big picture, role studies rely on one central dichotomy: roles as given and existing expectations versus roles as diverse constructions. In the studies of Max Weber (see e.g. Weber, 1922), who did not actually describe roles through the concept of a role but was interested in status positions and ideal types, the individual's position and role in society were seen as aspects of ready-made structures. Weber particularly examined the formation of capitalism, organizations, and power in modern society. His concept of the *ideal type* refers to a clearly structured analytical model, such as the ideal type of bureaucracy, based on a position of authority in which an individual's status is determined by rules, hierarchy, and the division of tasks. In this context, the role is not negotiable by the individual; rather, it is constructed through the expectations and structures that come with the position.

The importance of role expectations is also central to George Herbert Mead's role theory (1934). Mead viewed the individual as adopting roles through the expectations of others, reflecting on them "through the eyes of another" and constructing the self in interaction with the social environment. Mead's analysis is located at the micro level, while Weber's approach represents a macro-level structural perspective. Moreover, Mead focused more explicitly on the interactive processes through which expectations are internalized, whereas Weber considered the structural conditions that define them. Nonetheless, both approaches converge in viewing roles as shaped by external expectations rather than individual choice. Thus, the individual acts in relation to social structures and social expectations, which ties both views to the first perspective of the dichotomy presented earlier (i.e., roles as given and based on expectations). This approach is also visible in organizational role research, which emphasizes the guiding influence of organizational structures and rules on individual actions (Nyström et al., 2014): The individual accepts the role given in the workplace and fulfills the expectations associated with it. From this perspective, roles are determined through organizational tasks and responsibilities.

The theories described above have been criticized for presenting overly static, generalizable, and individual-centered views of roles and action. Thus, more recent sociological and social psychological literature has emphasized roles as socially and culturally constructed, negotiated, and changing constructs. The modern constructionist trend retains the idea of the relationship between the individual, the community, and society, but the individual's role in the formation of roles, and in shaping the structures influencing roles, is seen as more central. According to Peter Berger and Thomas Luckmann (1966), individuals participate in the construction of roles through a process in which thoughts and patterns of action go through three stages:

- *Externalization:* The individual articulates their ideas and practices, which become visible through social interaction.
- *Objectification:* The community begins to perceive these practices as real and stable, leading to their institutionalization.
- *Internalization:* Individuals adopt these practices as part of their own thinking and actions, making them an integral part of culture and everyday structures.

In this perspective, roles are not simply given; rather, they are shaped in continuous interaction between individuals and communities. Similar thinking is found in sociologist Anthony Giddens's (1984, 1991) description of role construction. For Giddens, roles are behavioral patterns and expectations associated with particular societal positions and are thus shaped by social norms, cultural values, and institutional structures, but they are not permanent or predetermined; instead, roles are constantly renewed through individuals' actions. In Giddens's model, roles provide a framework whereby individuals not only navigate social situations and interact with others but also actively construct their roles through their everyday actions and choices. Through their actions, individuals can shape and redefine role expectations, thus influencing social change. Giddens emphasized the importance of reflexivity in the construction of roles, referring to the ability of individuals to reflect on and evaluate their own actions and their consequences, question existing roles, challenge social norms, and envision alternative ways of being and acting.

Nyström et al. (2014) identified three ways of understanding roles as constructed rather than predetermined tasks in organizational practice and research. The first is the symbolic interactionist perspective in which roles are not given; rather, they are actively taken over by individuals and shaped by their own goals, experiences, and social contexts (Callero, 1994; Nyström et al., 2014). In other words, a role is not determined by position but by how a person acts and interprets a situation and by how others respond to their actions. The second is the resource-based approach, emphasizing that roles are constructed in relation to the resources that individuals possess and that are available to them, such as social networks, cultural capital, and material conditions (Baker & Faulkner, 1991; Nyström et al., 2014). In this perspective, a role is also a tool, allowing an actor to utilize, strengthen, or expand their own resources within the organization. The third perspective, based on action, emphasizes that roles arise through practical action and interaction. Thus, rather than being a permanent position, a role is constantly shaped according to how actors participate in joint work and the achievement of goals (Heikkinen et al., 2007). Common to these perspectives is the idea of roles as reciprocally and interactively constructed phenomena: Individuals not only fulfill the roles assigned to them in the workplace, but they also create and shape them as part of the organization's everyday practices and innovative activities.

In innovation research, the structure and formation of roles have so far been examined only to a limited extent. Most studies have focused on identifying roles either at different stages of the innovation process or on an individual basis, describing individuals based on their characteristics as different *innovation actors* regardless of the situation. Particular attention has been paid to those individuals who act in visible and exceptionally active roles. For example, Roberts and Fusfeld (1980) described how the role of idea developers is emphasized in the early stages of the innovation process. They are followed by so-called champions (see also Murray & Ron, 2010) who take new ideas forward, present them to management, and act as bold leaders or use various strategies to get members of the organization to support the idea. These champions have been described as risk takers and as proactive individuals who have a decisive influence on innovation's success or failure (Howell et al., 2005; Rost et al., 2007). One of the roles mentioned is that of gatekeepers (or boundary spanners), who act as information brokers between the organization's internal and external environments. Gatekeepers monitor new technologies, market changes, and external trends and make this information available for the organization's use (Roberts & Fusfeld,

1980). In addition to these, research has described role of so-called promoters, whom Gemünden et al. (2007) considered to be key supporters of innovation activities. The promoter model they presented has four informal roles: expert promoter, who reinforces technical expertise; power promoter, who utilizes hierarchical position and resources; process promoter, who supports networking and knowledge sharing within the organization; relationship promoter, who builds and maintains collaboration with actors outside the organization (Mansfeld et al., 2010).

What these roles have in common is that they are not tied to formal organizational positions: They can occur at the top-management, middle-management, or even expert level (Murray & Ron, 2010). Although these descriptions highlight the central figures in innovation activities, they are often based on an individualistic perspective, focusing attention on the characteristics and actions of individuals. Such an approach leaves less attention to the environment, situation, and context—how roles are constructed through interaction, change over time, and are related to employees' learning, growth, and experience. Furthermore, traditional role research emphasizes roles that are easily observable and visible, such as idea developers, champions, and promoters. This limits the visibility of many other potentially significant roles that can support innovation at the everyday level and thus enable a more diverse starting point for organizational development. Therefore, research should also pay attention to latent and evolving roles, which reflect the active agency of employees and the dynamic construction of roles in everyday organizational life.

2.1.2 Agency in Embodying Innovation Roles

From Giddens's (1984) perspective, a role is constructed in the interaction between individual agency and social structures. In this approach, agency is an individual characteristic or an individual's active action, structures represent the social and institutional contexts of an action, and a role is something that is constructed in the interaction between the two. However, in the study of professional agency, agency itself has been understood as being formed in the interaction between the individual and the environment (e.g., Eteläpelto et al., 2013), with the individual's abilities, background, and social relations overlapping with the structural conditions. From this perspective, agency can be seen as a phenomenon largely corresponding to Giddens's definition of a role—or even as a concept describing a role in itself. Professional agency refers to employees' participation and active involvement in working life, enabling them to influence, build, shape, and maintain their own (career) paths, work identities, and work-related practices and environments rather than simply adapting to the prevailing circumstances (Eteläpelto et al., 2013). Thus, agency at work focuses on both development and renewal, but also on maintaining what exists (Vähäsantanen & Eteläpelto, 2015).

Professional agency has been conceptualized as both a capacity and an activity (e.g., Goller & Paloniemi, 2017, 2022). The capacity perspective emphasizes self-initiated and goal-oriented activity in working life, guided by an individual's inclinations, abilities, and competences. Based on capacity perspective, agency is seen as a relatively permanent characteristic—in the same way as in the role types described above—that is attached to personality. When agency is understood mainly as an individual's capacity, the effects of the work environment and its sociocultural opportunities are largely ignored (Goller & Harteis, 2017). Goller and Paloniemi (2022) illustrated how agency should not be conceptualized as a permanent trait or capacity, but as a process that is attached to the context, mediated through interaction and reflection. In addition to examining agency at the individual level, sociocultural research on agency has focused on the individual's opportunities to act and participate in their work (e.g., Eteläpelto, 2017), given that an individual's intentions and aspirations are not only internal to the mind or linked to knowledge and abilities but also in multiple connections with other people and operating environments (Hakanurmi et al., 2021; Vanhalakka-Ruoho & Ruponen, 2013). In this case, agency is not something that people can have (e.g., a characteristic, ability, or competence) but something that people do, implement, and achieve within the possibilities and limitations offered by the work environment (Biesta et al., 2015). Action is thus not detached from the context but manifested in the interaction between the individual and the environment.

The subject-centered sociocultural perspective on agency developed by Eteläpelto et al. (2013) is based on the idea of professional agency at work, with individuals and communities influencing work by using opportunities for influence. This considers individuals' experience, competence, and expertise as well as motivations, interests, and ideals as part of agency, while recognizing that agency is expressed for a specific purpose and within the historically shaped sociocultural and material conditions of the workplace. Therefore, in research, the individual and social perspectives on agency can be seen as analytically separate but mutually constructive. From a sociocultural perspective, professional agency is expressed in terms of choices and intentional actions related to work tasks (Eteläpelto et al., 2013). In this case, agency is understood as actions that are directed at work (Forsman, 2023; Priestley et al., 2012) or through which professionals influence their work and organization (Eteläpelto et al., 2013).

In this book, I limit the examination of agency specifically to innovation work. The examination of agency in innovation work is appropriate, as agency has been described as specifically required to improve working conditions and to learn at work (Eteläpelto et al., 2013). It has been seen to manifest as active, positive initiatives aimed *at developing* work practices (Messmann & Mulder, 2017) or as a critical attitude opposing externally proposed reforms (Vähäsantanen & Billett, 2008). In development work, practicing agency through active participation in social practices is seen as a starting point (Goller & Billett, 2014). In this book, I approach agency as influencing the organizational innovation activities through which I see innovation roles being built. Therefore, I focus on so-called *innovation agency*. I consider innovation agency as a subcategory of professional agency, as the majority of innovation occurs within organizational and professional contexts. It can be sharply defined as agentic actions aimed at achieving innovation-related goals within the framework of institutional structures and constraints.

The concept of innovation agency comes close to the concept of transformational agency, which refers to the employee's ability and desire to actively change their own or their community's work based on their everyday experiences and perceived needs (Kerosuo & Jokinen, 2023; Tuominen & Lehtonen, 2017). This can be considered a special form of professional agency, focusing on the relationship with change and change work. However, transformational agency is often defined in relation to change (e.g., Hyrkkö & Kajamaa, 2025), not necessarily in relation to novelty. For this reason, restorative or reconstructive action can be understood as transformational agency if it focuses on modifying existing practices—albeit toward a previous model. The key difference between transformational and innovation agency is therefore related to the emphasis on novelty value and change value. On the one hand, innovation agency requires the production of novelty—an activity that creates something that has not previously been used in the context in question. On the other hand, transformational agency can focus on any change, in which case it is important to note that not all change is innovation. While innovation is often associated with change more generally (Kerosuo et al., 2010), as new things are seen as drivers of change, Martins and Terblanche (2003), for example, observed that a change in practices can also be a return to the old and familiar—not always the introduction of something new. For this reason, this chapter further limits the examination of agency within transformational agency to innovation agency, although it is not yet an established or widely accepted concept in the research literature.

Since agency is socioculturally constructed, formal positions, statuses, and job descriptions also influence how individuals perceive their capacity to exercise agency, that is, how strong their sense of agency is (Eteläpelto et al., 2013; Goller & Paloniemi, 2017). For example, employees in supervisory positions tend to demonstrate stronger agency at work than nonsupervisory employees. Moreover, the forms of agency differ: Supervisors often display *developmental agency*, whereas employees more commonly exhibit *survival* or *adaptive agency* (Hökkä & Vähäsantanen, 2014). According to Billett (2014), a higher occupational position also provides greater *agentic affordances*, meaning opportunities to act independently. However, research on the connections between professional agency, employee roles, and formal positions remains limited, and little is known about the forms of innovation agency exercised by employees in different positions.

2.2 Role Construction Through Innovation Agency in Police and Technology Work

In the EDLI research project, I examined innovation roles and their construction in the technology organization and in the preventive work of the Finnish police from the perspective of innovation agency. The starting point was the idea of agency as a relational and context-dependent phenomenon (Eteläpelto et al., 2013; Glăveanu, 2015). Innovation agency was analytically defined as an individual-driven desire and active influence that is related to the opportunities offered by the environment (organization and work)—that is, the context. Thus, the object of examination was both the individual's action and the context of the action, which together determine the innovation agency that is being constructed. In the EDLI research project, I wanted to find out what forms of innovation agency appeared in the target organizations, what kinds of innovation roles the research participants had at the time of the research, and how these roles were seen as being constructed through different levels of agency.

2.2.1 Open, Seeming, and Rebellious Innovation Agency

The interviews with police and technology personnel revealed different forms of innovation agency, depending on how the individual's influence on development work was expressed in relation to the opportunities offered to them. Based on the analysis, innovation agency can manifest in three ways: *open*, *seeming*, and *rebellious*.

2.2.1.1 Open Innovation Agency

Open innovation agency is enabled by the job description and the situation in relation to the individual's efforts to influence. It is active, visible, direct, and enabled agency that is also externally observable. Open innovation agency is established in situations in which the individual's desire to participate in innovation meets the opportunities offered to them. The most typical *opportunities* described in the data consist of an attentive and open discussion culture in a team or group, which was seen to offer experiences of truly being heard and thereby influencing development activities:

> It is often the case that when we start doing something completely new, we think about where it could start. We have had a good culture of free discussion. Everyone [in this team] has been able to say whatever comes to mind. (PP12, Police)
>
> We [in the team] took on a development target, such as meeting practices. [...] For that [development], we took a short pause so as we could discuss together. (PP19, Police)
>
> In my opinion, ideas have been listened to and taken into account quite well here, and they've asked [...] what changes are needed. Surprisingly well, I've actually been able to share my own views. (TP29, Technology)

In both organizations, in addition to a culture of discussion and asking for opinions, the space, time, and places provided for influencing were emphasized. This space can be a formally organized opportunity for co-development or a practice for collecting ideas that is integrated into the organization's processes:

> We [police officers doing a certain type of work from different locations] spent two days in [location where they gathered] going through this [our work], and we also took some good practices from there. And there was talk that this would become a regular event, that we would gather twice a year to develop this activity. (PP17, Police)

> We have this initiative system where we can make a proposal, and then they're rewarded if it's feasible […] I think it's a really good system; people use it for work in general, even if it doesn't directly concern their own tasks. There have actually been some really good ideas that have come from it, and a few have even been implemented. (TP12, Technology)

As can be seen from the above quotations, the opportunities focus on spaces for sharing ideas and thoughts, but also on the supervisor's attitude, stance, and role as a provider of opportunities. The supervisor's accepting attitude toward new ideas is thus central to the construction of open innovation agency:

> Here, people can bring ideas. There have been team meetings where superiors lead by saying, "Hey, come and tell us what you think." And then people get the experience that this is taken seriously, especially if it can be shown that it has actually been implemented. (TP3, Technology)

> We are specifically allowed to develop this preventive activity here and do our own projects. [For example,] projects have been done with schools based on what has been considered important in this area, and we also do not burden the supervisor, because for him it is a reporting matter—that "we have done this and this and this." (PP17, Police)

2.2.1.2 Seeming Innovation Agency

Seeming innovation agency refers to agency that is built in situations in which an individual is willing and active in terms of development and influence, but their work only partially or seemingly enables it (See also Welling, 2025). Seeming innovation agency is reflected in the fact that an individual's innovation efforts are not fully enabled by the environment and structures, but they are not directly neglected either. Seeming innovation agency includes the idea of a slight conflict between the individual's actions and desires and the structures. This was emphasized in situations in which, in principle, one can express one's own opinions, but according to one interviewee, "nothing follows" from this:

> I have even separately gone to discuss this with the department management, sharing the observations I've made. However, overall, it has sometimes felt like things are falling on deaf ears. (PP14, Police)

In the technology organization, seeming innovation agency is constructed in situations in which an individual's formal role (e.g., title or described areas of responsibility) may suggest that they are responsible for innovation and influencing development work; however, in reality, the person does not subjectively feel that their position provides corresponding opportunities because of various organizational structures, values, or modes of operation. The next quotation illustrates a case in which a person formally has the possibility to present ideas, yet real opportunities for influence are lacking. Innovation thus becomes more of a rhetoric of participation than genuine influence. The speaker's ironic tone reflects an awareness of this contradiction:

> We do express our opinions on things quite honestly, but there's a contradiction in that I don't really know what kind of weight they carry. I mean, I'm "just" here as a [mentions title and position, which in principle could also include innovation activities], so what do I have to say about it [said sarcastically]? Some of the suggestions we've made […] have

> been completely ruled out [...]. I have a lot of these creative ideas. [...]. Sometimes when I've thought about those decisions, I've joked that there must have been torches and black robes involved when they were made, because there's no other logic to it, and nobody knows anything about [the decision-making processes]. (TP6, Technology)

In the police organization, surveys or other practices that collect information from personnel but are not actually utilized in the development of the organization reflect seeming agency. In such situations, the individual is offered a formal opportunity to express their views, but these views have no real impact on decision-making or the direction of development, or at least it does not become visible to the employee. It is possible that the employee's view has been considered, but the feedback loop does not function, meaning that the organization does not clearly communicate how employee's initiative has been realized. For the individual, this appears as an experience of not having any real agency in the development process. Seeming innovation agency is also established in situations in which the individual participates in, for example, a development meeting but has no opportunity to be heard. Thus, participation appears to be symbolic rather than an activity enabling real participation and influence:

> No one bothers to respond to [the surveys] anymore, because the results are just damn terrible: People are exhausted and overworked. Those [results] are always somehow nicely twisted [by higher management] into something like, "well, the staff must have misunderstood the question." (PP22, Police)

In the police organization, it was observed that opportunities to participate in training that can provide new ideas and thereby tools for developing new practices often materialize as tasks performed alongside one's regular work, but their content and implementation are inappropriate or superficial (see Lemmetty, 2024a). This reflects a form of seeming agency:

> Such things are done alongside regular work or on a designated day when you're clicking through these [online courses], but in reality, they're just fulfilling the letter of the law—"everyone has now been informed about this and given the opportunity to familiarize themselves with these regulations." In that way, the organization can, in principle, wash its hands of it, saying the matter has been handled, but no genuine, deeper learning actually takes place. (PP20, Police)

In general, seeming innovation agency emerges in situations in which the nature of work or its processes can, in principle, enable innovation, influence, and the expression of one's voice, yet, for one reason or another, this does not occur in practice. This becomes evident in situations in which individuals lack the time to perform or develop their core work in ways that they personally consider meaningful or that their formal job descriptions would suggest are possible:

> The pressure for investigations is intense, limiting other activities, but if there were more time available, we could design projects and shape our work to a greater extent. (PP8, Police)

2.2.1.3 Rebellious Innovation Agency

Rebellious innovation agency emerges in situations in which an individual advances innovation efforts that they personally consider important, but they do so indirectly or in ways deemed unacceptable from the organization's perspective, as the existing structures do not allow for direct, rule-compliant, or formal participation at all. The individual actively seeks to contribute, express their views, and develop new ideas, yet structural constraints hinder these efforts. In such cases, agency is expressed indirectly or even manipulatively, and it may appear as a violation of rules, guidelines, or established operating models, especially from an upper-level perspective.

In the police, rebellious innovation agency more clearly contradicts the organizational operating models, as because of bureaucracy and hierarchies, the direction of operations should in principle be clear and set in stone. In the following quotation, rebellious agency manifests in terms of circumventing power and structures instead of directly challenging them, as directly challenging is not seen as having real effects. Through agency, weaknesses in the system (e.g., the leader's need to own ideas and appear to be the decision-maker) are exploited to promote an innovative goal. Participation thus occurs invisibly, but it was perceived as more effective than striving for direct influence:

> [The] leaders who are responsible for these [certain things] up there in the ivory tower: They don't know what police work is like in the field today, when it's four in the morning and people are coming out of bars. They are far removed from it, but they are the people who make decisions about these matters. Then they form a working group from that fossilized base, and someone is appointed to lead that working group. I've also been in such working groups, where, in my opinion, very innovative, good ideas have been proposed that could be developed further, but they don't [progress] if the idea doesn't belong to the leader of that working group. So I've found a tactic to "sell" it as their own idea, in which case it might get approved. This is our system. (PP22, Police)

The context of the technology sector is more flexible with regard of innovation agency. Thus, rebellious agency does not necessarily appear as manipulation or actual violations of rules or processes (the rules and processes being less strict), but rather as neglect of a commonly accepted or typical way of operating or as a decision to act independently, even if the idea does not receive wider support:

> There would still be an opportunity to influence things, and if it would make the work of [the other department] easier, then it would be worth doing. And I think it should be done. If they don't believe it, I'll do it myself. (TP24, Technology)

Rebellious agency is, by nature, even more determined and self-directed than open or seeming agency. It often manifests as independent decision-making in situations in which rules or guidelines do not provide clear direction or are even highly ambiguous, as in the exploitation of so-called *loopholes*:

> Because these are again such multidimensional issues, the law may say one thing, but we also have to consider what this will cause [...]. It leads to a longer-term reflection on what my actions in this time and place will then cause for those [people]. (PP1, Police)

2.2.1.4 Summary

In the context of innovation activity, agency can take the following forms in the interaction between the individual and the environment:

1. *Open*—the individual's aspirations and the organization's possibilities are in harmony; thus, the role is consistent from the perspective of both the individual's activities and the environment.
2. *Seeming*—the individual formally influences innovation activity, but their influence is symbolic and limited to the level of speech; thus, the role becomes contradictory and unclear.
3. *Rebellious*—the individual seeks to participate in innovation activity contrary to prevailing structures, norms, or hierarchies or in questionable situations; thus, agency is placed in a tense relationship with the organization's official practices and can appear questionable or violate common acceptance. In such cases, roles manifest as hidden or shadowy positions.

Open innovation agency was the form of agency most strongly observed in both the police and technology organizations. It represents the ideal version of innovation agency, in which an individual's motivation and proactivity align with the opportunities provided by the organization. Typically, descriptions of open agency were contextualized in one's own work, the team's work, and everyday practices. By contrast, *seeming* innovation agency was more pronounced in the police organization, in which agency appeared more conflicted than in the technology organization. Rebellious innovation agency was not particularly common, but it occurred more frequently in the police, in which it was strongly contextualized within bureaucratic and hierarchical decision-making that did not always allow for employees' open innovation agency. Rebellious innovation agency is an especially interesting form of agency from an ethical perspective. In the police organization, it was reflected in, for example, balancing the law, regulations, and guidelines against one's own moral judgment and reasoning.

2.2.2 *Drivers, Advocates, Ideators, and Thinkers*

The forms of innovation agency described above are situational rather than inherent individual traits: In one situation, agency may be open, while in another, it may be rebellious, depending on the balance between the individual's interests and aspirations and the opportunities afforded by the context. When attention shifts to understanding roles in relation to innovation activity more generally, the examination of innovation agency becomes less situational and more stable.

In the EDLI project, a cross-sectional analysis was conducted of the target organizations' current innovation roles: What kind of innovation role did each research participant appear to occupy in their organization at the time of the study? Based on this analysis, four innovation role types were constructed. Although the typology aimed to generalize individuals' roles at that moment, these roles were viewed not as permanent or based on individual traits but as emerging through agency developed over time. Agency was understood here as evolving. A central aim was to identify the determinants explaining why individuals fell into different role types. The following section presents the innovation role types identified in the data, based on differing levels of agency.

2.2.2.1 Drivers

Drivers are employees who represent a strong innovation role. They are individuals who act as an internal engine and trend setter within the organization. They strive to promote development and renewal at the level of the entire organization, viewing innovations as broad, future-oriented wholes. Their actions are based on a vision and a desire to build a long-term organizational direction. Their speech is directed at others—colleagues, teams, and management—rather than at their own work:

> [I act] kind of like the driver, in terms of content. I don't have managerial responsibility as such […] it's a natural role with other teams; we collaborate closely with everyone, and it's quite natural—there's not much asking whether something needs to be done. If something is agreed on, it has to be done, and that creates a bit of a managerial role. But for me, my work is [focused on] engineering, design work related to products, and closer to collaboration between management and various company departments […] so a kind of intermediary role, where in daily work I act as an interpreter for people, trying to understand the big picture and articulate all the time what the company wants. I feel that it's my role to be there correctly, not going against what someone in management thinks. (TP15, Technology)

The role of a driver is typically built on long experience and deep organizational knowledge. Drivers have often gradually progressed to their current position. Their own activism has provided them with opportunities to participate. Over time, this shapes the structures around them, increasing both their credibility and their ability to influence. They operate at interfaces, connecting different units and stakeholders and striving to create an open and inclusive atmosphere in which others can develop and innovate:

> I have been at the police department [describes work as a chief]. We haven't had [this kind of work] before, so I've had very free hands to develop and invent, and then I've given free rein again to the unit and function leaders, because they know their own operational environment. I've given the message: Innovate, be open, and make suggestions. Even though I have long police experience and experience in many roles, it's been a long time since I've been out on the beat. (PP3, Police)

In practice, drivers guide and support others, gather information from different sources, and form broad conclusions and visions based on it. Their role is strategic and future-oriented: They strive and are able to shape structures and processes that support the renewal and continuous development of the organization. In this way, they act as drivers of development—as showers of direction and maintainers of change. The agency of drivers is therefore strong at the organizational level: They have influence over the organization's strategic decisions and development policies as well as over other members of the community, often across unit and team boundaries. From their perspective, the organizational structures appear to be open and capable of development.

In the police, the role of a driver is achieved through a formal position and title: long work experience, position and training together provide the opportunity to act as a decision-maker and influencer. By contrast, in the technology organization, the role is not so much based on a formal position; rather, the role of a driver is likely to be achieved through a long career and extensive experience, a broad understanding of the cultural and historical nature of the organization and product development, and the development of interpersonal relationships:

> I don't have managerial responsibilities, but the company still uses me as a kind of consultant, someone whose job is to drive things forward. (TP20, Technology)

2.2.2.2 Advocates

Advocates represent an innovation role in which an individual acts as a mediator of information, messages, and views between different teams and sometimes also departments. They focus primarily on current and near-future work and examine innovations on a more limited scale than at the organizational level, most often from the perspective of their own team, group, or operating unit. Innovation work is primarily aimed at improving internal practices and the smoothness of everyday life, although they also justify development through broader organizational goals. Advocates see innovation primarily as practical solutions that facilitate, enhance, and renew existing work:

> Some colleagues say, "What about this?" and then I can either tell them that they can contact someone themselves, or I will take the matter forward. (TP12, Technology)

> If there is something that is wrong or could be done differently, it's not always that I tell them, "Don't do it this way; do it this way instead," but I expect that some ideas will also come from the employees. (PP9, Police)

Advocates describe their role as information gatherers and communicators who convey views in different directions within the organization. Their task is to listen, ask questions, and convey the experiences and observations of different parties to support decision-making. Their work is strongly linked to the development culture defined by the drivers: They make what the drivers are striving for at the strategic level a reality in practice. This makes their role very practical, closely linked to everyday work, experimentation, and the implementation of small development steps:

> I repair a lot; if something breaks [they come to tell me], somewhere between heaven and earth, I go and replace it with a new one. You don't always know in the morning what you will have to do in the evening, as far as the so-called urgent things are concerned. (TP17, Technology)

Often, advocates have worked on the same team or task for several years and have thus gained a deep understanding of the everyday work and a sufficiently extensive organizational network. They use this experience to highlight employees' perspectives and forward them to management or other units. They can make decisions on internal matters within their own team, but larger changes often require approval from higher levels. Their innovation agency is moderate from an organizational level: They get their messages heard at many organizational levels and are thus able to influence innovations, but they do not have opportunities to make large-scale decisions within the organization. Structures appear to them as enabling—as something that creates space for initiative.

In both the police and technology organizations, the role of an advocate is typically attached to a formal immediate supervisor or a team leader position. The position is achieved through work experience.

2.2.2.3 Ideators

Ideators represent an innovation role in which an individual critically examines their own work, its practices, and the organization's operating models from their own perspective. Their role is more focused on thinking, evaluating, and generating new ideas than on large-scale development work or decision-making. Ideators constantly reflect on the meaning of their work and the possibilities for improving it. They actively present their own views, suggestions, and experiences, especially to their closest colleagues. They often feel that they influence the organization's operations, for example, by providing feedback to their superiors or through formal development processes:

> Some new ideas have come up, and then we sort of examine whether they are of any use. But of course, the routine tasks are also running alongside that. (TP23, Technology)

The innovation role of ideators is critical in nature: They evaluate other people's ideas and organizational practices and changes, bringing their own views to the discussion. Their thinking and actions are often more reactive than proactive, relating to everyday problems, customer needs, or colleagues' observations. They actively defend their own work and their own views on it. The role is built on different career backgrounds and experiences: Some have worked for only a few years, and others for over a decade, but what they have in common is the desire to participate and influence the development of the work:

> In a way, the decision-making side has been outsourced, but in practice, knowledge is power. (TP18, Technology)

Ideators operate within existing structures and feel that their current position is sufficient: Broader decision-making is seen as the responsibility of management or other people. When their own ideas do not progress or are not considered more widely, they may experience their efforts as frustrating or burdensome. However, they actively utilize official feedback channels and other opportunities for influence:

> After all, we ourselves are thinking about how to do it and what we could try in it and what would work, but of course within the framework. (PP5, Police)

The innovation role of ideators is therefore fundamentally critical and reflective. They act as everyday developers who highlight problems and opportunities in their work and challenge established practices. Structures seem to guide them, offering orientation and influence but limiting their participation in broader development work. Although their influence is limited and guided by structures, their continuous idea generation and evaluation maintains the potential for organizational renewal and critical thinking. Their innovation agency seems critical because they actively see and communicate the problems they observe in the organization, which is important in organizational development work. However, they do not necessarily want or are not enabled to develop organizational-level solutions for problems, which limits their influence in organizational-level innovation activities:

> I wish that someone would always think about these things, so that I don't have to [in this position] go and say, "Are you really sure?" (TP21, Technology)

> In the bigger picture, some changes should be made so that this thing stays together; I guess those gentlemen are thinking a lot about how to get out of this. (PP18, Police)

2.2.2.4 Thinkers

Thinkers represent an innovation role in which the individual's participation in development is minimal or invisible, albeit with the potential for innovative thinking and participation. They do not usually actively participate in development or innovation work, but they can use their own influence when specifically asked to share their views. The potential innovation agency of thinkers thus appears in moments when they reflect on their work practices, consider development opportunities, or react to questions and suggestions posed by others. The passivity of the role is often related to the limited or unclear opportunities for work development. The work is primarily perceived as practical and doable, even though thinkers have a good understanding of the challenges and development needs of the work:

> The supervisor has asked [for opinions], saying, "Now tell us any suggestions that come to mind [...]". We are doing [this work], so we know it anyway. [...] We do talk [among colleagues] a bit. We do exchange ideas, like this could be done this way or that, but then they get forgotten [and are not carried forward]. (TP26, Technology)

Thinkers typically have a short work history in the organization, often only 1 or 2 years, and their previous work experience may not be related to the same field. They recognize some formal channels for influencing, including team meetings, feedback surveys, and ideation processes, but self-initiated participation in them is rare. Thinkers reflect on and justify work practices among themselves, but they do not usually actively seek to change them. They mainly bring forward their views when requested to do so by a superior or a person responsible for development.

The innovation role of thinkers is characterized by low initiative, and their potential agency is not yet fully realized: They do not set out to develop the organization or its operations on their own initiative, and the organizational structures do not yet offer this to them:

> Usually we do this work as we are told, [which is] why it [innovation] is a difficult question in this work. (TP27, Technology)

Their participation is largely based on external encouragement, questions, or calls for development. They often feel that their job description does not actually fall within the scope of development or innovation. The role of thinkers is therefore potential: They have capabilities and views, but their emergence requires the organization's active invitation and support.

Thinkers were only located in the technology organization: There was not a single thinker among participants carrying out preventive work in the police. This probably reflects the higher individual responsibility of the own work and proactivity of preventive work, in which at least one's own everyday work is inevitably renewed. By contrast, some of the routine-like work positions in the technology organization basically enabled developmental passivity whereby work could only be carried out based on the instructions given.

2.2.2.5 Summary

Through the innovation role analysis, it was observed that innovation agency develops over a long period of time (see Fig. 2.1) as an individual's actions expand from their own work to various organizational areas. Through formal—or informal—career development and broadening expertise and experience, agency develops from the potential agency of thinkers toward the strong agency of drivers.

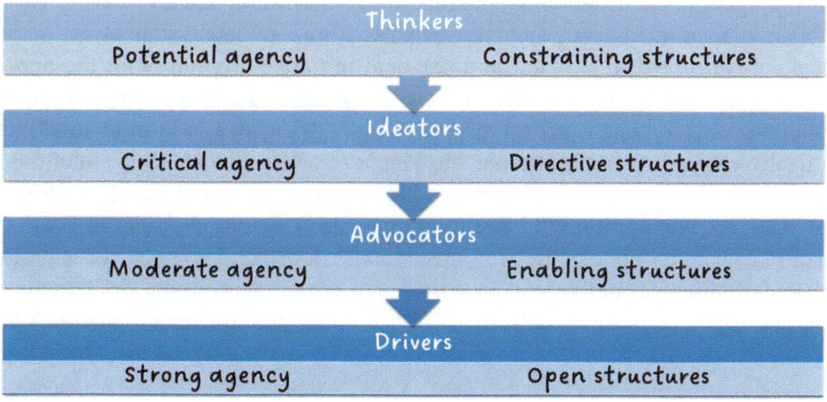

Fig. 2.1 Developing innovation agency

Since drivers and advocates have typically worked in the organization for a long time, they have had the opportunity to witness and experience the long-term outcomes of previous innovation processes at either the group or organizational level. They thus see opportunities for development as broader, viewing their involvement more positively. Moreover, they have learned to recognize hidden processes within the organization. As a result, they tend to view structures as more flexible, are better able to leverage them, and have gained positive experiences from participating in innovative activities, which has strengthened their agency. Thus, over their long careers, they have actively *cleared* the path toward their current level of agency through experiences. By contrast, the agency of thinkers and ideators is more strongly defined by organizational structures. Ideators approach innovation activities in organizations critically, perceiving more conflicts and issues in structures than representatives of other groups. Thinkers have very limited agency and do not actively seek to strengthen it themselves, but they participate in innovation work when straightly asked. Thus, the agency of thinkers is strongest through structures, appearing as potential agency that is not realized in direct action. The majority of organizational actors are ideators making their role particularly central at the organizational level.

2.3 From Static Role Conceptions to Evolving Innovation Agency: Lessons Learned

Based on the EDLI project, this chapter finds that employees' roles in innovation are constructed and conveyed through participation in everyday work. By examining the speech of personnel in the police and technology organizations, it was possible to understand how innovation agency—which manifests as influence and participation (i.e., an individual's desire to influence and the opportunities for influence provided by the organization)—can take different forms. The chapter identifies three main forms of agency: open, seeming, and rebellious innovation agency.

Open innovation agency can be seen as a kind of ideal state, with an individual's desire for development and personal initiative aligning with the opportunities provided by the organization. This corresponds to a subject-centered sociocultural perspective on agency (cf. Eteläpelto et al., 2013), in which individual factors (motivation, expertise, commitment, etc.) interact with organizational structures and resources. In this way, agency emerges that is constructive and visible both for the individual and the community. Seeming innovation agency, by contrast, reflects a situation in which opportunities for agency exist in principle but do not materialize into actual influence. Individuals take up the offered opportunities, yet structural or cultural barriers prevent the activity from becoming genuine development. Agency thus remains superficial and is often confined within organizationally defined boundaries. It is formally active but practically ineffective. Rebellious innovation agency emphasizes the individual's capacity to act independently and creatively within and at the edges of organizational structures. Such agency is not guided or controlled by the organization; it is based on the individual's willingness to question established practices and to perceive latent opportunities for change. Rebellious agency exhibits traits similar to the transformational agency acts described by Haapasaari and Kerosuo (2015), such as resisting management or development structures when they obstruct work-related innovation. All forms of innovation agency share a focus on action: the desire and effort to change work in one way or another. Differences arise in how this effort relates to organizational structures and culture—sometimes compatibly and visibly, sometimes superficially and within limits, and occasionally outside norms, autonomously, and through acts of resistance.

By examining agency at a more general level—not as isolated situations but as participant-specific approach related to the organization's innovation activities as a whole—it is possible to identify employees' current innovation roles based on their own descriptions. These roles can be arranged along a continuum ranging from more passive *thinkers*, who voice their opinions mainly when asked, to *drivers*, who actively lead organizational renewal. This role typology partially resembles classifications presented in previous innovation research. The role of drivers corresponds to innovation champions, while the role of advocates aligns with promoters within the organization (cf. Gemünden et al., 2007; Howell et al., 2005). In this study, a particularly central role was found to be that of the *ideator*, which was the most common role in both the police and technology organizations. The ideator's role is not immediately the most influential (idea generators do not have direct impact on organizational-level decisions). However, it is significant because previous research has indicated that critical thinking, raising issues, identifying problems, and considering alternative solutions can serve as a springboard for organizational innovation. The ability to critique can thus be interpreted as a gateway mediated by agency to initiative taking and, consequently, to creative development (cf. Engeström & Virkkunen, 2007; Haapasaari & Kerosuo, 2015).

This study's focus is not limited to describing roles; rather, it is primarily directed at the innovation agency developing behind these roles—how individual activity and organizational structures change and evolve over time. From the perspective of Giddens's (1984) structuration theory, a role can be understood as a process built through continuous interaction between the individual and organizational structures. A key observation is that the development of innovation agency is particularly supported by the accumulation of individual experience and expertise (cf. Eteläpelto et al., 2013), the broadening of organizational understanding, and one's position within the social community, which is built either through substantive expertise (in the technology sector) or formal position (in the police organization). In practice, this means that employees' innovation agency can be strengthened not only through personal initiative or direct organizational positions but also by accumulating extensive organizational experience and deep professional competence in one's field, thereby enhancing both one's status and influence in organizational innovation activities.

2.3.1 Summary of Findings by Context

Examining agency and roles within the context of innovation provided not only generalizable insights but also context-specific understanding, forming a basis for comparing police and technology organizations. Table 2.1 presents a concise summary of the contextually distinct elements related to agency and roles.

As have been said before, formal position does not automatically lead to a driver role in innovation, although it can theoretically provide opportunities for broad participation and influence (cf. Billett, 2014). This was evident in the *technology-sector organization*, in which leadership position was not the primary factor in shaping innovation agency or roles. Instead, roles were more strongly determined by a background in product development, deep expertise, and long organizational experience (cf. Billett, 2014; Hökkä & Vähäsantanen, 2014). This can be explained contextually: In the *technology sector*, innovations are primarily understood as technological. Consequently, the position of product development experts naturally becomes strong within the organization, and their agency gains institutional recognition. A leadership position does not automatically imply the status of an innovation driver, as management work may focus more on administrative and routine tasks rather than on supporting creative or participatory innovation. This highlights an interesting tension within organizational structures: Innovation roles do not always follow the formal organizational chart but can develop alongside it or even outside of it, forming a kind of shadow role structure. Such informal structures can promote agility and novel thinking, but they may create ambiguity in processes and decision-making if they are not recognized or supported by the organization. While the formal decision-making structure may be traditionally hierarchical, actual decision-making power and opportunities to be heard do not rely solely on titles. In practice, whose voice is heard and who can influence outcomes are determined by expertise, credibility, and networks, not just formal positions. The role appeared to reflect agency at both the individual and organizational levels in the technology organization, but opportunities for participation were intentionally safeguarded for all personnel through various institutionalized practices. Examples of these practices, designed to make participation in innovation activities visible also at the organizational level, included ideation forums, feedback channels, and meeting practices.

Table 2.1 Summary of findings by context: innovation agency and roles across organizations

Theme	Police	Technology
Open agency	• Enabled by team-level discussion culture and receptive immediate supervisor • Strong in preventive policing; autonomy embedded in everyday work • Formal spaces (co-development days etc.) enabling visible, consequential participation	• Supported by participative leadership and lower hierarchy • Established ideation channels (initiative systems, open forums) • Team rituals and clear "time & place" for influence enabling visible agency
Seeming agency	• Input invited via surveys/meetings; effects symbolic; broken feedback loops • Training modules fulfilling formal requirements without deeper learning • High caseload/time pressure limiting actual influence	• Titles implying influence without decision rights • Participation rhetorical rather than effective • Ideas voiced but perceived limited weight in decisions
Rebellious agency	• Ideas advanced indirectly when structures block open influence • Negotiating at rule margins; discretion used in ambiguity	• Independent "I do it anyway" actions • Fewer normative risks due to flexible processes
Drivers	• Strategic shapers; formal position plus long tenure and broad organizational knowledge • Connecting units, legitimizing development efforts; enabling open agency at scale	• Internal engines not necessarily in management roles • Influence built via long experience, deep product/organizational knowledge, networks • Translating vision into enabling structures and practices
Advocates	• Immediate supervisors or seasoned practitioners moving information across levels • Influence concentrated at team/unit level; hierarchy constraining scope	• Team leads or senior experts converting vision into everyday adjustments • Autonomy to act and coordinate across teams
Ideators	• Everyday developers surfacing problems and alternatives; critical stance common • Influence limited by structures despite active ideation	• Largest group; prolific in identifying issues tied to work and customers • Requiring managerial sponsorship for organization-wide progress
Thinkers	• Not observed in preventive policing; work requiring constant adjustment	• Present; reflective, low-initiative participation • Views voiced mainly when asked; often linked to short tenure or narrow roles

The *police organization's* strong hierarchical structure partly guides role formation through positional authority (see M. Weber, 1922). In this context, formal position significantly explains the distribution of decision-making power and influence and thereby the different forms and levels of innovation agency—from moderate to strong and from open to rebellious. In other words, innovation potential is, on the one hand, enabled by formal positions (those who attain official status gain the opportunity to influence); on the other hand, it is constrained by the same positions (those without formal status remain outside the sphere of influence). This arrangement clearly reflects Weber's ideal type of managerialism, in which power and decision-making are concentrated at higher levels of the hierarchy. This manifests in police as limited innovation activity when viewed from the perspectives of organizational structures and formal decision-making.

In this context, innovation appears not as open or shared but as controlled and hierarchically defined. Interestingly, when police officers' discourse shifts from the organizational level to the context of their own work and daily routines, the descriptions of agency become more individually driven through discretion and everyday problem-solving. Discretion is an essential part of police work because not all situations can be precisely regulated by law; therefore, police officers constantly make choices, for example between intervening, issuing a warning, or making an arrest (Charman & Bennett, 2022). It is therefore natural that they have a degree of freedom in their work and everyday practices, and this freedom also extends to development activities. From this perspective, agency appears strong and active: officers describe themselves as proactive and capable of making decisions and developing their own work. This observation also reinforces the view that the particular nature of preventive policing creates space for autonomous and reflective action (cf. Lemmetty & Collin, 2022). The work is inherently such that it is not strictly governed by clearly defined rules or predetermined processes; employees must continuously make decisions, plan, and develop their work independently. Notably, not a single police officer interviewed described themselves as passive or as participating in innovation only when requested. This highlights how innovation agency in preventive police work is not exceptional but part of the nature of the work, even though its extension to the organizational level is constrained by hierarchical structures, organizational practices, limited resources, a traditional organizational culture, and so-called *hard values,* which sometimes continue to maintain control and inhibit the spread of new ideas.

2.3.2 Concluding and Practical Perspectives

According to Finnish research, transformational agency strengthens both well-being and productivity, enables EDI, requires sufficient autonomy and support, and manifests in the emergence of new roles and job descriptions (Ylisassi et al., 2016). My analysis of police and technology organizations extends these findings. Based on the results, it is justified to question ideal-type, hierarchical approaches to roles, in which agency and influence are primarily linked to formal positions. Instead, it is important to examine, including in practical work and organizational contexts, different actors as active, participatory, and contextually learning subjects, whose innovativeness can be consciously supported and strengthened by developing the sociocultural environment. Such a perspective generates value not only at the individual level but also for the community and the organization as a whole.

In practice, organizations may need to identify innovation roles, forms of agency, and the associated potential and opportunities by engaging in discussions with staff about, for example, their expectations, possibilities, willingness, and capabilities regarding participation in innovation activities. Such identification and reflection can be carried out through self-assessment or joint discussions between a supervisor and an employee. If the expectations, possibilities, willingness, and capabilities align with the opportunity to engage, learn at work, further development of their innovation role is possible in the future. If any of these elements are lacking, it is important to pause and consider the underlying reasons. If the possibilities or expectations do not seem realistic, reflection may reveal organizational practices or cultural aspects that hinder participation in innovation activities. Conversely, if expectations and possibilities exist but the individual lacks the willingness to participate, such observations may point to factors related to broader issues of well-being, motivation, or engagement. In this way, discussions about innovation agency can serve not only as a tool to strengthen innovation agency but also as a practice that supports work development and employee well-being. The aim of this reflection is not to push, coerce, or unilaterally direct staff into innovation activities, nor to try to turn all employees into *drivers*. Rather, the goal is to enhance participation and interaction in innovation activities more broadly to enable the organization and its innovations to be developed through multiple perspectives.

In both the technology organization and the police, the foundation and development of innovation agency are partly a matter of individuals' competence and continuous development: In the technology sector, competence appears as a building block of the innovation role regardless of position, whereas in the police, competence enables the attainment of formal positions that expand the innovation role. But what kind of competence is required for innovation activities? Competence develops through learning, so what kind of learning underlies innovation activities? In the following chapter, we turn to these questions.

References

Baker, W., & Faulkner, R. R. (1991). Role as resource in the Hollywood film industry. *American Journal of Sociology, 97*(2), 279–309.

Berger, P. L., & Luckmann, T. (1966). *The social construction of reality: A treatise in the sociology of knowledge*. Anchor Books.

Biesta, G., Priestley, M., & Robinson, S. (2015). The role of beliefs in teacher agency. *Teachers and Teaching, 21*(6), 624–640. https://doi.org/10.1080/13540602.2015.1044325

Billett, S. (2004). Workplace participatory practices: Conceptualising workplaces as learning environments. *The Journal of Workplace Learning, 16*(6), 312–324. https://doi.org/10.1108/13665620410550295

Billett, S. (2014). Mimesis: Learning through everyday activities and interactions at work. *Human Resource Development Review, 3*(4), 462–482. https://doi.org/10.1177/1534484314548275

Callero, P. L. (1994). From role-playing to role-using: Understanding role as resource. *Social Psychology Quarterly, 57*(3), 228–243.

Charman, S., & Bennett, S. (2022). Voluntary resignations from the police service: The impact of organisational and occupational stressors on organisational commitment. *Policing and Society, 32*(2), 159–178. https://doi.org/10.1080/10439463.2021.1891234

Ellström, P.-E. (2010). Practice-based innovation: A learning perspective. *Journal of Workplace Learning, 22*(1/2), 27–40. https://doi.org/10.1108/13665621011012834

Engeström & Virkkunen: Engeström, Y., & Virkkunen, J. (2007). Muutoslaboratorio – kehiävän työntutkimuksen uusi vaihe [The Change Laboratory—a new phase of developmental work research]. In E. Ramstad & T. Alasoini (Eds.), *Työelämän tutkimusavusteinen kehittäminen Suomessa: lähestymistapoja, menetelmiä, kokemuksia, tulevaisuuden haasteita* [Research-assisted development of working life in Finland: Approaches, methods, experiences, future challenges] (Raportteja/Kansallinen työelämän kehittämisohjelma No. 53). Työministeriö.

Eteläpelto, A. (2017). Emerging conceptualisations on professional agency and learning. In M. Goller & S. Paloniemi (Eds.), *Agency at work: An agentic perspective on professional learning and development* (pp. 183–201). Springer.

Eteläpelto, A., Vähäsantanen, K., Hökkä, P., & Paloniemi, S. (2013). What is agency? Conceptualizing professional agency at work. *Educational Research Review, 10*, 45–65. https://doi.org/10.1016/j.edurev.2013.05.001

Forsman, P. (2023). *Luovuus muuttuvassa työorganisaatiossa – etnografinen tutkimus toimijuudesta ja luovuuden kehittymisestä* [Creativity in a changing work organization: An ethnographic study of practiced agency and emerging creativity]. Doctoral dissertation, University of Jyväskylä.

Gemünden, H. G., Salomo, S., & Hölzle, K. (2007). Role models for radical innovations in times of open innovation. *Creativity and Innovation Management, 16*(4), 408–421. https://doi.org/10.1111/j.1467-8691.2007.00453.x

Giddens, A. (1984). *The constitution of society: Outline of the theory of structuration.* University of California Press.

Giddens, A. (1991). *Modernity and self-identity: Self and society in the late modern age.* Stanford University Press.

Glăveanu, V. P. (2015). Creativity as a sociocultural act. *Journal of Creative Behavior, 49*(3), 165–180. https://doi.org/10.1002/jocb.94

Goller, M., & Billett, S. (2014). Agentic behaviour at work: Crafting learning experience. In C. Harteis, A. Rausch, & J. Seifried (Eds.), *Discourses on professional learning: On the boundary between learning and working* (pp. 25–44). Springer.

Goller, M., & Harteis, C. (2017). Human agency at work: Towards a clarification and operationalisation of the concept. In M. Goller & S. Paloniemi (Eds.), *Agency at work: An agentic perspective on learning and development* (pp. 85–103). Springer. https://doi.org/10.1007/978-3-319-60943-0_5

Goller, M., & Paloniemi, S. (2017). Agency at work, learning and professional development: An introduction. In M. Goller & S. Paloniemi (Eds.), *Agency at work* (pp. 1–14). Springer. https://doi.org/10.1007/978-3-319-60943-0_1

Goller, M., & Paloniemi, S. (2022). Agency: Taking stock of workplace learning research. In C. Harteis, D. Gijbels, & E. Kyndt (Eds.), *Research approaches on workplace learning: Insights from a growing field* (pp. 3–28). Springer. https://doi.org/10.1007/978-3-030-89582-2_1

Haapasaari, A., & Kerosuo, H. (2015). Transformative agency: The challenges of sustainability in a long chain of double stimulation. *Learning, Culture and Social Interaction, 4*, 37–47. https://doi.org/10.1016/j.lcsi.2014.07.006

Hakanurmi, S., Palonen, T., & Murtonen, M. (2021). Digital stories representing agency enhancement at work. *Adult Education Quarterly, 71*(3), 251–271. https://doi.org/10.1177/0741713621989990

Heikkinen, M. T., Mainela, T., Still, J., & Tähtinen, J. (2007). Roles for managing in mobile service development nets. *Industrial Marketing Management, 36*(7), 909–925. https://doi.org/10.1016/j.indmarman.2007.05.014

Hökkä, P., & Vähäsantanen, K. (2014). Agency-centred coupling: A better way to manage an educational organization? *International Journal of Leadership in Education: Theory and Practice, 17*(2), 131–153. https://doi.org/10.1080/13603124.2013.783932

Howell, J. M., Shea, C. M., & Higgins, C. A. (2005). Champions of product innovations: Defining, developing, and validating a measure of champion behavior. *Journal of Business Venturing, 20*(5), 641–661. https://doi.org/10.1016/j.jbusvent.2004.03.003

Høyrup, S. (2010). Employee-driven innovation and workplace learning: Basic concepts, approaches and themes. *Transfer: European Review of Labour and Research, 16*(2), 143–154. https://doi.org/10.1177/1024258910364102

Hyrkkö, S., & Kajamaa, A. (2025). Teachers' transformative agency in a Change Laboratory in a Finnish elementary school. *Teaching and Teacher Education, 159*, 105011. https://doi.org/10.1016/j.tate.2025.105011

Kerosuo, H., & Jokinen, E. (2023). Transformative agency and the cultivation of innovations in frontline homelessness work. In N. Hopwood & A. Sannino (Eds.), *Agency and transformation: Motives, mediation, and motion* (pp. 311–335). Cambridge University Press.

Kerosuo, H., Kajamaa, A., & Engeström, Y. (2010). Promoting innovation and learning through change laboratory: An example from Finnish health care. *Central European Journal of Public Policy, 4*(1), 110–131. Retrieved from https://doaj.org/article/9ea8e1c1aee64b6dbe573ec4a6bee528

Kesting, P., & Ulhøi, J. P. (2010). Employee driven innovation: Extending the license to foster innovation. *Management Decision, 48*, 65–84. https://doi.org/10.1108/00251741011014463

Lemmetty, S. (2024a). Real-time and long-term challenges of remote learning and innovation: Cases from police and technology organisations. *Vocations and Learning, 17*, 565–587. https://doi.org/10.1007/s12186-024-09354-1

Lemmetty, S., & Collin, K. (2022). Co-occurrence of sociocultural elements and self-direction in learning situations: A police organization case study. *Adult Learning, 34*(4), 220–229. https://doi.org/10.1177/10451595221094072

Mansfeld, M. N., Hölzle, K., & Gemünden, H. G. (2010). Personal characteristics of innovators: An empirical study of roles in innovation management. *International Journal of Innovation Management, 14*(6), 1129–1147. https://doi.org/10.1142/S1363919610003033

Martins, E. C., & Terblanche, F. (2003). Building organisational culture that stimulates creativity and innovation. *European Journal of Innovation Management, 6*(1), 64–74. https://doi.org/10.1108/14601060310456337

Mead, G. H. (1934). *Mind, self, and society: From the standpoint of a social behaviorist*. University of Chicago Press.

Messmann, G., & Mulder, R. H. (2017). Proactive employees: The relationship between work-related reflection and innovative work behaviour. In M. Goller & S. Paloniemi (Eds.), *Agency at work: An agentic perspective on learning and development*. Springer. https://doi.org/10.1007/978-3-319-60943-0_8

Murray, R., & Ron, E. (2010, November). Innovation roles in SME internationalization. In *2010 International Conference on Management Science & Engineering 17th Annual Conference Proceedings* (pp. 1389–1397). https://doi.org/10.1109/ICMSE.2010.5719972.

Nyström, A.-G., Leminen, S., Westerlund, M., & Kortelainen, M. (2014). Actor roles and role patterns influencing innovation in living labs. *Industrial Marketing Management, 43*(3), 483–495. https://doi.org/10.1016/j.indmarman.2013.12.016

Priestley, M., Edwards, R., Priestley, A., & Miller, K. (2012). Teacher agency in curriculum making: Agents of change and spaces for manoeuvre. *Curriculum Inquiry, 42*(2), 191–214. https://doi.org/10.1111/j.1467-873X.2012.00588.x

Roberts, E. B., & Fusfeld, A. R. (1980). *Critical functions: Needed roles in the innovation process.* Alfred P. Sloan School of Management, Massachusetts Institute of Technology. Retrieved from https://hdl.handle.net/1721.1/47154

Rost, K., Hölzle, K., & Gemünden, H. G. (2007). Promotors or champions? Pros and cons of role specialisation for economic process. *Schmalenbach Business Review, 59*, 340–363. https://doi.org/10.1007/BF03396754

Tuominen, T. M., & Lehtonen, M. H. (2017). The emergence of transformative agency in professional work. *Organization Studies, 39*(11), 1601–1624. https://doi.org/10.1177/0170840617717093

Vähäsantanen, K., & Billett, S. (2008). Negotiating professional identity: Vocational teachers' personal strategies in a reform context. In S. Billett, C. Harteis, & A. Eteläpelto (Eds.), *Emerging perspectives of workplace learning* (pp. 35–49). https://doi.org/10.1163/9789087906450_004

Vähäsantanen, K., & Eteläpelto, A. (2015). Professional agency, identity, and emotions while leaving one's work organization. *Professions and Professionalism, 5*(3), 1394. https://doi.org/10.7577/pp.1394

Vanhalakka-Ruoho, M., & Ruponen, R. (2013). What do the participants gain? Group counselling to enhance agency at work. *International Journal for Educational and Vocational Guidance, 13*(3), 217–231. https://doi.org/10.1007/s10775-013-9248-9

Weber, M. (1922/1978). *Economy and society: An outline of interpretive sociology.* Berkeley: University of California Press.

Weber, M. (1946). *From Max Weber: Essays in sociology* (H. H. Gerth, & C. Wright Mills, Eds. & Trans.). Oxford University Press. (Original work published 1917).

Weber, M. (1980). *The Protestant ethic and the spirit of capitalism* (T. Parsons, Trans.). Routledge & Kegan Paul. (Original work published 1904–1905).

Welling, M. (2025). *Ennalta estävää työtä tekevien poliisien ammatillinen toimijuus - Kriittinen diskurssianalyysi toimijuuspuheesta poliisityön kehittämisen kontekstissa.* [Professional agency of police officers working in preventive policing – A critical discourse analysis of agency talk in the context of police work development.] Master's thesis. University of Eastern Finland. Retrieved from https://erepo.uef.fi/items/1bcc1a78-8534-4853-8d5e-9f3082a1ad44

Ylisassi, H., Hasu, M., Heikkilä, H., Käpykangas, S., Saari, E., Seppänen, L., & Valtanen, E. (2016). *Työntekijöiden kehittämistoimijuutta edistämässä: Kehittämismenetelmäkokeilujen tuloksia vanhuspalveluissa.* [Promoting Employees' Development Agency: Results of development method experiments in elderly care services]. Työterveyslaitos. Retrieved from https://urn.fi/URN:ISBN:978-952-261-605-0

Chapter 3
Process of LBI: Competence and Learning in Innovation

Abstract This chapter presents innovation as a continuous learning process, forming the foundation for understanding Learning-Based Innovation (LBI), in which phases of adaptive and innovative learning alternate across individual, group, and organizational levels. The chapter defines the concepts of professional competence and workplace learning in relation to innovation activities and provides empirical examples from two fields: policing and technology. It also explains the type of competence required to support innovation activities, particularly in police and technology work, and illustrates how competence diversity operates as a key driver of workplace innovation. Furthermore, the chapter conceptualizes the innovation process as a continuous, learning-based phenomenon grounded in learning practices and the diverse competence of those involved in the process.

Keywords Learning-based innovation · Adaptive learning · Innovative learning · Innovation · Professional competence · Workplace learning · Police organization · Technology organization

The importance of knowledge and competence for innovation cannot be overstated. How can we create something truly new if we lack the understanding and ideas to build upon? How can we approach problems from multiple perspectives without a reservoir of experience to spark *aha* moments, the ability to transfer previously acquired knowledge to new contexts, or the capacity to question assumptions critically? Innovation, at its core, relies not just on creativity but on the rich interplay between what we know, what we have experienced and learned, and how we apply both in novel ways. Based on previous studies as well as empirical data from the EDLI project, the aim of this chapter is to clarify what is meant by competence and what types of competence are valuable from the perspective of innovations occurring in working life. Moreover, the chapter describes more precisely the types of learning processes and practices through which new knowledge flows and competence develop, becomes visible, and ultimately transforms into innovations.

S. Lemmetty, *Learning-Based Innovation*,
SpringerBriefs in Education, https://doi.org/10.1007/978-3-032-26911-9_3

3.1 Competence in Innovation

In this work, we are in a certain way in the middle ground between art and science and at their interfaces. Much of that innovation is intuitive. You must have enough knowledge, understanding, and experience in the matter to be able to justify to yourself and others why you do what you do. That intuitiveness is based specifically on tacit knowledge of the identity of this company—some kind of feeling or idea of what is right or wrong. On the one hand, research, measurement, and facts play an equally central role here. We aim to do background work—we even do research ourselves—as the basis for the innovations. On the other hand, we also measure how any prototype works or what kind of effects the finished innovation has.

"The balance of facts and intuition": innovation type story, previously created and published as part of the EDLI project based on its data from the technology organization (Lemmetty, 2024b, p. 141).

Innovation, as a human activity, emerges from everyday work and interactions within organizational contexts. Its foundation lies in the understanding, knowledge, and ideas of those who engage with practical tasks, including employees and stakeholders who encounter problems, identify development opportunities, and generate new insights (Buhl, 2018; Ellström, 2010; Kesting & Ulhøi, 2010). Employees are key holders of knowledge and competence, but how do we understand *competence*, and what kind of competence is actually needed for innovation?

3.1.1 Competence as a Combination of Knowledge, Skills, and Attitudes

According to Mulder (2014, p. 111), "professionals are competent when they act responsibly and effectively according to given requirements." Professional competence is seen as a general, integrated, and internalized ability to act in sustainable and effective ways in developmental work (problem-solving, implementing innovations, and creating change) within a *specific professional domain, task, role, organizational context, or work situation.* Professional competence is thus the ability both to maintain sustainable functioning in the work context and to promote change within one's professional field (Mulder, 2014).

Competence is often structured into different competence areas (i.e., competences) (Mulder, 2014). It is common to distinguish between job-specific competence and generic competence (e.g., Kyndt et al., 2013). Job-specific competence refers to task-related and domain-specific knowledge, skills, and understanding, while generic competence includes knowledge and skills required across various professions, including problem-solving, communication, organizational, and teamwork skills (Mulder & Winterton, 2017). Each specific competence area focuses on a defined set of abilities related to a particular role, task, or function, describing the overall capacity to act within a given domain. As this book focuses on innovation, it is relevant to note here that some literature also suggests that innovation competence can be seen as a distinct area of competence. For example, in their literature review, Hero et al. (2017) examined individual-level innovation competence as a type of generic competence, defining it as "a set of personal characteristics, knowledge, skills (or abilities) and attitudes that are connected to creating concretized and implemented novelties via collaboration in complex innovation processes." They understood innovation competence as a distinct competence, consisting of personal characteristics, such as self-leadership, as well as future orientation, creative thinking, and project-management skills. This approach excludes the situated perspective (see Mulder, 2015), which has long been emphasized in professional competence research, according to which the context determines, influences, and guides the meanings and construction of competence.

Competence consists of *knowledge*, *skills*, and *attitudes* (Mulder, 2014; Baartman & de Bruijn, 2011), enabling individuals to carry out their work and achieve the desired outcomes (Ellström, 2010). According to Davenport and Prusak (1998), *knowledge* is

> a fluid mix of framed experience, values, contextual information, and expert insight that provides a framework for evaluating and incorporating new experiences and information. It originates and is applied in the minds of knowers. In organizations, it often becomes embedded not only in documents or repositories but also in organizational routines, processes, practices and norms. (p. 5)

A *skill* refers to a special ability to do something (Cambridge Dictionary, 2025). It may be seen as a capacity to *use* and *apply* existing knowledge to achieve results, thus referring to doing or acting in practice (Baartman & de Bruijn, 2011). *Attitudes* can be defined as context-bound affective orientations that influence an individual's choices and actions in specific situations (Baartman & de Bruijn, 2011). They represent dispositions formed through both long-term socialization and short-term contextual experiences. They connect an individual's knowledge and skills with concrete behavior in professional or everyday tasks. Attitudes can reflect relatively stable personality traits, but they are dynamically constructed *in the moment* according to the demands of situations. In this way, they act as a mediating factor between the individual's potential and the demands of the environment (Ellström, 1998).

In this work, competence is approached broadly as an integrated whole of knowledge, skills, and attitudes that can be applied and developed in innovation activities in professionals' daily work. The examination is contextual, analyzing the competence needed in innovation work in the police and technology organizations.

3.1.2 Competence Required for Police and Technology Work Innovations

In the EDLI research, participants were asked to describe what kinds of competence their work—and the innovation activities occurring within it—require. The descriptions of competence were highly diverse; for example, the police interviews alone revealed over 50 distinct competence descriptions. Across both the police and technology sectors, the competence required for innovation activities can be broadly categorized into three main groups, although their specific content is shaped by the respective contexts:

- *subject-matter and practical competence*;
- *organizational and cultural–historical competence*;
- *attitudinal and motivational competence.*

3.1.2.1 Subject-Matter and Practical Competence

Subject-matter and practical competence can be understood as encompassing all the knowledge and skills that participants associate with their profession or its various content areas. This type of competence includes both theoretical and practical knowledge and skills acquired through formal education as well as broader life experience, everything an individual perceives as necessary for carrying out and developing their core work tasks, whether building trust with young people or designing electronic components for a new product. This competence category covers both knowledge and understanding, as well as their application: the ability to translate knowledge into practice at work. From the perspective of employee-driven innovation (EDI) processes promoted in everyday work, subject-matter and practical competence directly target innovation: one must first deeply understand subject-matter and practical foundations of the work, so as the development of content, practices or products at work becomes possible.

In the context of preventive *police work*, subject-matter and practical competence encompasses knowledge of legislation, professional rules, theories and methods of policing, proficiency in tools and systems used in the work, and skills related to coercive measures and the use of force. Because preventive work is inherently interactional, taking place within networks and directly engaging with clients, subject-matter competence includes communicative and interpersonal skills, the ability to encounter people, and cultural awareness, as well as understanding how these manifest in everyday practice.

> That scale is broad, and it requires those collaboration skills, and then you have to have 'substance' [subject-matter knowledge] that you know and are clear about things [...] All of that has an impact; there are those precise articles and precise facts that regulate it, and it is easier for the investigating officer, for example, to inform them when they know those criteria. (PP2, Police)

The specific knowledge and skills that constitute subject-matter and practical competence depend entirely on the nature of the tasks and may vary significantly among police officers with different roles and responsibilities. While understanding social media, youth activities online, and digital skills may form the core of development work for one officer, another may need to focus on expertise related to pre-trial investigation processes or the local crime situation. However, police work rarely focuses on a single, narrowly defined area. For this reason, the descriptions of subject-matter and practical competence among officers engaged in preventive work often emphasize the need for broad and comprehensive knowledge:

> [The work] requires that specialization [...] it requires that you simply cannot go and do or study these things if you don't understand the whole thing and what it all involves. [...] We should be those hybrid people, jacks of all trades, who know everything. (PP2, Police)

Subject-matter and professional competence in the *technology organization* appeared to participating experts and professionals as a core competence, focused on each expert's or unit's central task area:

> Many of us are experts in our own field. (TP30, Technology)

Such competence areas include, for example, automation competence (understanding the phases and laws of robotization and automation), electronics and software competence (understanding product integration, problem identification, and software development), and communication and marketing competence (e.g., branding and the meanings and methods of external and internal communication):

> My core competence is probably in designing digital [...] or running some optimization algorithm [with a certain program], which is a very narrow but important [area] for the company. (TP19, Technology)

> Then there's what you need to know and understand in terms of substance, all of these. [...] in a way, if you're not a coder, [...], you're coding in the wrong way. You're making the wrong choices and so, [...] In a way, I've improved a lot in that in the last few years; I'm making much more sensible and editable and maintainable code that can be reused. (TP18, Technology)

From an innovation perspective, subject-matter and practical competence is a key comparison target in relation to competitors: Personnel assess what specific competence in their own core area the organization has—something that competitors do not master—and in which areas they are lagging behind their competitors. In this way, subject-matter and practical competence appears not only as the basis for individual and team work but also as a means of competitive differentiation in the technology sector:

> A good general understanding of [one's own area and its] different means that can be utilized. One must also understand at least a little bit about our products, including the technical side and the solutions that our competitors offer. (TP2, Technology)

Subject-matter and practical competence appears as a two-level phenomenon in both police and technological innovation work: On the one hand, it represents a deep understanding and knowledge base related to the work; on the other hand, it involves the application of this knowledge in practical work situations. These forms of competence develop in parallel and reinforce each other.

3.1.2.2 Organizational and Cultural–Historical Competence

The need described by participants to understand and be aware of the organization's structural conditions, processes, operating methods, strategy, goals, and values—in whose direction innovation activities are carried forward—is structured as organizational and cultural–historical competence. This was described as both visible and hidden things, structures, and practices, awareness of which is important in innovation activities:

> You need to know history—where it came from, why it is like this—so that you can build something new on it. I think that's essential. (TP19, Technology)

In the police, the emphasis is on understanding the goals of the organization and of one's own work—what is meant by prevention in the police? (see Chap. 5)—viewing structures and hierarchies as both enabling and limiting development (see Chaps. 2 and 5), and comprehending decision-making processes and one's own formal role in this whole. These formal structures show the police the big picture of the *sandbox* within which they can operate in their own preventive work. However, the sandbox was often described as quite broad and sometimes as unclear. In terms of organizational competence, this is an area in which one must understand how different starting points are applied in different areas and units and what opportunities different police stations provide, reflecting regional differences and resources:

> A police department or station in a big city is very compartmentalized, and it is clearer there who does what. [...] There can be no overlaps, no skipping. It doesn't work here in smaller towns because we don't have those resources. Everyone has to do a little bit of everything. Understanding that [the differences and organizational differences] is key. Sometimes there are challenges because we can get, for example, instructions or orders that are unreasonable here [...]. I know, for example, that in a big city [with regard to certain activities] the police's hands are more tied than mine here in a small town. We get to do more multi-agency cooperation, also with the third sector. We get to plan our own working time more for these surveillance events and patrols. (PP23, Police)

The key element is awareness of what it is appropriate to do in the organization and in each operating environment and what the accepted and institutionalized practices that guide the promotion of operations are. Particularly in the *technology organization*, understanding the history, traditions, and culture of the organization—perhaps of the entire industry—is crucial from an innovation perspective, as a strong contextual understanding serves as the basis for defining the novelty and value of innovations. Through history and customers, it is possible to understand what constitutes innovation in a given organization:

> It is important to understand the roots and what has happened and how we have got to this point, what kind of path we have been on, what kind of clients we have. (TP2, Technology)

Historical knowledge also involves understanding innovations and failures in hindsight. By looking back, it is possible to understand what mistakes have been made, what has already been tried, and what is not innovative in this context:

> You can see it afterwards, the failure—which can be the future success—so if you can afford to spend the time, it is quite valuable for us to learn what doesn't work and not repeat it next time. (TP15, Technology)

Organizational and cultural–historical competence is linked to an understanding of an organization's structural conditions, routines, and historical development paths as well as its future direction. Such competence is central to directing and implementing innovations in the context of one's own work, as well as to defining their value and making development-related decisions.

3.1.2.3 Attitudinal and Motivational Competence

Attitudinal and motivational competence relates to people's attitudes, motivations, and values in relation to the task at hand or development work. It is more difficult to observe, document, or articulate, but it emerges in descriptions of ways of thinking and attitudes.

> A huge curiosity and interest in the world, not just technology but in general. When [a certain person asked him] in a postgraduate course, he asked if you could build [a specific product] and then [this person from the company] first said yes and then asked what it was. (TP5, Technology)

In the *technology organization*, such competence can be seen as, on the one hand, a childlike creative experimentation and, on the other hand, a healthy (self-)criticism toward one's own thoughts and actions. This competence includes understanding that one's own ideas may be flawed and that critical discussion—sometimes even debate—is useful for decision-making and developing innovations. This requires the ability to regulate emotions and an attitude that values others. Related to attitudes is the ability to refrain from decision-making based solely on intuitive first impressions; instead, one should spend time re-examining an idea or reflecting on it together with colleagues:

> A flawed line of thinking or a wrong idea can sometimes end up producing huge consequences. Once [in a situation with a colleague] I said to them: 'I've got this thought, and it really needs to be shot down, shut it down, because is there really any sense in it? [...] Of course, you also need to be the kind of little boy who can sometimes think wrongly, so to speak. In other words, in a different way, like "can't this be done in a different way?" In other words, why can't this be done this way? [...] Not always according to what comes to mind first or what would be the most logical way. (TP24, Technology)

The courage to make independent decisions in everyday life and a personal interest and motivation in one's work were also viewed as essential:

> Self-initiative, that I want to solve this problem [...] an open attitude to a little bit of everything [...] I would say that a good engineer is one that when you give it a problem, [...] that's what it does, that it gets strength from it, how to solve it. (TP15, Technology)

In police preventive activities, the key attitudinal competences were described as an open attitude toward one's customers, colleagues, or stakeholders, empathy, and the ability and desire to *put oneself in the other's shoes*, as well as critical examination and awareness of one's own and others' prejudices:

> When dealing with young people, it's not the same basic police attitude that may be on display at some point or in public, so it doesn't work that way. You have to be very open and experienced yourself, not like a growling or a snarling informant, but someone who can have a conversation. I don't know if you even have to be empathetic or understanding, but something that gets the young person interested and then creates that conversation. And yes, there are also more and more young people with an immigrant background as clients, not because they commit crimes, but because more and more of them are coming here to Finland and [to our region] and you see them in the villages there too. So yes, you have to throw your prejudices in the trash right away so that the matter can move forward with them. If there were any prejudices at all. (PP8, Police)

Because the boundaries of work sometimes appear unclear and the organization of everyday work is sometimes very autonomous, the police saw the importance of their own motivation to develop their work even when they would choose not to do so. This also describes their initiative in organizing their own work:

> If there was a day when there was nothing [mandatory], I would go to places like schools or downtown where young people gather. I would chat, and it was completely up to me. I could also have sat in the office and twiddled my pen and threw chewing gum at the ceiling, but that's so much based on the person. (PP22, Police)

3.1.2.4 Toward Shared Competence

Competence at work is not only an individual characteristic; it is also above all a collective and shared phenomenon built in knowledge communities, social structures, and work and market environments. In today's increasingly complex working life, in which problems are solved in communities and networks—not alone—, in addition to individual competence, it is essential to understand competence at the level of communities:

> The sky is the limit here [in terms of] what [competence] can be used here. We have noticed that my colleague is incredibly skilled in these IT matters, where I am, frankly, absolutely crap. [...] and then again I have a nursing education [specifies education], which then supports this tremendously and gives that side of knowledge to this work [...]. So we are such a [pair] fortunately that we have our own skills, and then we rely on each other. (PP17, Police)

Innovations are built on the heterogeneity of community skills and group-level competence diversity (Ness & Søreide, 2014; Ramstad, 2009; Walrave et al., 2024; Wang et al., 2020). Perceiving competence diversity as a value for innovation is linked to broader discussions on the importance of diversity among work community members, especially for sustainable and socially responsible innovation activities (e.g., Jones et al., 2020). In an organizational context, diversity generally refers to the intentional inclusion of individuals from a wide range of identities, backgrounds, and experiences (Stahl & Maznevski, 2021). The starting point is the idea that individuals with different backgrounds bring different perspectives and different understandings to the group, which, when combined, form a new kind of multi-perspectival and creative thinking, being a good starting point for building innovative processes and outcomes. Patrick and Kumar's (2012) study comparing the problem-solving abilities of homogeneous and heterogeneous (i.e., diverse) teams found that heterogeneous teams with similar competence levels were more creative than their homogeneous counterparts.

> We need each other. None of us can do the whole set alone so well that we can proudly present it. When people have special competences, they are happy to contribute what comes naturally to them and what they are good at. And then they also think in the same way that it is not worth everyone learning any special skills separately, because it is not efficient that "I do this because I can, and then you do that because you can." Together we can make it as good as possible. (TP15, Technology)

Therefore, the competence set in a community or organization should be examined at a high level: What kind of expert groups are formed in the organization? How is competence shared? How can different people learn from one another and create something new and useful—innovative—together?

3.2 Learning Within Innovation

> *Here, ideas develop, refine, transform, and build into innovations. There can be many diverse ideas in various stages of the process. We, as experts, possess a lot of knowledge and are, in a certain way, confident, wanting to create something new. In such a perspective, it's important to be able to feel that you've accomplished something and say, "I've come up with or developed a product or a new way of doing things." In this viewpoint, there are also dangers of self-centeredness that have emerged in the history of this organization, especially when the significance of individuals was more pronounced and stronger. Excessive ambition or selfishness is not good because it leads to conflicts within the group. It's also not a good thing because in today's world, innovation—such as a new product or approach—cannot be developed from start to finish by a single person in such an organization. Developing innovations is so much more complex and requires much more diverse and specific expertise nowadays, so few individuals can possess such skills. Therefore, it's important that we fundamentally understand these innovations as shared and collective. They come about through compromises, refinement, collaboration, comparing and blending of ideas, and communal learning. Excessive humility—never expressing one's opinion or offering criticism to others—is also not beneficial. The essence of innovation is not whose idea a particular thing is or whether someone receives a personal reward for it, but rather the shared experience of success and significance—understanding one's role as part of something larger. Thus, the focus should be on what has been created, rather than emphasizing who created it.*

"Personal but shared": innovation type story, previously created and published as part of the EDLI project based on its data from the technology organization (Lemmetty, 2024b, p. 136).

Although competence diversity is central to innovation (Billett, 2012; Darsø & Høyrup, 2012; Høyrup, 2012), it is important to understand that competence alone does not automatically translate into innovation; it becomes a driver only through *collective learning* at the group level. Thus, a learning process through which individuals share their experiences, ideas, knowledge, and competence in interaction generates new understanding for the entire group, enabling ideas to transform into innovations with broader organizational impact (Castaneda & Cuellar, 2020; Ness & Søreide, 2014). We can see that competence underlies individuals' creative ideas, but for these ideas to evolve into innovations that engage a wider audience, complementary competences must circulate across different actors, including employees within the organization and institutions at the network level (Allen & Stephen, 2013; Castaneda & Cuellar, 2020; Ramstad, 2009; Wang et al., 2020). Next, we examine how this collective learning can be structured and approached in the context of innovation activity.

3.2.1 Learning in the Innovation Process as Continuous and Situated

As described in the introductory chapter, in EDI activities, learning can be divided into two complementary forms: *adaptive* and *innovative* learning (Ellström, 2010). Adaptive learning refers to learning something *already known*, acquiring existing knowledge, and adjusting to external demands, while innovative learning involves the *creation of new knowledge*, understanding, or ways of working (Høyrup, 2010). These forms of learning are not separate but form a *continuous process* in which previously acquired knowledge—and innovations produced based on it—serves as a resource for new learning and innovation (Lemmetty, 2025; Lemmetty & Billett, 2023). Adaptive learning occurs when individuals and groups develop an understanding of something that has already been invented and is known. This adaptive learning then serves as a resource and building block for further innovative learning, which takes place when individuals or groups learn—individually or socially—something genuinely new that does not yet exist. This, in turn, is a prerequisite for the emergence of new innovations, which are then 'taken up' (learned) adaptively, so that the process becomes continuous. This view shows that innovation does not mark the end of the process but rather the beginning of further development. Learning and innovation are thus dualistic in nature: They are both the consequence and the prerequisite of each other.

This process can be further described through the idea of *continuous learning*. Continuous learning refers to a process in which learning extends beyond and between individual learning situations through the ongoing application of knowledge and the integration of prior and new understandings (Albinsson & Andersson, 2012; Tractenberg et al., 2016). It is sustained by reflection, which links earlier experiences with new ones and enables individuals to combine, reinterpret, and apply their understandings in novel situations (Høyrup, 2004; Bound, 1985; Huber et al., 2005). From the perspective of continuous learning, the essentials are prior experiences and an understanding of what already exists, upon which new competence is built. At work, this means that individuals gradually learn to handle the tasks and tools belonging to them (Lave & Wenger, 1991), making workplace learning *situated* in context, community, and practice.

This kind of *situated learning*, according to Fleming (1994), is based on the community's everyday methodical practices. According to them this process could be analytically structured in three phases: first, identifying how activities are organized and constructed (structural anatomy); next, understanding how methodical practices are applied (functional anatomy); finally, examining how different elements—descriptions, facts, and processes—together produce an intelligible explanation of the phenomenon under study. Fleming's (1994) model is grounded in the understanding and adoption of existing activities and structures, making it closely aligned with adaptive learning (Ellström, 2010). However, it also contains elements that open pathways toward innovative learning. When the learning process involves questioning why things are done in particular ways and how activities might be structured differently, learning becomes critically reflective and may generate new ways of acting.

While learning changes individual thinking, it also depends on interaction with the environment and the community; only when knowledge is accepted and integrated into collective practice does individual learning translate into organizational-level innovation, turning individual competence into a shared resource for development (Lemmetty & Billett, 2023; Castaneda & Cuellar, 2020). In this way, learning becomes an ongoing social process in which knowledge is circulated, constructed, and expanded across the organization by transforming individual expertise into shared competence, so that individual- and group-level learning progress together and one person's development contributes to all (Nonaka & Takeuchi, 1995; Sessa & London, 2006; Kira & Frieling, 2007). Consequently, learning in innovation contexts is both social and contextual in its processes and outcomes (Kerosuo et al., 2010; Slappendal, 1996). Next, we examine these processes and outcomes in the light of the EDLI project.

3.2.2 Adaptive and Innovative Learning in the Police and Technology Organizations

The EDLI project outlined various stages and practices of learning at work as part of a innovation process, especially from the perspective of shared and thus collective competence. The description of innovation as an activity implemented through continuous adaptive learning, innovative learning, and innovation construction, which emerged from the review conducted as part of the project's background (Lemmetty & Billett, 2023; see also Chap. 1 of this book), created a starting point for locating different learning stages and practices based on the project data. Next, I describe what are the stages of innovation from the learning perspective; how competence is used and built in these stages and; what kind of learning practices are attached to the different stages of the innovation process in police and technology work.

3.2.2.1 Adaptive Learning

In the police and technology data, adaptive learning appears as a phase in the innovation process in which the existing competences of participants are made visible, shared, and collectively combined. Adaptive learning thus incorporates two key elements: the existing competence of the actors, and the learning practices through which this competence is combined. Thus, existing competence is a starting point for adaptive learning, which is realized in learning practices related to participation, through which competence is shared and combined.

The police's existing professional competence is shared both in the work between close colleagues and in group activities with one's own team and stakeholders. Typical triggers for adaptive learning are situations in which a police officer feels that their expertise is weak and actively seeks to learn new information from a colleague, who in turn acts as a guide and example:

> Creating social media is not easy for me. For example, I wanted to get rid of my habit of educating and instructing people through updates, when social media could be so much more. A communication intern who worked here over the summer has brought a lot of good tips on how to use social media in the police. Following her updates and the discussions we have had together has given me good ideas and a new approach to communication. (PP13, Police)

Adaptive learning occurs, for example, in situations in which there is no ready-made model for action, but informal methods of action have already been developed by colleagues. Before developing the actual new method of action (i.e. innovation), getting to know the practice already created by a colleague is important. Adaptive learning takes place in these situations by *following* a colleague's work or *discussing* it together. It is essential to combine the experiences, views, and understandings of others regarding the topic with one's own competence:

> That [certain area of work] is still so new in the organization that there is no [clear process and instructions] for it yet. But it is based on what I have learned from my colleague who has done that work. And then I apply what I have learned from him to my own [expertise] [...]. We each have our own strengths and different educational backgrounds. In addition to the police degree, so to speak. Everyone gains understanding from the other person, also from their other education, when they share that information with each other. That is how it works when there is no specific template for how we operate. (PP13, Police)

Likewise, existing professional competence in the *technology sector* is conveyed and shared in everyday work, for example, by concretely *demonstrating* how work is done and by actively *observing* the work of others. Thus, current practices and methods of operation—and the knowledge embedded in them—become visible and tangible:

> When you watch something for an hour or two, follow a production process, see how it works and make notes for yourself, you'll quickly start to see the pain points [...] it is probably a pretty effective way to learn what the current situation is. (TP19, Technology)

Utilizing the views and experiences of people working in different units and departments is evident. The aim is to build a knowledge base regarding the experience and understanding of many people as the background for development activities:

> I've tried a lot to encourage people from [another department] to be involved, for example, in [certain types of] projects, so that [people in certain roles] can be involved early on or someone else from [another department]. Purely for learning purposes. (TP3, Technology)

Thus, adaptive learning is concretized as collective practices: professional competence, both one's own and others', is shared through participatory activities such as observing, discussing, questioning, and demonstrating in practical situations, forming a combined competence base that enables innovative learning.

3.2.2.2 Innovative Learning

Innovative learning in the police and technology organizations also involves two key elements: The combined competence (formed through adaptive learning) is *concretized* as a new body of competence, described through a shared vision or decision, a documented or concretized intermediate outcome, or an initial model. This new but still raw entity is a launching pad for innovative learning practices, which participants described as learning by doing, including experimentation and, in the technology sector, prototyping:

> It requires a physical object, a rough prototype, so that it is understandable what I or others are aiming for […]. It's always at the heart of the job—what the concrete intermediate result is […] How do you make it kind of flesh out the idea? Because that's what people then start to take forward. (TP15, Technology)

Innovative learning is embodied in both fields as experiments: Through a testing process, the initial idea is tested, providing knowledge and understanding of the functionality of the practice or product being developed that are new to all parties. In this way, completely new knowledge is built, based on something that has not been known before:

> So, for example, we try different approaches [to the target group]. Now, as one example, in the spring [gives an example]. We tried how it works, how it gets people to participate. Then last fall, a similar experiment was conducted [gives another example]. Yes, we try different ways of working […] and I would like more direct feedback. Then over there [in the other work area], we have to constantly think and try different things, because the challenge is that those criminals quickly learn our way of working […]. But now in this [related to the first-mentioned experiment], we are trying to get our entire team [to that target] in the future. The feedback from that experiment was really positive. (PP23, Police)

> A good rule here is always […] don't say it works until you've tested that it works […]. For the most part, it is the experimentation: that first you take it [gives an example] [then you state] that you can't do it this way, how you can make it work, and then you just try it out to see what works. For each experiment, we record how the experiment was done, and then we see what a good way would be to do it […] The result is saved, and then we do another experiment and the same thing again. (TP20, Technology)

> We demonstrated, made cardboard models of just where it is located there, so that it would be good to use it there. We looked at it with a group of people, and we rotated it quite a lot, but I think it turned out pretty good. (TP17, Technology)

Experimentation and prototyping are above all *learning by doing*, confirming and deepening the new understanding and competence that have been formed:

> In other words, learning by doing, in a way, seals and deepens that competence. (TP14, Technology)

3.2.2.3 Evolving Innovation

Innovative learning gives rise to *innovative outcomes*, which, although based on analysis, do not appear to be final or the end of the process; rather, they are *products or results* providing a starting point for future development processes. These outputs appear in themselves as new and valuable outcomes for individuals, teams, and the organization, concealing within them the competence created in the precending learning processes. This outcome and competence embedded in it in turn becomes part of the organization's cultural history, appearing as a starting point for future adaptive learning processes (see Lemmetty, 2025; cf. Lemmetty & Billett, 2023):

> Not everything is necessarily new, for example, in products. You do not have to have cutting-edge innovation in every little part, but the combination is something new or better. (TP16, Technology)

Innovative outputs are not created, nor do they remain static; they are constantly evolving through the organizational actors' evaluation, experimentation, and improvement, reflected in the data as learning. The innovative outcome is therefore often unfinished and context-bound; its value and functionality are only built through practical application and evaluation.

> With a little work or change like this, it became really beautiful [presenting the product.] There is nothing like it in the world. [...] all these [stages] are formed [...] that learning is like a stream. All these details, but then how much [knowledge] has been applied to this and then also learned from this drop by drop? (TP1, Technology)

> More has been [mentions certain stakeholders] before with the so-called [mentions a specific opportunity that was developed earlier], so it was no longer a new idea in itself; the concept already existed, which defined what we do [...] but we felt [...] that we would start to influence [...] and go through it together and then a little bit about how it [this activity] could be improved. (PP8, Police)

3.3 Innovation Based on Learning: Lessons Learned

> When you look back at the end and see where you left off, it may be something completely different to where you are and what you have got left. You just must accept that there's some kind of journey and learning process that you have to do [...] It's quite rare that you can foresee that outcome. (TP2, Technology)

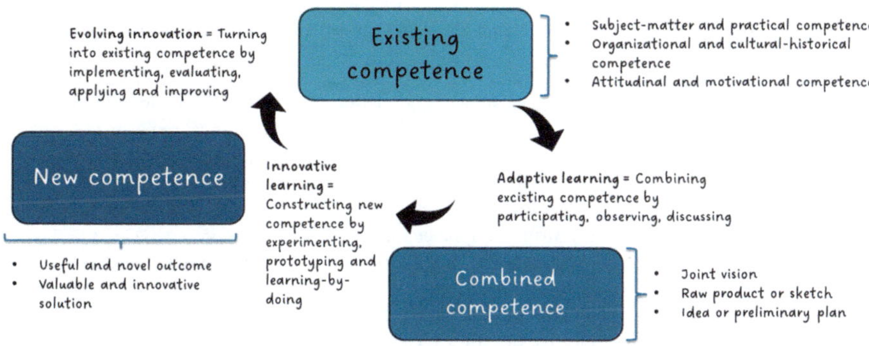

Fig. 3.1 Expanding competence through learning practices in different phases of the innovation process (modified and expanded from Lemmetty, 2025, p. 8)

This chapter examined the competence required in innovation activities and the innovation process from the perspectives of different stages and practices of learning. Based on the analysis, the innovation process can be described as a continuous process in which qualitatively different forms of learning (adaptive and innovative) vary and competence is shared, combined, and applied at the community level, assuming different forms at different stages (Fig. 3.1).

The examination of adaptive and innovative learning from both organizations produced an understanding of innovation as a continuous process in which competence, which is not only a prerequisite for innovation but also its output, develops through various adaptive and innovative learning practices (see also Lemmetty, 2025). These practices manifest in following ways: as participation, which combines discussion and observation and builds on existing competence; learning by doing, which involves prototyping and experimentation to construct new competence, and; implementation, including evaluating and improving the developed practice, model, or product, thereby turning new competence into existing competence.

3.3.1 Summary of Findings by Context

Although the study enabled a theoretical, cross-context description of the innovation process as constructed through competence and learning, the substantive and operational characteristics of both competence and learning practices are emphasized somewhat differently in policing and in the technology sector. Table 3.1 compiles the key contents regarding competence domains and learning practices by context.

In this chapter, innovation was found to rely simultaneously on three interrelated domains of competence: subject-matter and practical competence (task- and field-specific knowledge and skills), organizational and cultural–historical competence (awareness of structures, processes, values, and traditions), and attitudinal and motivational competence (motivational and value-based orientations relevant to one's

Table 3.1 Summary of findings: competence domains and learning practices across organizations

Theme	Police	Technology
Subject-matter and practical competence	• Broad, hybrid knowledge base: legislation; coercive measures; preventive methods; communication; interaction; clients; networks • Strong emphasis on situational judgment and trust-building • Multi-domain coverage; "jack of all trades"	• Deep, domain-specific technical expertise (automation, electronics, software, marketing, production, depending on the core tasks) • High specialization; competitive advantage from unique mastery
Organizational and cultural-historical competence	• Understanding of organizational goals, hierarchy, structures, regional variation • Awareness of "the sandbox": limits, legitimacy, permissible action • Cultural-historical understanding shaped by bureaucracy and legacy practices	• Understanding of long organizational history, product lineage, culture • Knowledge of customer base, market competition, past successes/failures • Cultural-historical framing of what qualifies as innovation in the industry
Attitudinal and motivational competence	• Empathy; openness to diverse clients; suspension of prejudice • Motivation essential for self-directed activity • Personal initiative in ambiguous environments; contextual behavioral adjustment	• Curiosity; playful experimentation; tolerance for failure; critical discussion • Intrinsic motivation for problem-solving • Ability to challenge assumptions, revisit ideas, regulate emotions
Adaptive learning	• Peer guidance, shadowing, informal sharing • Triggered by recognizing limits and seeking others' know-how • Observing colleagues' practices when formal models absent	• Observation/demonstration of processes; cross-sectional discussions • Expertise gathered across teams to identify current problems ("pain points") • Collective, experiential sense-making before new ideas
Innovative learning	• Experimentation in preventive activities; trying new approaches with clients/partners • Testing in real contexts; interpreting feedback; adjusting methods	• Strong emphasis on prototyping, testing, learning by doing • Use of material artifacts (models, prototypes)

work and professional community) (cf. Baartman & de Bruijn, 2011). As innovation is deeply situated within specific professional and organizational contexts, the forms and applications of these competences differ across fields. While both the police and technology sectors share overarching elements, particularly in attitudinal competence (e.g., openness and motivation), their enactment varies notably. For instance, playful experimentation and tolerance of failure, considered central to in technology work, would appear inappropriate within police practice, in which the situational adaptability and the ability to select effective interactional strategies are important.

In police officers' subject-matter and practical expertise, it was, perhaps unsurprisingly, the technical and tactical skills, as well as legal knowledge, that stood out, but also a remarkably broad form of "knowing everything." Interestingly, police officers viewed interaction skills particularly as a form of subject-matter competence. This highlights not only the importance of interaction in police work but also its distinct characteristics: interaction competence is not merely a generic skill, but a form of specialized competence within preventive police work. In terms of learning, police work appears collaborative and continuous due to its built-in reliance on cooperation. Earlier research (Doornbos et al., 2008) has indeed shown that police officers learn extensively on the job, through everyday conversations with colleagues—acquiring not only information in general but also culture and shared understandings of the organization as a whole (Lundin & Nuldén, 2007; Wieslander, 2019). In police work, collaboration with external stakeholders enables exposure to different ways of acting and thinking (Janssens et al., 2017), which in this study appeared as learning that advances innovation processes.

In the technology sector, subject-matter competence was tied less to broad knowledge and more clearly to the one's own core tasks and the specialized knowledge required within specific field (see also (see e.g. Lemmetty, 2020). Interestingly, however, cultural-historical knowledge of the organization also emerged as an important dimension of competence, which can partly be explained by the company's strong identity and its roots as a family-owned business. In terms of attitudinal competence, what stood out was not only playfulness and the generation of "crazy ideas," traits typically associated with creative work (see also Craft, 2011), but also an explicit appreciation of the value of challenging one's own ideas and engaging in critical, collective evaluation. This was understood as an attitudinal competence in which individuals must be ready, and even willing, to receive critical feedback from others, including comments suggesting that their ideas should be "shot down." Such practices were seen as enhancing multi-perspectivity, which in turn was viewed as essential for ensuring the quality and robustness of innovations in otherwise uncertain processes. Learning in the technology sector was characterized by strong interaction related to both product development and production processes. Concrete material artefacts, such as prototypes, played a central role: the competence built collectively within the organization was seen as embedded in these artefacts, which then served as vehicles for advancing the innovation process further.

3.3.2 Competence for Innovation and Its Visibility in Learning Practices

The competence descriptions found in this study are in line with professional learning research viewing competence, knowledge, skills, and attitudes as context-bound in nature (Baartman & de Bruijn, 2011; Mulder, 2014). In the context of innovation activities, knowledge, skills, and attitudes form a functional entity, whose relevance and adequacy are situationally determined through work, the community, and their interaction. The development of attitudes and contextual understanding largely reflects the socialization process whereby learning is shaped by both the social environment and the institutional boundaries of the activity (Baartman & de Bruijn, 2011). The centrality of cultural–historical competence supports this: Organizational and often implicit competence can only be acquired by participating in the organization's practices and cultural activities. Simultaneously, theoretical and conceptual subject-matter knowledge—reinforced by education and theoretical knowledge (e.g., Svensson et al., 2004)—is reflected in the sector- and task-specific specialization of work in both fields. The competence required by innovations is thus specialized, situational, continuously evolving, and culturally transmitted.

According to this chapter, competence first became visible in employees' practices in innovation activities, being *shared*. Participation through observations and discussion were seen in the study as learning practices through which people gained information and understanding from one another, thus learning adaptively (cf. Ellström, 2001; Fenwick, 2003; Høyrup, 2010). Shared and combined competence became visible as concrete outputs, transmitted as visions, models, ideas, and preliminary products (cf. Davenport & Prusak, 1998) that merged also into physical, material artifacts. Combined competence created the starting point for innovative learning. Based on this combined competence, the artifact (whether a method, a tool, or a product) or idea was tested for functionality. In this process, participants learned something that was not previously known. Thus, the initial idea or output was further developed, through learning by doing, until it was collectively accepted as the final result i.e. innovation—a method or a product that could be adopted, disseminated, or scaled in organization. This innovation became part of the everyday life of the organization, community, or group—a cultural–historical entity—serving in turn as the starting point for future adaptive processes (i.e., something that must first be understood to be developed further). Thus, the theoretical description (Lemmetty & Billett, 2023) of the innovation process as employee-driven and learning-based received empirical confirmation. This study emphasizes the importance of everyday learning opportunities in organizations, especially sharing knowledge and promoting community learning, for supporting innovation activities. This is consistent with previous research suggesting that a company's innovation capacity is better the more it encourages knowledge sharing and the more that tacit knowledge is transferred (Cavusgil et al., 2003).

From a *learning perspective*, the innovation process appeared to be a *continuous* process: The final result created in the previous phase formed the starting point for the following processes. In the technology sector, this was evident in the historical phases of product development: It was discovered that the current product was in practice a version of the first prototype that was gradually improved over decades, which itself was based on an earlier product from another manufacturer. Thus, the organization's innovation process was linked to previous innovations in the industry, combining the expertise of people working within the organization at different times.

3.3.3 Concluding and Practical Perspectives

This study examined competence by understanding it as a combination of the knowledge, skills, and attitudes needed to develop and do work (Mulder, 2014). The competence areas identified emerged as inherently context-bound (cf. Mulder, 2015), directly embedded in participants' everyday work practices. Examining the competences behind innovation activities did not produce a description of a specific context-independent *innovation competence* (cf. Hero et al., 2017) as such, as in participants' speech, competence was always structured around work and its specific situations, even when they spoke about the things like future orientation or creativity. This is because innovation was described as a process formed in a specific cultural–historical context and in the interaction between individuals, in which specialized subject-matter competence and contextual understanding are central. These findings align with the *situated professionalism* (Mulder, 2015) approach, understanding professional competence as a context-bound phenomenon. Thus, the same description of a competence area often means different things to employees in different jobs. According to Mulder (2015), in this approach, the desired competence is determined by what key stakeholders in the professional context expect from the activity, which was evident in the technology organization's monitoring and comparison of competitors and in the police's emphasis on strong stakeholder work.

The findings here thus challenge the prevalent competence discourse in organizations and, more broadly, in society. The professional competence areas observed as underlying innovation activity are broad, experiential, and situationally and contextually bound combinations of skills, knowledge, and attitudes, and therefore do not readily fit into predefined, unit-based "skill lists" commonly used in workplaces to map employees' 'competence'. This reinforces the understanding that success at work is not determined solely by a sum of various generally and technically described skills (see Sandberg, 2000), but strongly by how work is understood and structured in different situations in relation to one's experiential background and learned knowledge as well as organizational and operational environment. The findings of this book support the view that the focus of professional competence assessment should shift from checklist-style metrics toward making processes, experiences and context visible: how knowledge, skills, and attitudes are integrated in participation, experimentation, and implementation, and how competence accumulates through adaptive and innovative learning processes.

It thus also challenges the prevailing societal view of competence, which risks, for example in EU and OECD reports, narrowing to generalizable meta-skills or "thinking skills" as competence (the EU's skills first policy; see Milana et al., 2025). In these kinds of approaches, an individual's standardized and measurable skills and competences that are "not limited to a specific domain, activity, subject, or area" (European Commission, 2025) highlight a psychometric perspective in which test-measured individual characteristics are seen as key factors in adaptation to future demands and even as world-shaping abilities. The future competences defined by the OECD and other twenty-first-century projects are understood as metacognitive, higher-level abilities (e.g., social skills, thinking skills, and self-direction) that are not tied to specific content (see Miettinen, 2019), but "transferable". This conceives competence primarily as thinking skills excludes cultural, contextual, and content-knowledge dimensions of competence. However, in examining professional competence and learning, content knowledge, context, and culture appear—based on the previous literature and this chapter—to be essential conditions for how general thinking skills, such as creativity or problem-solving, can actually be applied within each field to advance innovation.

With regard to the examination of innovation processes, descriptions and models of linear innovation processes (Sossa et al., 2019; see also Meissner & Kotsemir, 2016) typically end with a phase in which the innovation (i.e., the final result) is completed. However, a learning-based examination of innovation allows for a perspective in which the implemented innovation *continues* to develop, serving as the basis for new innovations. This perspective assumes that the understanding produced in the previous process serves as a building block for future processes (Lemmetty & Billett, 2023). Rehn and Vachhani (2006) emphasized the importance of such continuity, criticizing the view of innovation as a single event with a beginning, an end, and a value defined in the present. They based their criticism on ontological considerations regarding the novelty value of innovation that essentially includes a view of temporality: the question of what is valuable in the present. In emphasizing the present, the historical and future development of innovation is ignored. Thus, innovation processes should be understood as a continuously evolving cycle in which what appears worthless at one moment may become valuable at another, and in which the replication of the old may become new when situated in a new context. Because innovations must always be interpreted within their cultural-historical and social contexts, including reflection on what counts as innovation in a given setting (for example, in relation to culture, stakeholders, and organizational history), their nature and value vary across organizations. Thus, with these contextual variations in mind, we next turn to examining the nature, types, and value of different innovation projects.

References

Albinsson, G., & Arnesson, K. (2012). Team learning activities: Reciprocal learning through the development of a mediating tool for sustainable learning. *The Learning Organization, 19*(6), 456–468.

Allen, T., & Stephen, J. (2013). Innovation: A knowledge transfer perspective. *Production Planning & Control, 24*(2–3), 208–225. https://doi.org/10.1080/09537287.2011.647875

Baartman, L. K. J., & de Bruijn, E. (2011). Integrating knowledge, skills and attitudes: Conceptualising learning processes towards vocational competence. *Educational Research Review, 6*(2), 125–134. https://doi.org/10.1016/j.edurev.2011.03.001

Billett, S. (2012). Explaining innovation at work: A socio-personal account. In S. Høyrup, M. Bonnafous-Boucher, C. Hasse, M. Lotz, & K. Møller (Eds.), *Employee-driven innovation: A new approach* (pp. 92–107). Palgrave Macmillan.

Buhl, A. (2018). Do it yourself: A lean startup toolbox for employee-driven green product innovation. *International Journal of Entrepreneurship and Innovation Management, 22*(4–5), 526–544.

Cambridge Dictionary. (2025). *Skill*. Retrieved from https://dictionary.cambridge.org/dictionary/english/skill

Castaneda, D. I., & Cuellar, S. (2020). Knowledge sharing and innovation: A systematic review. *Knowledge Process Management, 27*(3), 159–173. https://doi.org/10.1002/kpm.1637

Cavusgil, S. T., Calantone, R. J., & Zhao, Y. (2003). Tacit knowledge transfer and firm innovation capability. *Journal of Business & Industrial Marketing, 18*, 6–21. https://doi.org/10.1108/08858620310458615

Craft, A. (2011). *Creativity and education Futures: Learning in a digital age*. Sterling: Trentham Books.

Darsø, L., & Høyrup, S. (2012). Developing a framework for innovation and learning in the workplace. In H. Melkas & V. Harmaakorpi (Eds.), *Practice-based innovation: Insights, applications and policy implications* (pp. 135–254). Springer. https://doi.org/10.1007/978-3-642-21723-4_8

Davenport, T. H., & Prusak, L. (1998). *Working knowledge: How organizations manage what they know*. Harvard Business Press.

Doornbos, A. J., Simons, R., & Denessen, E. (2008). Relations between characteristics of workplace practices and types of informal work-related learning: A survey study among Dutch police. *Human Resource Development Quarterly, 19*(2), 129–151. https://doi.org/10.1002/hrdq.1231

Ellström, P.-E. (1998). The many meanings of occupational competence and qualification. *Journal of European Industrial Training, 22*(6), 266–273. https://doi.org/10.1108/03090599810230678

Ellström, P.-E. (2001). Integrating learning and work. Problems and prospects. *Human Resource Development Quarterly, 12*(4), 421–435. https://doi.org/10.1002/hrdq.1006

Ellström, P.-E. (2010). Practice-based innovation: A learning perspective. *Journal of Workplace Learning, 22*(1/2), 27–40. https://doi.org/10.1108/13665621011012834

European Commission. (2025). *Defining 'skill' and 'competence'*. Retrieved from https://joint-research-centre.ec.europa.eu/projects-and-activities/skills-and-competences/defining-skill-and-competence_en

Fenwick, T. (2003). Innovation: Examining workplace learning in new enterprises. *Journal of Workplace Learning, 15*(3), 123–132. https://doi.org/10.1108/13665620310468469

Fleming, J. (1994). Recognising learning in work: A perspective on the relationship between work and learning. *Journal of European Industrial Training, 18*(8), 30–37. https://doi.org/10.1108/03090599410068036

Hero, L.-M., Lindfors, E., & Taatila, V. (2017). Individual innovation competence: A systematic review and future research agenda. *International Journal of Higher Education, 6*(5), 103–122. https://doi.org/10.5430/ijhe.v6n5p103

Høyrup, S. (2004). Reflection as a core process in organisational learning. *Journal of Workplace Learning, 16*(8), 442–454. https://doi.org/10.1108/13665620410566414

Høyrup, S. (2010). Employee-driven innovation and workplace learning: Basic concepts, approaches and themes. *Transfer: European Review of Labour and Research, 16*(2), 143–154. https://doi.org/10.1177/1024258910364102

Høyrup, S. (2012). Employee-driven innovation: A new phenomenon, concept and mode of innovation. In S. Høyrup, M. Bonnafous-Boucher, C. Hasse, M. Lotz, & K. Møller (Eds.), *Employee-driven innovation* (pp. 3–33). Palgrave Macmillan.

Huber, M. T., Hutchings, P., & Gale, R. (2005). *Integrative learning for liberal education*. Carnegie Foundation for the Advancement of Teaching. http://www.gallery.carnegiefoundation.org/ilp/uploads/PRSUFA05-IL.pdf

Janssens, L., Smet, K., Onghena, P., & Kyndt, E. (2017). The relationship between learning conditions in the workplace and informal learning outcomes: A study among police inspectors. *International Journal of Training and Development, 21*(2), 92–112. https://doi.org/10.1111/ijtd.12095

Jones, G., Chirino Chace, B., & Wright, J. (2020). Cultural diversity drives innovation: Empowering teams for success. *International Journal of Innovation Science, 12*(3), 323–343. https://doi.org/10.1108/IJIS-04-2020-0042

Kerosuo, H., Kajamaa, A., & Engeström, Y. (2010). Promoting innovation and learning through change laboratory: An example from Finnish health care. *Central European Journal of Public Policy, 4*(1), 110–131. Retrieved from https://doaj.org/article/9ea8e1c1aee64b6dbe573ec4a6bee528

Kesting, P., & Ulhøi, J. P. (2010). Employee driven innovation: Extending the license to foster innovation. *Management Decision, 48*, 65–84. https://doi.org/10.1108/00251741011014463

Kira, M., & Frieling, E. (2007). Bureaucratic boundaries for collective learning in industrial work. *Journal of Workplace Learning, 19*(5), 296–310.

Kyndt, E., Govaerts, N., Verbeek, E., & Dochy, F. (2013). Development and validation of a questionnaire on informal workplace learning outcomes: A study among socio-educational care workers. *British Journal of Social Work, 44*(8), 2391–2410. https://doi.org/10.1093/bjsw/bct056

Lave, J., & Wenger, E. (1991). *Situated learning: Legitimate peripheral participation*. Cambridge University Press.

Lemmetty, S. (2020). *"Self-learning is present every day—In fact, it's my job": Self-directed workplace learning in technology-based work*. Doctoral dissertation. University of Jyväskylä.

Lemmetty, S. (2024b). Explaining the innovation dichotomy: The contexts, contents, conflicts, and compromises of innovation stories. *Frontiers of Narrative Studies, 10*(1), 126–149. https://doi.org/10.1515/fns-2024-2007

Lemmetty, S. (2025). "Failure is future success": Expanding knowledge through learning practices in a continuous innovation process. *Innovation*. https://doi.org/10.1080/14479338.2025.2573102.

Lemmetty, S., & Billett, S. (2023). Employee-driven learning and innovation (EDLI) as a phenomenon of continuous learning at work. *Journal of Workplace Learning, 35*(9), 162–176. https://doi.org/10.1108/JWL-12-2022-0175

Lundin, J., & Nuldén, U. (2007). Talking about tools: Investigating learning at work in police practice. *The Journal of Workplace Learning, 19*(4), 222–239. https://doi.org/10.1108/13665620710747915

Meissner, D., & Kotsemir, M. (2016). Conceptualizing the innovation process towards the "active innovation paradigm": Trends and outlook. *Journal of Innovation Entrepreneurship, 5*(14). https://doi.org/10.1186/s13731-016-0042-z

Miettinen, R. (2019). 21. vuosisadan kompetenssit. OECD Kasvatuksen kielen uudistajana. *Kasvatus, 50*(3), 203–215.

Milana, M., Brandi, U., Hodge, S., Hoggan-Kloubert, T., & Morris, T. H. (2025). Skills, skills, skills! The European Commission's endorsement of a *Skills-First* approach and the future of adult education and lifelong learning. *International Journal of Lifelong Education, 44*(2), 127–130. https://doi.org/10.1080/02601370.2025.2472553

Mulder, M. (2014). Conceptions of professional competence. In I. S. Billett, C. Harteis, & H. Gruber (Eds.), *International handbook of research in professional and practice-based learning* (pp. 107–137). Springer. https://doi.org/10.1007/978-94-017-8902-8_5

Mulder, M. (2015). *Professional competence in context: A conceptual study*. Retrieved from https://www.mmulder.nl/wp-content/uploads/2011/11/150406-Paper-Competence-and-Context.pdf.

Mulder, M., & Winterton, J. (2017). Introduction. In M. Mulder (Ed.), *Competence-based vocational and professional education: Bridging the worlds of work and education* (pp. 1–43). Springer. https://doi.org/10.1007/978-3-319-41713-4

Ness, I. J., & Søreide, G. E. (2014). The room of opportunity: Understanding phases of creative knowledge processes in innovation. *Journal of Workplace Learning, 26*, 545–560.

Nonaka, I. and Takeuchi, H. (1995). *The knowledge-creating company: How Japanese companies create the dynamics of innovation*. Oxford University Press.

Patrick, H. A., & Kumar, V. R. (2012). Managing workplace diversity: Issues and challenges. *SAGE Open, 2*(2), Article 2158244012444615. https://doi.org/10.1177/2158244012444615

Ramstad, E. (2009). Developmental evaluation framework for innovation and learning networks: Integration of the structure, process and outcomes. *Journal of Workplace Learning, 21*(3), 181–197. https://doi.org/10.1108/13665620910943924

Rehn, A., & Vachhani, S. (2006). Innovation and the post-original: On moral stances and reproduction. *Creativity and Innovation Management, 15*(3), 310–322. https://doi.org/10.1111/j.1467-8691.2006.00390

Sandberg, J. (2000). Understanding human competence at work: An interpretative approach. *Academy of Management Journal, 43*(1), 9–25. https://doi.org/10.2307/1556383

Sessa, V. I., & London, M. (2006). *Continuous learning in organizations: Individual, group, and organizational perspectives*. Taylor & Francis.

Slappendal, C. (1996). Perspectives on innovation in organizations. *Organization Studies, 17*(1), 107–129. https://doi.org/10.1177/017084069601700105

Sossa, J., Rebolledob, J., Manuel, J., Hincapiéc, M., & Zartad, R. (2019). Innovation management models: A literature review. *International Journal of Innovation, Creativity, and Change, 10*(6), 175–194.

Stahl, G. K., & Maznevski, M. L. (2021). Unraveling the effects of cultural diversity in teams: A retrospective of research on multicultural work groups and an agenda for future research. *Journal of International Business Studies, 52*, 4–22. https://doi.org/10.1057/s41267-020-00389-9

Svensson, L., Ellström, P.-E., & Åberg, C. (2004). Integrating formal and informal learning at work. *Journal of Workplace Learning, 16*(8), 479–491. https://doi.org/10.1108/13665620410566441

Tractenberg, R. E., Rochette, S., FitzGerald, K., & Collman, J. (2016). Evidence of sustainable learning from the mastery rubric for ethical reasoning. *Education Sciences,* 41, 400–413.

Walrave, B., van de Wal, N., & Gilsing, V. A. (2024). Knowledge diversity and technological innovation: The moderating role of top management teams. *Technovation, 131*, Article 102954. https://doi.org/10.1016/j.technovation.2024.102954

Wang, L., Li, S., & You, Z. (2020). The effects of knowledge transfer on innovation capability: A moderated mediation model of absorptive capability and network reliance. *Journal of High Technology Management Research, 31*(1), Article 100372. https://doi.org/10.1016/j.hitech.2020.100372

Wieslander, M. (2019). Learning the (hidden) silence policy within the police. *Studies in Continuing Education, 41*(3), 308–325. https://doi.org/10.1080/0158037X.2018.1497592

Chapter 4
Accumulation of LBI: Types and Values of Employee-Driven Innovations

Abstract This chapter highlights various types of innovation projects and categorizes them according to the nature of the innovations, the specific content they address, and the forms of employee participation. Drawing on previous research, the chapter emphasizes that the value of innovation extends beyond economic benefits to include social, cultural, and well-being outcomes. It further demonstrates that innovations can be evaluated not only in terms of their situational novelty but also through their cumulative development over time. The empirical examples illustrate the nature of employee-driven innovations in both police and technology organizations, showing how they can be classified, what kinds of value they generate, and how incremental improvements made by individuals may lead to substantial long-term outcomes.

Keywords Employee-driven innovation (EDI) · Innovation value · Type of innovation · Police organization · Technology organization

> *Big innovations, those products or truly significant organizational changes that have a major impact on the development of this company, are seldom celebrated. That's why it's difficult to grasp innovation as a whole. Innovation in this work involves solving small problems as part of a larger whole. We break down individual problems or complexities into smaller parts and seek the best solutions for them. The difficulty then lies in the fact that our experience is not that we innovate or build innovations. These small pieces, small advancements, don't feel meaningful or valuable from an innovation perspective. Instead, the value and sense of achievement should come from the journey of continuously learning a little, moving step by step forward. Sometimes you must pause to look at that journey—to see the leaps forward that all those small parts and steps have taken you. We have a lot of staff who have had long careers in this organization. They can see that journey and the bigger picture and understand the significance of individual steps. Individual products or end results are always built on the background of new products or outcomes. Temporally, it's an evolution. It's about constantly innovating, but in small steps.*

"Evolution in steps": innovation type story, previously created and published as part of the EDLI project based on its data from the technology organization (Lemmetty, 2024b, p. 139).

S. Lemmetty, *Learning-Based Innovation*,
SpringerBriefs in Education, https://doi.org/10.1007/978-3-032-26911-9_4

When we talk about innovation research, it is important to consider what actually makes something an innovation. When can we approach a phenomenon, outcome, or solution as *innovative*? Throughout the history of innovation studies, the two perspectives of *novelty* and *value* have consistently stood out as key features of innovation, underpinning its definition. Novelty is not an objective and absolute characteristic, but a relative and context-dependent assessment. As individuals, we often perceive innovation in relation to our own knowledge base and experience: What is foreign to us appears new. For example, educational scientists can easily accept a quantum technological breakthrough as an innovation because it is outside their expertise; its background, development stages, and practical applications are mostly unknown to them. Instead, something closer to them, such as a new pedagogical solution, may seem less innovative precisely because they see it as a continuation of previous practices and theories, not as a radical change. The same applies to examining an innovation's value, albeit from the reverse perspective. For example, in terms of *utility value*, we accept a new output developed in a context familiar to us as valuable because we can concretely see and understand its benefits. Perceiving the utility value of an innovation in another field can be more challenging, as we do not understand what its meaning actually is in practice.

Thus, an innovation's *novelty* and *value* arise not solely from the idea's content but also from the observer's position and interpretative framework. In innovation research, this has been described as relative or contextual novelty (e.g., Høyrup, 2010; Slappendal, 1996), with novelty, and value more broadly, being assessed in relation to a specific social or organizational context. But what does *value* actually mean in concrete terms in different contexts? In this chapter, I examine different types of employee-driven innovations (EDIs) and the kinds of value that they generate within police and technology-sector organizations. The purpose is to provide an overview of the nature and types of EDI *projects* and the ways in which value is defined within them.

4.1 Innovation Types and Values

When we talk about product innovations—or organizational innovations that promote product development or production—we are of course talking about money. A company must produce in order to ensure its existence, but the essential question is by what means this financial return is achieved. This organization has grown tremendously over the years, and it poses challenges for certain types of family assets. Before, everyone knew each other; it was easy to build trust, and thus humanity was self-evident in all activities. Now we must consciously strive to maintain this humanity. On the other hand, there are opportunities here to develop your own work from the point of view of your own well-being: If you have to bang your head against a wall because of a way of working day after day, and if it can be solved with your own ideas, then you can solve it. These everyday solutions develop operating methods to be humane, but they also bring efficiency. A person is a creative being, and it is important that that creative potential is put to use. At the same time, work that does not require a human can be automated. This has been done and will be done, and it does not mean

> *that the work will stop. Human resilience is a key value in innovation also because many innovations are based on long experience—a long working career—and thus it is important that these working careers can be maintained. It has not always been successful, but it is worth striving for. Learning is created through competence and well-being, which in itself is already a value in innovation.*

"Humanely effective": innovation type story, previously created and published as part of the EDLI project based on its data from the technology organization (Lemmetty, 2024b, p. 142).

In the organizational context, an innovation's value is typically examined in relation to the work and the organization's core mission. Because innovation can mean different things in different industries and organizations, its types and value should be examined in relation to the organization's operational, strategic, cultural, and historical contexts: What is new and valuable in this particular organization? Who decides what counts as new, valuable, or useful? Is something innovative if it is new and valuable only to an individual? Must it be entirely new to the world? Or is it enough that it brings value to an organization? These questions lie at the heart of understanding innovation as a sociocultural phenomenon.

4.1.1 How Can We Typify Employee-Driven Innovation Projects?

EDI can be approached in terms of different kinds of projects in which employees play central roles. These projects involve several dimensions that help us understand their nature and significance for organizational operations. In this section, I present three analytical angles through which EDIs can be approached and typified: the nature of the innovations, the specific content addressed, and the forms of employee participation involved.

In terms of their *nature*, innovations can be structured into technological and product innovations, marketing innovations (strategic or methodological innovations), social innovations (new practices responding to societal challenges), and organizational innovations (e.g., new organizational models or management philosophies) (e.g., Armbruster et al., 2008; Crossan & Apaydin, 2010; Edwards-Schachter, 2018). In particular, organizational innovations are central in that they enable and support the emergence and embedding of other forms of innovation, including product and service innovations. Different types of innovation are therefore interdependent: Organizational innovations create the structural and cultural prerequisites for other innovations, thereby influencing the organization's overall success (Alves et al., 2018). For example, the introduction of a new service may require significant changes in work practices, organizational structures, or management approaches (Caroli & Van Reenen, 2001; Damanpour, 2014). At first glance, organizational innovations may appear to aim primarily at improving organizations and work practices internally and externally, reflecting the principle of generating social value (Armbruster et al., 2008; Crossan & Apaydin, 2010). However, the primary value of such innovations may lie in how they make organizational operations more purposeful by enabling people to learn and adopt new practices. In turn, this renders production more effective and makes technological outputs and products possible, thereby indirectly contributing to economic value through subsequent product development.

The *content perspective* describes an innovation's objective and scope (e.g., an individual's own work and professional activities or a broader development or strategic change project). Billett et al. (2023a) identified three types of innovations that differ in terms of scope, extent, and impact. These types—strategic, work practice, and procedural innovations—describe how innovations arise, who initiates them, and what kinds of impact they have on organizational operations:

- *Strategic innovations* are significant changes in the organization's direction, basic operational principles, and key practices. Typically initiated and approved by management, they affect what work is done and how it is done.
- *Work practice innovations* concern the ways in which work is organized and carried out. Often initiated by management, their practical implementation is carried out by operational personnel.
- *Procedural innovations* are improvements or changes to everyday work practices initiated by employees themselves. They may involve streamlining work, solving problems, or developing operating methods. They are usually approved and supported by superiors or other responsible individuals.

According to Billett et al. (2023a), procedural innovations are the purest EDIs, as they are initiated, implemented, and monitored entirely by employees themselves, offering opportunities for diverse learning. Through these processes, employees develop the knowledge needed to respond to changes (e.g., by assessing the effectiveness of their own practices). Employees also participate in strategic innovations and work practice innovations; however, in these innovations, employees' discretion, participation, and freedom of action are more limited, although different forms of learning may emerge (Billett et al., 2023a).

Billett et al., (2023a) findings are underpinned by Høyrup's (2012) typology for examining the degree of *employee participation.* According to this typology, EDIs can likewise be structured into three categories based on an employee-participation perspective:

- In the first level (*bottom-up innovations*), innovations are implemented from the bottom up and are completely initiated and implemented by employees.
- In the second level (*a blend of bottom-up and top-down innovations*), employees initiate the innovation processes, which are supported by management.
- In the third level (*top-down innovations*), innovation processes move from the top down; the innovation process is initiated by management, but within it, there is delegation to employees, who are involved in the process at different stages.

Employee participation relates to where an innovation originates and in which direction it progresses in the organization (e.g., a reform implemented from the organizational level to employees or an innovation arising from employees' ideas and initiatives and progressing to the organizational level). Through this typology, it becomes possible to examine how strongly an innovation project is driven by employees.

4.1.2 Theoretical Perspectives on the Value of Employee-Driven Innovations

In innovation research, individual innovation processes resulting in concrete innovations (e.g., products) have traditionally been categorized as either radical or incremental innovations based on their impact and novelty value (Tushman & Anderson, 1986; see also Henderson & Clark, 1990). Radical innovations, based on significant technological or scientific breakthroughs, open up completely new markets for organizations and can form the basis of entirely new industries (Tushman & Anderson, 1986). By contrast, incremental innovations are small improvements made to existing products that strengthen the organization's position and can lead to significant impacts over time (Hollander, 1965; Nelson & Winter, 1982). EDI has been primarily seen as incremental (Høyrup, 2010; Voxted, 2018), reflecting how an innovation does not always involve creating something completely new but often means restructuring or applying existing knowledge, practices, or ideas to new contexts, with novelty and value arising from the process of change itself.

Billett et al. (2023b) distinguished three types of innovation based on their novelty value: (1) *de novo* innovations that are completely new, requiring new skills and ways of thinking; (2) innovations based on the extension of existing concepts, applying previous knowledge to new situations; (3) innovations related to the promotion or integration of processes, adapting existing knowledge to new circumstances. The literature has shown that these types of innovation overlap. Small developmental steps can, over time, lead to larger solutions with novelty value at the organizational level (Holmquist & Johansson, 2019; Høyrup, 2010; Lemmetty & Billett, 2023; Tidd & Bessant, 2009). These kinds of continuous and complementary processes blur the line between radical and incremental innovations.

An innovation's value is not confined to economic factors but can include social, cultural, human, and environmental aspects (Edwards-Schachter, 2018). In the EDI context, Kristiansen and Bloch-Poulsen (2010) proposed that EDIs should produce value through new shared and *sustainable* practices, presenting three EDI criteria:

- bringing value to the organization;
- improving the organization of work;
- improving working-life quality from the employee's perspective.

Kristiansen and Bloch-Poulsen (2010) argued that the last of these criteria is the most important, as new practices (i.e., EDI outcomes) should improve working-life quality, which can relate to employment, well-being, or organizational culture (Høyrup, 2010). If this value is not realized, the outcome cannot be seen as an innovation. Thus, EDI is essentially a humanistic and social innovation, although, as stated by Høyrup (2010), it can generate economic value, including through reduced costs, increased employment, and improved well-being at work.

4.2 Innovation Projects and Values in the Police and Technology Organizations

In the EDLI research project, I classified innovation projects into different types to show (a) the nature of EDIs in the police and technology organizations, (b) the content of EDIs in these contexts, and (c) the forms of employee participation in the various innovation projects. Furthermore, I analyzed these projects from the perspective of the value generated both at the end of the project and in later developmental stages, as projects become interconnected and innovations accumulate.

4.2.1 Four Types of Employee-Driven Innovations

In the EDLI project data, the nature of innovations appears differently in the police and technology organizations. In the police context, social innovations are prominent, especially related to interaction among stakeholders, clients, and colleagues, as well as the resolution of locally occurring problems within communities or regions. By contrast, in the technology sector, technological innovations naturally dominate, including the development of the company's core product, the technological advancement and automation of various production processes, and the construction of specific technical solutions. Notably, both contexts emphasize the strong role of organizational innovations, viewed as foundational for social innovations in police work and for technological innovations in the technology organization:

> We develop working methods. We develop programs. We develop products. We develop personnel cooperation. I think innovations start there, with the development of working methods. (TP7, Technology)

More specifically, innovation projects were categorized in the EDLI project based on Høyrup's (2012) typology of bottom-up, blended, and top-down innovations and Billett et al.'s (2023a) classification of procedural, work practice, and strategic innovations. The aim was to form an understanding of innovation projects and their diversity, making visible the various kinds of innovations simultaneously occurring in everyday work. Four types of innovation projects were identified:

- *individual EDIs*—bottom-up procedural innovations;
- *group EDIs*—bottom-up work practice innovations;
- *unit/regional EDIs*—blended work practice innovations;
- *organization-driven EDIs*—top-down strategic innovations.

Next, I describe in more concrete terms what these different types of innovation projects look like in preventive policing (PP) and the technology company.

4.2.1.1 Individual EDIs—Bottom-Up Procedural Innovations

These EDIs are small development activities of an individual or a team, whose purpose is to improve existing daily practices. Centered on individual ideas, learning, and experimentation, they gradually develop through everyday tasks. They arise from problem-solving situations, self-identified areas for improvement, mistakes, feedback from supervisors, colleagues, or clients, and emerging work needs. A key factor is the employee's initiative in finding, recognizing, and addressing their development needs. These EDIs progress through individual learning processes, requiring the development of new understanding, knowledge, and skills related to one's work. Often emerging through everyday ideas, self-directed experimentation, knowledge gathering, and reflection, they lead to changes in one's actions:

> Even if you do it alone, there is always the possibility of taking the other point of view—to see if this is the right thing to do or if there is something else that could be better to achieve the goal. (PP13, Police)
>
> In the beginning, it was very difficult because I didn't have much experience and skills as a police officer [...] Now I have learned to be a bit creative and to see my own strengths and how I could do my job best. (PP15, Police)

In the police, these projects include developing social media communication, adapting to new roles (e.g., new duties), improving client and colleague interactions, and managing work time through task organization:

> I've tried to develop my [own] social media communication myself [...] It has been a kind of trial and error. It's been more about trying out what feels right—by experimenting. Trying out different things to see what works and what doesn't. [Police]

In the technology sector, these EDIs similarly emerge from individuals' everyday work, primarily aiming to make employees' own tasks easier. They involve ways of organizing one's work, approaches to communication or interaction, efforts to strengthen one's own agency, and small technical solutions and improvised inventions that accelerate work processes and make the work more meaningful:

> These are the kinds of very small innovations we've made. For example, when you're supposed to cut this kind of fuel hose, you'd normally take a measuring tape every time, mark it, and cut it with scissors. I came up with this instead: I just attached a utility-knife blade here. When you cut the hose through, there's a stopper, and by doing it like this, it always comes out the right length. These are little improvised solutions I've invented myself. (TP10, Technology)

> I don't really know about any big development initiatives, but sometimes employees give comments, like why are we doing this or whether it could be done differently, and then they had looked into it. [...] So the employee had noticed or thought while doing the work that, to make the job easier and faster, maybe it could be done this way. And then the change actually happened for real. [TP12, Technology]

4.2.1.2 Group EDIs—Bottom-Up Work Practice Innovations

Group EDIs are also strongly employee-driven (i.e., bottom-up) but focus on developing team or group (e.g., multidisciplinary teams in the police) work practices and methods. They are typically collective improvements relating to meeting practices, time management, and tools, systems, and processes for collaborative group work and intra-group communication. Each group member is portrayed as an active participant in the development:

> The creation of this whole group—we as members have been developing the activities of this group, so it is already an innovation. (PP4, Police)

Group innovation emerges as a process deeply rooted in team-level learning, with each group member's contribution being essential:

> Often it starts with us doing something completely new and thinking together about where it starts. We've had a pretty good and free culture of discussion. Everyone has been able to say what comes to mind. And then everyone has had a lot of experience and know-how, which we have then used together to take it forward. (PP12, Police)

> For this kind of innovation, it's just not possible that I now walk here, present you this, and that is that, but you have to start talking together as a group about whether it would be better to do it this way. Usually in this, there then also comes resistance, as some do not want it, and there are counter-arguments as to why it should not be like this. They don't come by themselves. (TP28, Technology)

Group-level innovation appears as an interactive and negotiated process rather than a one-directional solution proposed by an individual. An innovation emerges only through discussion, argumentation, and the handling of potential counter-arguments, requiring the confrontation of different viewpoints within the group and the construction of compromises. Through this process, the innovation becomes socially constructed, as solutions must be justified and defended.

In both organizations, group-level innovations appear to be similar, characterized as interactive activities focusing on developing team or group practices and systems. Such innovations typically begin with a perceived problem or an idea raised by an individual. A key feature of these solutions, capturing the essence of employee-driven and group-driven innovations, is that the group does not wait for managerial instructions but takes the initiative to improve its own ways of working. Innovation thus emerges from the collective exploration of a problem and shared decision-making, with the group seeking to develop more efficient and purposeful routines for its everyday work:

> Our group is new, and we are still developing its working methods. We have a work queue, which is a kind of tracking system for our work. Despite this system, it happens from time

to time that on different days the same request is handled by several people in the team. To avoid duplication of work and waste of time, we in the group decided to improve our ways of working. [PP4, Police]

It was a kind of joint result of the team, meaning that we thought it through together and defined how the guidance should be carried out. (TP30, Technology)

4.2.1.3 Unit/Regional EDIs—Blended Work Practice Innovations

These EDIs typically have some organizational basis, model, or starting point in the background, which is, however, loose in nature, allowing for quite strong EDI. They require the participation of a group larger than one team, as they often develop models, processes, and methods between several regional partners (as in police) or units (especially in the technology organization):

Some time ago, we launched an innovation team. The idea is that it will be something we run regularly, so we are now developing a process and a way to handle those matters or ideas. There are people in it [from different parts of the company], and the idea now is that the early phase of the innovation would work so that the idea is examined to see whether it has potential. (TP30, Technology)

In the police, these innovations include the creation or further development of multidisciplinary cooperation processes with partners (often youth services or social and health authorities), cooperation projects with local schools, projects related to the changing security situation in the area, and improvements in how police units or teams work or interact. These innovations are typically triggered by feedback and observations that various actors (partners, residents, stakeholders, supervisors, colleagues from other groups, etc.) bring to the police's attention. However, police officers themselves actively identify new phenomena and needs that require the launch of wider development and action projects. Essential to these innovations are interactions between representatives of different groups, the sharing of understanding and knowledge, the creation of a shared vision of the situation based on discussion, and the implementation of measures decided jointly. This knowledge sharing and collaborative working—and through this, a new understanding—is a collaborative learning process for achieving the best outcome for the target (e.g., the area). These innovation projects are often larger, longer-term, and more resource-intensive projects and developments than individual or group projects. As they are more demanding and time-consuming, their implementation is determined by the resources and opportunities available. These resources and opportunities are often provided by management:

There was no such clear national model and structure, so we created it ourselves [as a group]. We analyzed our operations and situations and started building what is currently our model, the way we work, how we do it, and we have been able to define different skills—what it requires. In other words, we are partly a self-created unit, as there has not been a framework for what our mission requirements and abilities are. [PP2, Police]

In the technology organization, unit-level innovations are development processes involving members from different teams and addressing a broader phenomenon, problem, or need that concerns several units. In this context too, a central feature is the multiplicity of perspectives, with the aim of achieving the best possible outcome that serves multiple actors and units. The development work is thus grounded in the experiences and insights of employees with different tasks and areas of expertise, but often behind it there is also management's perspective, proposal, or encouragement for development. The impact of these innovations is stronger than that of individual- or group-level innovations, reaching further across the organization and influencing the work of multiple actors:

> We had a brainstorming meeting, like okay, this has come up, how would we solve it? We started looking for solutions together. We made a kind of draft based on the very first meeting [...]. We were just the three of us at that stage. We thought about how we would do it. [...] We each put together our own sort of proposals, and then we went back to talk with the production people about how this would fit their work. [...] And once it kind of took shape, okay, this could be the concept, and now it seemed to please everyone. (TP15, Technology)

4.2.1.4 Organization-Driven EDIs—Top-Down Strategic Innovations

These top-down actions include organizational strategic decisions and structural changes, as well as the implementation of policies and practices enabling these innovations to be embedded across the organization. They typically require coordinated leadership commitment and resource allocation to ensure that the strategic intent translates into organization-wide impact:

> Those bigger lines, what is done so that it is just that and is just followed, very little can influence them. (PP20, Police) (See Chap. 5 for more examples.)

In the police, the national development of different functions, including major policy decisions and resource allocation, shapes organizational-level innovations by setting the strategic direction. Those working as senior constables or sergeants tend to detach themselves from them, stating that while organizational policies and decisions greatly affect their work, they themselves have little opportunity to influence the progress of these development projects. By contrast, police officers at the commissioner level are involved in development groups and projects, including at the national level and between police departments. As the police is a hierarchical organization, formal management determines much of the involvement in organizational-level development work. These innovation projects originate in decision-makers' and managers' initiatives at higher organizational levels and are typically described as top-down processes. As such, they are about communicating and introducing new policies. This can be seen as one-way (from the organization to the staff) organizational learning, with the whole staff being involved in internalizing the new, institutionalized practices decided at a higher level:

> This [organizational development project] started in such a way that the organization decided to develop this [...] and all the managers of the sectors and units were consulted, and there was a preparatory working group that found out if this is possible at all and if there is a need for this, and then, a decision was made—that we will try. And then we looked for people to do it. [PP1, Police]

In the *technology organization*, these organizational-level innovations are initiated by management, but employee involvement typically appears stronger than in the police organization. These initiatives were often also triggered by ideas, needs, or wishes expressed by employees, on the basis of which management launched a development project. Participation provides practitioners and specialists with the freedom and opportunities to engage in the development work from its early stages onward:

> [The development of a new flagship product is] right at the very beginning. I mean, we are designing something that will again define what we are for the next 20 years. Everything is like [...] I have no idea yet what form it will eventually take, probably in a couple of years, but we have the freedom to rethink absolutely everything. (TP16, Technology)

In the technology organization, organization-driven strategic innovations are associated not only with major product development projects (entirely new product entities, as illustrated in the quotation above) but also with organizational changes involving simultaneous modifications to the structures, responsibilities, role allocations, or work organization of several teams. These processes are described as long and multifaceted. Although employees, and especially key personnel, are involved, managerial steering remains strong. This sometimes appears challenging, particularly when expectations of participation exist, but decisions are nevertheless made sporadically by management alone:

> Group interview (Technology):
>
> Participant 1: So the company wants to somehow change or improve the product development organization—and probably the whole organization. Our way of working is supposed to develop now [...]
>
> Interviewer: How did this organizational change take place? If you were to describe it, who carried it out and how?
>
> Participant 2: We started talking about it maybe about a year ago for the first time. [Manager 1] was strongly involved. [Manager 2] took a pretty quiet role. When we talked with them, we discussed things together. It was kind of a compromise team effort. And it changed somewhat from the original idea.
>
> [Off-topic discussion]
>
> Participant 1: We talked very openly. I was maybe more ready than you to make the change, because in a way the change was already underway.
>
> [Off-topic discussion]
>
> Participant 1: At some point, we looked at things and said, "everything's fine, yes, let's do it this way." A week later, management suddenly made a U-turn on their own, and it was communicated really poorly.
>
> Participant 1: But the old tasks and everything still have to be completed, so we're moving very slowly here. Yes. So someone should ensure that we have a roadmap, that we have the right projects, that they follow the process, and someone should know where we are in all the projects and make sure the right people are informed.

4.2.2 Multiple and Cumulative Value of Employee-Driven Innovations

An innovation's value is grounded in the industry and purpose of the organization. In the police organization, innovations appear to possess *human value* when the focus is on improving how individuals or groups carry out their work and *social value* when the aim is to solve local problems or support regional development in collaboration with stakeholders. Examining value in organization-driven innovations proved challenging, as the interviews with employees and managers offered only limited explanations for the reasons and intended purposes behind these organization-wide changes. In addition to social value, the data reveal justifications related to efficiency and resource optimization, presented as the underlying drivers of various large-scale organizational transformation processes. In the technology sector, the value of many individual- and group-level innovations is likewise primarily human in nature—linked to making work easier or more meaningful. However, in the technology sector's value discourse, economic considerations also feature prominently. From an EDI perspective, these economic aspects emerge when initially human-value-producing individual innovations evolve into broader change projects that ultimately generate economic benefits through increased efficiency and enhanced well-being.

4.2.2.1 Value Vignettes

Next, we examine more closely the value of the kinds of EDIs described above. The vignettes below, drawn from the research data, are summaries of specific types of innovation projects, illustrating not only how a project progresses but also how and what kind of value is created. *The first vignette*, based on the police data, describes a unit-level or regional-level innovation project (cf. Section 4.2.1).

Vignette 1. Value of unit/regional EDI (blended work practice innovation) in the police

> Most typically, innovations in police work arise from various projects—often regional situations where a new phenomenon or problem is observed. For example, when we move around in the field and talk to young people, we may begin to notice signs of some ongoing change: Perhaps a high number of crime reports are coming in related to a certain activity, calls are coming in from schools or residents about the same concerns, or social media is filled with discussion around some new disruptive behavior.
>
> These small observations often set the whole process in motion. We begin to perceive that a phenomenon is emerging and that it should be addressed before it grows and becomes more complex. The phenomena can be very different—related to traffic safety, substance abuse, or disruptive behavior among young people—and no two cases are ever exactly the same.
>
> Once the problem has been identified, we in the police start to consider what could be done about it. Often, with a work partner or more broadly at the department level, we discuss how some actions are now needed. And because the police cannot solve community phenomena alone, we immediately involve a network: schools, social work, youth work, organizations,

> or other key actors. A multi-professional group is assembled, where observations are shared, key people are sought, and together we plan what actions could be tried to calm the situation.
>
> After that, we move on to doing. We as police officers operate with our own tools and perspective, and the other actors in the network implement their own measures from their own roles. This joint experiment—testing a new way of working—is, in a way, the innovation phase.
>
> Finally, we monitor the effects. If a new approach works, it is often very tangible: The number of crime reports and contacts decreases. For us, this is clear numerical evidence of success. But what people say is just as important—for example, feedback from schools or residents that the situation has calmed down. Our own experience in the field, when we see the changes in activities with young people, is also a significant part of the evaluation. Although not all effects can always be measured visibly, the feeling that our work is producing real change is an important indicator of a successful innovation for us.

As seen in this vignette, the value and impact of unit/regional EDI projects are both social and practical, extending from individuals' experiences to the wider work community and networks and including more effective and meaningful cooperation between stakeholders and within the police department, increased regional security, and reduced disruptive behavior.

Impact can be assessed both subjectively and objectively through qualitative and quantitative methods, considering both the experiential meanings of employees and stakeholders and concrete changes in operations and results. Thus, impact is not limited to a single organization but extends to its networks and operating environment:

> And we did get positive feedback from that [...] then in concrete terms [the developed activity] they calmed down a huge number of consultation calls and emails for us. (PP8, Police)
>
> The feedback that has been received from those who have started [the development work] has been positive. A lot of young people have been met, and the encounters have been positive on both sides. According to the city's technical measure, acts of damage have decreased in the city area. (PP23, Police)

The second vignette, based on the technology organization data, describes a project representing an initially individual bottom-up procedural innovation (cf. Sect. 4.2.1).

Vignette 2. Value of individual EDI (bottom-up procedural innovation) in the technology organization. (Previously created and published as part of the EDLI project based on its data and originating from the technology organization, see Lemmetty & Glaveanu, Forthcoming)

> A person working in a professional role in production work in the technology company began thinking about how to make their work easier—how to create "opportunities for laziness." They noticed how much time was wasted just walking across the hall to get materials or searching for tools placed in illogical spots. They asked themselves why things were arranged this way in the first place.
>
> They measured their daily steps and the time spent retrieving items. They then started planning a new layout for their workstation. After discussing the idea with a coworker and presenting it to management, they eventually received approval to reorganize the workstation.

> The changes were implemented, and the results were striking: Work became so efficient that one person could now handle tasks that previously required two. The initial aim of creating "laziness" didn't really materialize—but in the end, the work became more meaningful. Employees spent less time walking around the hall and more time on tasks that genuinely advanced the work, making their contributions feel more significant. At the same time, the improvements proved economically productive.

This vignette illustrates how innovations arising from personal local observations *accumulate* into organization-wide benefits. The process is initially driven not by the idea of increasing efficiency but by the *possibility of laziness*, motivating actors to reconsider how the work is carried out and organized. The first phase produces value for employees (working-life quality and meaningfulness), creating the basis for improving work organization and ultimately manifesting in measurable efficiency and economic value. This process demonstrates EDI's central principle: Enabling and supporting employees' observations and initiatives can lead to strategically significant organizational results that create economically sustainable solutions.

4.2.2.2 Analyzing the Values of Employee-Driven Innovations

When the innovation projects identified in the organizations are examined from a value perspective, it becomes possible to determine whether they are primarily activities supporting individual learning and well-being at work or broader initiatives affecting employees or stakeholders more widely. For the interviewees, describing the value of innovation was easiest when discussing individual-level innovations (Sect. 4.2.1), as the value in these cases is defined subjectively through one's own learning or through the facilitation of one's own work. The interviewees also described various value perspectives related to group- and unit-/regional-level EDIs. However, articulating the value of organizational EDIs appeared particularly challenging, as in these projects, the interviewees' personal roles and participation were either limited or restricted (in the police organization) or partly unclear (in the technology organization). Organizational EDIs were characterized as broad and long-term strategic change processes, perceived as somewhat *detached* from one's own work, and the responsibility for defining and assessing value was attributed more to management or *the organization* than to individuals. Therefore, the personnel's reflections regarding these projects were scarce.

In individual EDIs, value is reflected in terms of more efficient, more organized, and easier work, increased motivation, well-being, and skills, and higher-quality practices. In group EDIs, value is described in terms of more efficient and effective group activities, increased job satisfaction and meaningfulness, and more effective practices, processes, and tools. These projects are mainly assessed qualitatively, based on group members' collective experiences, but also through feedback from supervisors or close-contact groups. The effects of unit-level/regional-level EDIs are wider than those of individual and group EDIs. The value is reflected in more effective communication and interaction processes and practices between different units. In these projects, value can be assessed qualitatively based on factors other than subjective feelings or experiences. It can also be assessed quantitatively, including through the reduction of incoming contacts in the police organization and through increased work efficiency (e.g., observing the productivity of new working methods or production lines) in the technology organization.

Although *police officers* could easily describe the value of innovation projects, it is difficult to make the effects of individual-, group-, and unit-/regional-level EDIs visible at the organizational level. This reflects not only the nature of the projects and the preventive work behind them but also the organizational indicators used and the performance-based way of perceiving effectiveness (see Taponen, 2023; Lemmetty, 2024a). Performance orientation is evident in police officers' work and development work. This is a key challenge both for preventive activities, which are difficult to measure through performance, and for development, as effectiveness (the consequences, meaning, and value of development; see Chap. 5) rather than performance is at the core of innovation:

> The biggest problem with preventive action is how you prove that you did something that never happened. (PP6, Police)
>
> If we are successful in our work, do we hide the results of our work, by which we measure whether it didn't happen thanks to us or whether it didn't happen anyway? (PP7, Police)

Because the success of work and therefore development work in the police is measured statistically, statistics easily become a guiding factor in the work. They also guide where individuals direct their own development activities. The following quotation illustrates performance-drivenness and the turning of statistics against substantive value creation:

> The police play with statistics. I have always said that I am not here to work for statistics. [...] For example, we currently have our field patrols driving around in a police car. It is stipulated that they must do two 20-minute traffic control tasks during their shift. That is, record a traffic control task in our system—20 minutes at least per task. So that we can show at the end of the year that "Yes, our traffic control goal has been met." In reality, they beat that task and drive around the city, just like they do anyway, but they have to do that task so that we can get into the statistics, so that we can show that we have reached this goal, so that we get money. They have to come up with things like this to make the statistics look good. That is statistical gimmickry. (PP20, Police)

According to participants, PP, and perhaps police work more broadly, should be guided and examined not just in terms of performance but through broader indicators appropriate to the nature of the work. This would assist in making appropriate everyday decisions about what actions should be taken, how to apply what is already known, and in which direction to develop the activity. Appropriate indicators would make the results visible, enabling the motivation for the work and the learning from it to be concretized from the perspective of its perceptible benefits. However, the development of indicators was understood by participants as a demanding and challenging problem at the organizational level:

> This brings us to the heart of the problem of preventive work, in that we have no indicators to measure preventive work. None whatsoever. [...] And that is why resourcing, financing,

> getting training, everything is extremely difficult when it doesn't "produce anything." [...] We are dealing with people. We try to influence people's behavior, but when that person is not a static vase, they are shaped and changed. No one can say that if that "Ville-Petteri" comes to talk to us for an hour, he will no longer commit crimes because he talked to us. [...] Has our work had any significance, or has that person simply grown up and started to take on that responsibility? We cannot know. (PP1, Police)

In the technology sector, the need to make work or product easier, more meaningful, more effective or more high quality is strongly conveyed in the EDIs. This was often the reason behind the start of innovations (i.e., the basic reason why something was developed), as illustrated by a production expert:

> [It would be important] that we have those materials close enough to us at that workstation for ergonomic reasons. That's where the [development idea] came from, that this could be somewhere here, so that we wouldn't have to take it from the floor. Therefore we have a lot of ergonomic thinking in it. When the whole product is assembled at one workstation, there are an awful lot of different parts. And there were even work stages where we had to "pick up" [supplies] for each [different product] at this strange branch. So that's where we started refining how they could be "fed" to us. (TP3, Technology)

EDI's value was described as manifold in the technology organization, with its economic value coming primarily from its human and social value. The projects illustrate that EDI can simultaneously generate organizational value, develop work organization, and improve working-life quality. Thus, they meet the key criteria of EDI (Kristiansen & Bloch-Poulsen, 2010), showing that human and economic goals can support each other:

> If people are unwell, they are on sick leave, and that is not financially viable either. (TP12, Technology)

Based on the data, human and economic value creation does not occur instantaneously. Rather, especially in organizational innovations, economic value materializes as an innovation process, initially triggered by human needs, values (e.g. well-being, learning of meaningfulness), that gradually accumulates from an individual-level initiative into a broader group- or organizational-level innovation. This is strongly evident in the technology organization, whose innovation stories contain several descriptions of how an earlier version of a product or working method served as the foundation for a new, ultimately successful organizational invention:

> This first [certain part of the product] was a breakthrough in this [our whole] field, a really [certain part] that doesn't have [typical problems that usually exist]. [...] it became possible to do it because it's one surface, from which these current [versions] have kind of developed. [...] With that first [version] that was laborious, this [certain] product group has become possible. If that first one hadn't been invented, there wouldn't necessarily be the whole set. (TP24, Technology)

What is interesting in these examples is value's definition over time and the implications of failure for the process. Simultaneously, the examples convey reflections on the basis for evaluating technological product innovations. The economic perspective is a typical approach in innovation activities, but if a new product does not produce economic benefits, does that mean that the product is not innovative? The technology participants questioned this economic-related idea specifically from the perspective of the continuity of innovation: A product that is not financially successful can still be the most valuable innovation for the company, as the process provides a considerable amount of expertise and understanding of the background required for future processes that will have new opportunities to succeed, perhaps even financially:

> [Failed innovation] was our [certain] series [...] there were two models. It was not financially successful at all. As a product, it was incredibly good, but a few years after starting, [...] it was discontinued. [...]. These are the bigger [examples of failures] that come to mind, which have been started, and then it has been found that this didn't work at all. There were probably two identified or biggest reasons for that. Firstly, the fact that this industry was not ready for something like this—when it began to be marketed from a sustainable development perspective, that it was such a "sustainable decision"—no one paid any attention to that at the time. It [sustainability] has only recently become more significant. And then the second was the rather strong pressure to have a cheaper product. It wasn't even cheaper in relative terms, because we can't do that. But maybe the angle is that we weren't true to our identity. [...] but this is interesting because [it was a basis for] another [newer series], which was also not a financial success, but a [certainly successful] series was eventually planned based on it. So, how do you measure what constitutes failure? You could say that financially something was a complete flop, but by other metrics, it was [really important]. (TP5, Technology)

As this quotation shows, because of innovation's cumulative nature, defining value is challenging and a question of time (Rehn & Vachhani, 2006). So when is it relevant to consider an innovation's value at all? In this example, the value of the previous, so-called failed innovation is conveyed through new innovations created on its basis. This reflects both its economic value and its learning-based value. Learning took place in the unsuccessful innovation's development work, but the value of the learning was only later concretized at the organizational level. In the technology organization, there are similar descriptions of how mistakes and failures become valuable precisely because of learning, leading to the development of new products and outputs (see Chap. 3).

4.3 From Small Initiatives to Valuable Outcomes: Lessons Learned

This chapter provides an overview of the nature and types of employee-driven *innovation projects* and the ways in which value is defined within them. Innovation research has traditionally emphasized economic value, often viewing innovations as radical changes or significant breakthroughs or products that are evaluated through business-related measures (Høyrup, 2010). According to more recent work, this focus is too narrow, as innovations may also generate social, environmental, and cultural value (Edwards-Schachter, 2018) and support employees' learning, well-being, and employability (Høyrup, 2010), taking the form of incremental improvements or small-scale initiatives that initially benefit individuals or teams but later accumulate into broader organizational relevance (Voxted, 2018). Through the EDLI project, it was observed that many innovations arise from personally meaningful challenges experienced by employees or, at the group level, by various actors. These innovations tend to emerge in the flow of everyday work rather than solely through separate, purposefully structured activities (e.g., hackathons; Ellström, 2010; Flocco et al., 2022; Høyrup, 2012). This chapter makes visible the often-overlooked forms of value arising from employees' everyday innovation efforts, clarifying how such dispersed activities can collectively shape organizational and societal development.

4.3.1 Summary of the Findings by Context

In seeking to draw overarching conclusions about the nature, content, and value creation of EDI projects, this study highlights the importance of contextual examination, including contextual novelty (Høyrup, 2010) and, more broadly, the idea that an innovation becomes recognized as such only when its value is accepted and realized at the organizational level by organizational actors (Brandi & Hasse, 2012). Different types of innovative outcomes, whether product-, service-, or organization-related, create different kinds of value, often intertwined in complex ways. The outcomes' perceived value and impact depend on whose perspective we consider and when we make this consideration (see Glăveanu, 2015). Table 4.1 presents the key findings based on the organizational contexts, making visible how the results differ in emphasis when viewed side by side across the two settings.

In the police, the innovations were organizational (Armbruster et al., 2008) and social (e.g., Edwards-Schachter, 2018) in nature. Individual EDI projects, focusing on developing the individual's own work and individual learning, produced small-scale improvements in everyday task performance. Group EDI projects focused on developing practices within a specific team, necessitating collective action and learning at the team level. Unit/regional projects were broader processes connecting units or regional stakeholders and conveying learning collaboratively (see also Doornbos et al., 2008); based on this, new operating models were developed for institutionalization. Organizational projects appeared as organizationally oriented strategic projects in which employees' participation in the actual development was limited. The observation that police work—in this case, PP—involves a wide range of individual-, group-, and unit-/regional-level innovation processes embedded in everyday practice, in which activities are continuously developed and new approaches are created, challenges the traditional Weberian view of the police as a noninnovative organization with a monopoly on the legitimate use of force (Huotari, 2021; Filstad & Gottschalk, 2013; see also Chap. 6).

In the technology sector, innovation projects were organizational in nature, especially in the production and management employees' descriptions, or technological product innovations, especially from the product developers' perspective. Regarding product innovations, their evolutionary nature was strongly emphasized: In a continuous process of development, previous innovations, products, and related lessons

Table 4.1 Summary of findings: Innovation projects, outcomes and value across organizations

Theme	Police	Technology
Innovation projects	• Dominated by social innovations related to community problems, stakeholder collaboration, and regional phenomena (youth issues, safety, etc.) • Strong presence of unit-level/ regional-level EDIs (blended work practice innovations) involving multi-professional networks • Individual and group EDIs focusing on improving everyday work practices (communication, time management, interaction, etc.) • Organizational EDIs: mostly top-down, tied to national-level structures and decisions	• Dominated by technological innovations (core product development, automation, technical solutions, etc.) • Unit-level EDIs involving cross-team processes addressing organization-wide problems • Individual EDIs involving technical tweaks, workstation redesign, and process improvements • Organizational EDIs involving strategic reorganizations and major product development projects, typically management-initiated but with stronger employee participation than in the police
Innovation outcomes	• New cooperation models with schools, youth services, and social and health authorities • Improved regional safety, reduced crime reports, and smoother inter-unit processes • Enhanced team practices, communication, and workflows • Organizational outcomes are often taken for granted because of hierarchical structures	• New product versions, process improvements, and production-line innovations • Improved workflow efficiency, ergonomic redesigns, and less wasted time • Organizational outcomes involving the restructuring of teams, roles, and production processes • Evolutionary ("step-by-step") development
Innovation value	• Human value: improved work practices, better interaction, and increased well-being • Social value: solving local problems, enhancing community safety, and improving stakeholder cooperation • Organizational value: improved processes between units (sometimes measurable) • Economic value: rarely direct or visible, as preventive work is difficult to measure	• Human value: meaningful work, reduced physical strain, and smoother workflows • Organizational value: efficiency gains, optimized processes, and improved layouts and workflows • Economic value: emerges cumulatively as individual improvements evolve into wider organizational changes • Value is multidimensional, with learning, ergonomics, and well-being later producing efficiency and financial benefits
Manifestation of the accumulation	• Innovations expanding from an individual idea to the group to the unit to the region • Accumulation: less visible at the organizational level because of performance-driven metrics and difficulties in measuring prevention	• Individual tweaks, which form the basis for later organizational innovations and product breakthroughs • Failed innovations, which remain valuable as learning foundations for future solutions • Earlier versions of products and processes, which become platforms for subsequent innovations

accumulated into new, more advanced outcomes. This idea of continuous development and accumulation was visible in how technology personnel described innovations. Regarding organizational innovations, a similar accumulation perspective was emphasized, revealing processes that started with individual ideas and gradually expanded into development at the organizational level. Hence, individual employees' observations, ideas, and experiments formed the basis for broader changes affecting the organization's operating methods and structures. The results strengthened our understanding of both EDI's importance and its cumulative nature (Høyrup, 2010; Voxted, 2018).

4.3.2 Concluding and Practical Perspectives

Reflecting on both contexts' innovation projects in relation to Kristiansen and Bloch-Poulsen's (2010) criteria, it can be stated that the key EDI principles were implemented in many innovation projects from a value-creation perspective. First, the projects typically produced organizational value. For example, new spaces or work practices and the related changes increased efficiency by reducing transition time and optimizing work phases. These factors supported the organizations' financial or efficiency goals. Second, the projects improved the organization of work. New work arrangements and space layouts (in the technology company) and new collaboration practices (in the police) were designed in an employee-oriented manner, enabling a more logical workflow, smoother cooperation between actors, and more efficient handling of tools and technologies. Third, the projects typically had positive impacts on employees' working-life quality. Well-being increased thanks to new solutions or smoother and more meaningful work processes. Moreover, employees' experiences of participation, influence, and the broader significance of their own work grew as a result. All EDIs were likewise strongly characterized as being related to learning. In the individual EDI, the focus was clearly on individual learning; in the group EDI, on collective learning; and in the unit/regional EDI, on collaborative learning. In contrast, organizational-driven EDIs appeared as organizational learning processes (directed from the organization toward the individual). Thus, learning can also be defined as a criterion for an EDI: an EDI must include or promote a learning process at different levels in order to enable the creation of something new and further development (see also Chap. 3).

The literature has called for both research and practical insights into how employees' ideas develop and progress to implementation (Renkema et al., 2021) and how new practices become institutionalized as part of everyday life (Derrick, 2020). In the innovation projects described in both organizations in the EDLI project, it was evident that the processes were rarely totally separate or isolated initiatives. They were connected to both the past and the future, expanding from an individual to a broader group and then to the organization or region. The projects were interlinked with one another. Thus, innovation in police and technology-sector organizations can be characterized not as a set of discrete projects, but as an ongoing developmental process in which temporal dimensions and participants continuously shape the nature and direction of change:

> So that is something that is either the product or how the product is made, but then when you start making it, there can be continuous innovation there, if you count that as such. (TP28, Technology)

Consequently, it is important to recognize that while we can analytically examine innovations as separate projects and assess their value within each project's boundaries, in the bigger picture, innovation is a continuous process of creating something new and valuable through various projects and the outcomes and values produced. In this process, different projects and their phases become intertwined, with each preceding initiative serving as the basis for further development, expansion, and new ideas.

This study found that the value of EDI projects in both police and technology work can be social, human, and economic. Value often arises from *learning experiences* gained during innovation processes, which over time become starting points for new innovations. However, assessing impact is challenging when an innovation's primary and immediate value is a subjective experience (e.g., insight or learning something new) that only later becomes an objectively measurable result. However, if learning is a condition for future innovations, should it be assigned an intrinsic value? In an era increasingly dominated by data-driven management and a cult of measurement, this perspective challenges organizations to place greater trust in intuition, experiential knowledge, and professional competence. It invites recognition of the cumulative potential of small-scale improvements that are often invisible in formal metrics but are essential for sustaining learning, engagement, and innovation within everyday work practices. As this chapter shows, EDI can appear new to the actor, the workplace, the community, or society at large; it can thus be either radical or incremental (Høyrup, 2012).

Based on the EDLI research project, it is essential to investigate in which temporal dimension and from whose perspective the value of innovation is defined (Rehn & Vachhani, 2006). An individual's learning experience may seem small, but from a cumulative perspective, recognizing it is significant for organizations. EDI can begin with an individual's idea, small improvements, or application of new understanding, which, through communal learning and development, can grow over time into practices and changes at the workplace and organizational levels. Thus, while immediate benefits may emerge at the individual level, innovation is inherently dynamic and cumulative (Høyrup, 2010): As processes evolve, ideas mature, and contexts shift, the innovation itself may gain new forms, meanings, and layers of value.

The EDLI project made employees' initiatives, practices, and participation in various innovation processes visible. Understandably, when innovation projects are not formally structured development projects but continuous improvement taking place in everyday life, the roles and contributions of employees can remain invisible. Often, the original idea or its generator becomes obscured during the process, even though the final practice, product, or service is built on employees' input. Thus, understanding and making visible the role and participation of employees, especially in the context of continuous innovation, is essential. However, participation does not happen automatically. Next, we take a closer look at the barriers employees face in participating in innovation activities, and how organizations can support and enable their participation.

References

Alves, M. F. R., Galina, S. V. R., & Dobelin, S. (2018). Literature on organizational innovation: Past and future. *Innovation & Management Review, 15*(1), 2–19. https://doi.org/10.1108/INMR-01-2018-001

Armbruster, H., Bikfalvi, A., Kinkel, S., & Lay, G. (2008). Organizational innovation: The challenge of measuring non-technical innovation in large-scale surveys. *Technovation, 28*, 644–657. https://doi.org/10.1016/j.technovation.2008.03.003

Billett, S., Tan, J., Chan, C., Chong, W. H., & Keat, J. S. C. (2023a). Employee-driven innovations: Zones of initiation, enactment and learning. In W. O. Lee, P. Brown, A. L. Goodwin, & A. Green (Eds.), *International handbook on education development in Asia-Pacific*. Springer. https://doi.org/10.1007/978-981-16-2327-1_67-1

Billett, S., Yang, S., & Chia, A. (2023b). Innovations and learning at work. Local factors and contributions. In H. Bound, A. Edwards, K. Evans, & A. Chia (Eds.), *Workplace learning for changing social and economic circumstances*. Routledge.

Brandi, U., & Hasse, C. (2012). Employee-driven innovation and practice-based learning in organizational cultures. In S. Høyrup, M. Bonnafous-Boucher, C. Hasse, M. Lotz, & K. Møller (Eds.), *Employee-driven innovation: A new approach* (pp. 127–148). Palgrave Macmillan.

Caroli, E., & van Reenen, J. (2001). Skill-biased organizational change? Evidence from a panel of British and French establishments. *The Quarterly Journal of Economics, 116*(4), 1449–1492. Retrieved from http://www.jstor.org/stable/2696464

Crossan, M. M., & Apaydin, M. (2010). A multi-dimensional framework of organizational innovation: A systematic review of the literature. *Journal of Management Studies, 47*(6), 1154–1191. https://doi.org/10.1111/j.1467-6486.2009.00880.x

Damanpour, F. (2014). Footnotes to research on management innovation. *Organization Studies, 35*(9), 1265–1285. https://doi.org/10.1177/0170840614539312

Derrick, J. (2020). "Tacit pedagogy" and "entanglement": Practice-based learning and innovation. *Journal of Workplace Learning, 32*(4), 273–284. https://doi.org/10.1108/JWL-07-2019-0094

Doornbos, A. J., Simons, R., & Denessen, E. (2008). Relations between characteristics of workplace practices and types of informal work-related learning: A survey study among Dutch police. *Human Resource Development Quarterly, 19*(2), 129–151. https://doi.org/10.1002/hrdq.1231

Edwards-Schachter, M. (2018). The nature and variety of innovation. *International Journal of Innovation Studies, 2*(2), 1–15. https://doi.org/10.1016/j.ijis.2018.08.004

Ellström, P.-E. (2010). Practice-based innovation: A learning perspective. *Journal of Workplace Learning, 22*(1/2), 27–40. https://doi.org/10.1108/13665621011012834

Filstad, C., & Gottschalk, P. (2013). The police force: To be or not to be a learning organization? In A. Örtenblad (Ed.), *Handbook of research on the learning organization* (pp. 179–195). Edward Elgar Publishing. https://doi.org/10.4337/9781781004906.00020

Flocco, N., Canterino, F., & Cagliano, R. (2022). To control or not to control: How to organize employee-driven innovation. *Creativity and Innovation Management, 31*(3), 396–409. https://doi.org/10.1111/caim.12500

Glăveanu, V. P. (2015). Creativity as a sociocultural act. *Journal of Creative Behavior, 49*(3), 165–180. https://doi.org/10.1002/jocb.94

Henderson, R. M., & Clark, K. B. (1990). Architectural innovation: The reconfiguration of existing product technologies and the failure of established firms. *Administrative Science Quarterly, 35*(1), 9–30. https://doi.org/10.2307/2393549

Hollander, E. P. (1965). *Leadership and conformity in groups*. Oxford University Press.

Holmquist, M., & Johansson, A. (2019). Employee-driven innovation: An intervention using action research. *Technology Innovation Management Review, 9*(5), 44–53.

Høyrup, S. (2010). Employee-driven innovation and workplace learning: Basic concepts, approaches and themes. *Transfer: European Review of Labour and Research, 16*(2), 143–154. https://doi.org/10.1177/1024258910364102

Høyrup, S. (2012). Employee-driven innovation: A new phenomenon, concept and mode of innovation. In S. Høyrup, M. Bonnafous-Boucher, C. Hasse, M. Lotz, & K. Møller (Eds.), *Employee-driven innovation* (pp. 3–33). Palgrave Macmillan.

Huotari, T. (2021). *Innovaatio ja innovatiivisuus poliisitoimessa: esseitä historiasta, teoriasta ja filosofiasta* [Innovations and innovativeness in the police and policing: Essays on history, theory, and philosophy]. Police University College.

Kristiansen, M., & Bloch-Poulsen, J. (2010). Employee-driven innovation in team (EDIT): Innovation potential, dialogue and dissensus. *International Journal of Action Research, 6*(2–3), 155–195.

Lemmetty, S. (2024a). Real-time and long-term challenges of remote learning and innovation: Cases from police and technology organisations. *Vocations and Learning, 17*, 565–587. https://doi.org/10.1007/s12186-024-09354-1

Lemmetty, S. (2024b). Explaining the innovation dichotomy: The contexts, contents, conflicts, and compromises of innovation stories. *Frontiers of Narrative Studies, 10*(1), 126–149. https://doi.org/10.1515/fns-2024-2007

Lemmetty, S., & Billett, S. (2023). Employee-driven learning and innovation (EDLI) as a phenomenon of continuous learning at work. *Journal of Workplace Learning, 35*(9), 162–176. https://doi.org/10.1108/JWL-12-2022-0175

Lemmetty, S., & Glaveanu, V. (In Press). From possibility thinking to employee-driven organizational innovation. Accepted for publication in S. Lemmetty, I. Bäckström & M. Pajuoja (Eds.), *Employee-driven innovation in public and private organizations: How people shape change at work*. Palgrave Macmillan.

Nelson, R. R., & Winter, S. G. (1982). *An evolutionary theory of economic change*. Harvard University Press.

Rehn, A., & Vachhani, S. (2006). Innovation and the post-original: On moral stances and reproduction. *Creativity and Innovation Management, 15*(3), 310–322. https://doi.org/10.1111/j.1467-8691.2006.00390

Renkema, M., Meijerink, J., & Bondarouk, T. (2021). Routes for employee-driven innovation: How HRM supports the emergence of innovation in a formalized context. *The International Journal of Human Resource Management, 33*(17), 3526–3559. https://doi.org/10.1080/09585192.2021.1913625

Slappendal, C. (1996). Perspectives on innovation in organizations. *Organization Studies, 17*(1), 107–129. https://doi.org/10.1177/017084069601700105

Taponen, J. (2023). *Poliisin vaikuttavuus: Suoritteiden laskennasta vaikuttavuuden tutkimukseen* [Police effectiveness: From performance calculations to impact research]. Doctoral dissertation, University of Helsinki.

Tidd, J., & Bessant, J. (2009). *Managing innovation: Integrating technological, market and organisational change*. John Wiley & Sons.

Tushman, M. L., & Anderson, P. (1986). Technological discontinuities and organizational environments. *Administrative Science Quarterly, 31*(3), 439–465. https://doi.org/10.2307/2392832

Voxted, S. (2018). Conditions of implementation of employee-driven innovation. *International Journal of Entrepreneurship and Innovation Management, 22*(4–5), 471–488. https://doi.org/10.1504/IJEIM.2018.092974

Chapter 5
Pedagogy of LBI: Tackling Innovation Challenges at Work

Abstract This chapter examines how learning-based innovation (LBI) can be supported from the perspective of workplace pedagogy. It identifies the key challenges related to employee-driven innovation and provides insights into how these challenges can be addressed through pedagogical approaches within organizations. Drawing on qualitative data collected from police and technology sectors, the chapter focuses particularly on issues related to goal direction, co-creation, and participative leadership, which are viewed as essential conditions for fostering innovation activities. Building on the concept of workplace pedagogy and empirical examples from the EDLI project, the chapter presents core pedagogical approaches and practices that organizations can adopt to advance LBI, addressing both shared and organization-specific challenges.

Keywords Workplace pedagogy · Innovation pedagogy · Innovation challenges · Employee participation · Goal direction · Co-creation · Police work · Technology organization

> *A crappy product was born from a starting point where none of us wanted to do it the way we had to. There was creativity even in that situation, but that creativity isn't very motivating when we are forced to come up with ways to create something new or advance work within tight constraints. It's a bit like innovations forced by necessity during wartime. There, necessity motivates because there's so much at stake. However, this is not a war, so excessive compulsion adversely affects work motivation and leads to poor results. If this compulsion becomes too prevalent in the culture, people also learn to expect that all the answers are provided for them. On the other extreme are situations where you can do whatever you want. In the past, it was more common to have the freedom to work on things that were not directly related to a specific product. Nowadays, there is more urgency, which reduces freedom. Here, we have also seen that excessive freedom leads to individualism, and once again, we are on thin ice. Adequate courage and the opportunity to make decisions, to experiment, and even to play with ideas are important prerequisites, which fortunately are often realized in our work. In such cases, compulsion is in the right proportion, helping us understand expectations while also providing sufficient freedom and flexibility. Because we are talking about work where innovation is so crucial, creating something new is always more or less obligatory. Typically, these boundaries exist here; sometimes they could be more*

S. Lemmetty, *Learning-Based Innovation*,
SpringerBriefs in Education, https://doi.org/10.1007/978-3-032-26911-9_5

clearly defined, and there is enough freedom. Supervisors don't shout, and mistakes are not punished. In such a scenario, compulsion is motivating and acts as a driver for innovation.

"Motivating necessity": innovation type story, previously created and published as part of the EDLI project based on its data from the technology organization (Lemmetty, 2024b, p. 138).

As the previous chapters have shown, value-creating innovation is a continuous process in everyday organizational operations constructs through participation, competence and learning of personnel. Although employees' willingness to participate in and contribute to innovation is important, equally essential are the opportunities and support the organization provides for participation and innovation. Studies have found that even employees have creative potential and ideas, they do not lead to change, if employees are not given the authority or real opportunities to implement them (Voxted, 2018; Holmquist & Johansson, 2019; Lemmetty & Glaveanu, in press). Researchers have also noted that organizations have difficulties in engaging employees in innovation work, *which can appear separate* from their day jobs (Bäckström & Lindberg, 2018; Moosa & Panurach, 2008). This chapter takes a deeper look at the challenges of innovation activities, examining both the challenges to innovation work and participation, as well as the workplace pedagogical approaches through which these challenges could be addressed.

5.1 Workplace Pedagogy

In research on learning at work, learning in everyday work has long been described as an informal phenomenon, with workplaces viewed as informal learning environments in which learning is embedded in practices, often occurring as unconscious, incidental, and unstructured (Marsick & Watkins, 1990). However, this view has been criticized for overlooking the potential of developing pedagogical practices that support and guide learning at work. The pedagogical perspective on this is based on the premise that learning at work should not be merely *incidental* or *unconscious* but *intentional*—something with a purpose, direction, and goals (P. Weber, 2016). Billett (2002) pointed out that workplaces contain numerous pedagogical features that influence learning processes and employee engagement, but are these features visible and appropriate? Are they aligned with strategic goals of organizations or with individuals' starting points? And are they, in fact, based on a modern understanding of adult learning?

5.1.1 Understanding of Learning and Pedagogical Practices at Work

Guiding, supporting, and promoting learning comprise a workplace pedagogical issue that is fundamentally based on the *prevailing understanding of learning* within the workplace, which serves as the foundation for the *concrete pedagogical practices* (see e.g. Billett, 2002) as different conceptions guide different actions. For example, if the prevailing understanding of learning in the workplace is based on an understanding learning only as intrapersonal (i.e., cognitive) process, with learning occurring through external stimuli and associated responses, the workplace is likely to view the learner as a passive recipient of information, providing one-sided knowledge transfer to support learning (e.g., Lemmetty, 2024a). From the perspective of *sociocultural learning theory* (Vygotsky, 1978), this intrapersonal view on learning is not sufficient on its own; learning should be seen as an interactional process (P. Weber, 2016), which can occur everywhere and within all forms of interpersonal activity (John-Steiner & Mahn, 1996; Wenger, 1998). If a sociocultural understanding of learning prevails in the background of workplace pedagogy, emphasizing participation and interaction, learning will likely be supported by more diverse interactive, cultural, and environmental factors.

The sociocultural theory of learning (Vygotsky, 1978) highlights the individual's connection to their cultural, social, and institutional environment. It emphasizes that in the learning process, higher-order thinking skills are first learned at the social level and then transferred to the individual level (Vygotsky, 1978). The individual's interaction with other people and the environment is thus seen as central to the development of learning and thinking: It is essential that the person is able to perform intellectually demanding activities with the help of external support structures (Glăveanu, 2015; Vygotsky, 1978). In sociocultural learning, supported social interaction takes place using symbolic and physical tools. The tools used in learning can be linguistic or material objects that influence learning and form a central part of the interaction between the individual, the community, and the environment (Wenger, 1998).

Pedagogical practice refers to the ways in which learning processes can be influenced and is therefore linked to the question of how experiences gained at work can be enriched to promote learning (Billett, 2023). It can take the form of, for example, peer learning (i.e., learning from other, more experienced, individuals in the environment) or guidance, which take place through participation in culturally and situationally embedded activities (Halttunen et al., 2023) occurring between employees and supervisors (Keronen et al., 2025). From the perspective of sociocultural learning, mentoring and peers are considered essential because the learner is seen to develop by working either with the help of a more competent person or in collaboration with peers, acquiring models and shared understandings through interaction. In addition to these, learning in the workplace is best promoted in organizations with a trusting atmosphere, meaningful organization of work, and sufficient incentives (Lemmetty, 2020; Marsick, 2009).

Workplace pedagogy concerns both the individual's willingness and agency to engage in learning, and the opportunities for learning provided by the workplace (Billett, 2023). Pedagogy is therefore about aligning an individual's willingness to learn with the opportunities available to them, which in turn enables learning processes to progress through learner engagement and participation. In our previous research (Lemmetty et al., 2023), we found that adults working in police and technology-based work are engaged to and motivated by learning situations at work, when they:

- See and understand the concrete benefit or meaning of learning from the perspective of themselves, their clients, their community, or their organization (benefit orientation).
- Are able to utilize their own and others' experience histories in a learning situation, using what has already been learned as a resource and starting point for a new learning experience and linking new knowledge and understanding to existing knowledge (experiential orientation).
- Feel that they have been treated as self-directed actors by being given sufficient freedom, autonomy, and influence regarding the learning process and situation (self-directedness orientation).

Even though we know that work environment determines participation and commitment (see Lemmetty, 2020), general opportunities to learn at work do not automatically guarantee *what is learned* or *what kinds of goals are achieved through learning*. Therefore, workplace pedagogy must also pay attention to the goals and direction of learning.

5.1.2 Intentional Learning and Innovation Challenges

In the context of organizations, and especially innovation work, learning should not be seen as merely random but as intentional and emerging from participation in *goal-oriented activities* (P. Weber, 2016; Rogoff, 1995). Thus, the goals that direct learning processes are also a workplace pedagogical issue (P. Weber, 2016; Billett, 2023). The goals of workplace learning are shaped not only by the individual's personal interests but also by the organization's objectives, expectations, requirements, strategies, and values. Goals direct intentional learning through their definition, the selection of content through which the goals are pursued, and the tools and working methods used for learning (cf. P. Weber, 2016). The sociocultural understanding of learning challenges traditional top-down approaches to goal-setting by assuming that individuals (i.e., learners) themselves also actively participate in defining the goals. This means, that rather than absorbing ready-made goals, *learners construct the objects and meanings of learning during the process itself*. As workplace learning within innovation is seen as a reflective and communal process, the learner, the content of learning, and the goals of both learning and innovation are shaped and constructed through interaction. This, in turn, gives rise to a central pedagogical question concerning

LBI: How can organizations balance intentional guidance with the construction of goals throughout the process in ways that support employees' initiative-taking and their responsibility for LBI activities in everyday work?

Sociocultural construction of goal-setting and goal-directedness in learning, however, are not the only challenges organizations face in relation to enhancing innovation activities. Research shows that barriers to employee-driven (EDI) arise across organizational structures, practices, and cultures. It has been noticed that when employees lack genuine opportunities to participate, they may experience uncertainty, a sense of disconnection, and resistance, gradually distancing themselves from development efforts (Mitcheltree, 2021). It has also been noted that innovations may fail to materialize if the organization's decision-making structure is too hierarchical, if innovation is left solely to employees without managerial support (Studemund & Wallington, 2016), or if the organization lacks cross-organizational learning opportunities (Al-Saleem & Aldakheel, 2024). In addition, at a structural level, organizations often struggle with limited time for innovation due to demanding daily operations, rigid budgeting, and other administrative or legal constraints (Lidman et al., 2023). Hiltunen and Laitinen (2021) note that high work pace leaves little space for creative thinking, communication gaps restrict idea sharing, and employees may accept problems as fixed rather than seeking new solutions. Innovation thus tends to occur only sporadically. Cultural and relational barriers include risk-averse norms, organizational silos, and the fragility of innovation efforts that depend on only a few motivated individuals. In addition, inadequate support from managers, unclear incentives, and insufficient early-stage training can weaken employees' willingness or ability to engage in innovation (Lidman et al., 2023). As learning in organizations is seen as collective action (P. Weber, 2016), one of the key workplace pedagogical questions focus on how the participation to innovation work and learning within it is enabled and actually takes place in the time when interaction-related challenges have become increasingly central to innovation activities, reflecting the rise of remote work, technology-mediated communication, and more dispersed work communities (Lemmetty, 2024a).

Taken together, these findings suggest that EDI is challenged by a combination of structural constraints (e.g., budgets, legal frameworks, reorganizations), cultural and cognitive barriers (e.g., risk aversion, problem acceptance, ambiguity around innovation), and insufficient organizational support structures (e.g., managerial support, incentives, communication, training). At the same time, studies indicate that existing strengths—such as a positive work atmosphere, autonomy, employee willingness to contribute, and emerging participatory practices—form an important foundation for strengthening EDI. Because goals and activities are always context-dependent in organizations, pedagogical solutions or the challenges of innovation work cannot be precisely generalized across organizational boundaries. It is also typical that the challenges linked to innovation activities are described in research at a general level, even though, for the purposes of practical development and solutions, it would be important to understand these challenges more deeply and within the specific contexts in which they arise.

5.2 LBI Challenges and Pedagogical Solutions in Police and Technology Organizations

In the EDLI project, the challenges related to LBI were identified in both the police and technology organizations based on employees' descriptions. It was found that the key challenges for innovation in both organizations were, first, related to goals and, consequently, to the ambiguity of opportunities or to unsupported self-direction. Second, they were linked to participation and social relations, and thus to issues of trust and possibilities for influence. In the following sections, I examine these challenges of LBI in more detail and provide insights into the pedagogical means by which they can be addressed.

5.2.1 Challenges of Goal Clarity and Employee Participation in LBI

LBI relies on employees' ability to navigate evolving objectives and to actively contribute to the development of new practices. In the EDLI study it was found that unclear goals may lead to unsupported self-direction, whereas limited participation and the erosion of social ties weaken collective commitment and opportunities for influence. These factors challenge participation in innovation activities both directly and indirectly by undermining the communal learning processes at work. Next, I define these key challenges, highlighting how they manifest and are described in the contexts of police and technology work and why they are critical barriers to LBI.

5.2.1.1 Blurred Goals and Unsupported Self-Direction

Since innovation is created in everyday work through employees' learning and actions, work itself is its foundation. Innovation requires that the goals, principles, and tasks of work are understood at both the individual and community levels. In both organizations, a fundamental challenge concerned goals and their lack of clarity. In the police organization, this was linked to the goals of the work itself, whereas in the technology organization it was associated with the goals of innovation.

A central challenge for the innovation embedded within *preventive policing* (PP) is that the very content, tasks, objectives, and boundaries of preventive work remain loosely defined, leaving the field sometimes without a clear anchor or shared direction. This creates difficulties related to work planning, implementation, and development. While PP and the strategy guiding it have been recognized as part of national police work, its commonly shared and understood definition is challenged by its proactive starting point, which is fundamentally different from basic police work:

> An inherent thing in policing is that we are reactive. When something happens somewhere, we go there or investigate what has already happened. Whereas preventive action must be

> *proactive*, in that we should find potential locations or people who may have symptoms in advance and prevent those negative events from happening in advance so that nothing happens. (PP7, Police)

Participants in the EDLI study were unanimous in the fact that "after all, this preventive action is not basic policing" (PP8, Police), as "we do not think about an individual event but about the whole thing behind and in front of the person. We approach it from a different perspective" (PP13, Police). So what should preventive action—proactive policing—be? The problem of defining PP is described as nationwide, but it is concretized in terms of challenges to EDI and learning in individuals' everyday lives.

There are significant differences between police stations and regions in how preventive work is implemented. These differences are explained, first, by regional specificities: Different localities and regions experience different phenomena, crime trends, and security concerns; stakeholders and networks vary, as does the clientele. Second, dispersed organizational structures and resources affect implementation: In small localities, leaders—and sometimes even colleagues—may be far away, while in large cities, support is close by. Third, cultural differences shape the operation, as different institutions, communities, and regions have their own cultural and historical backgrounds, which are reflected in the practices and operating methods. Regional variation is inherent when discussing innovations in PP, because regionality is a central feature of PP: one of its core tasks is precisely local problem-solving. Thus the goal of PP is to develop methods that appropriately respond to the specific problems and situations of a given area:

> I made a conscious decision during the planning phase that we would not consider that [operating model] for this area. I have also told them [senior management] that this is our way, but the rest of you can do it however you see fit. (PP6, Police)

Altough variation is natural in PP, sometimes it becomes significantly large and problematic, creating conflicts at the organizational level and obscuring the role and scope of PP in general. The quotations highlighted below illustrate this through situations in which preventive action has been taken outside the technical, tactical, or principled guidelines of police work, as well as the views of two different actors regarding such activities.

> [Tells an example of the actions of PP police officer]. He had forgotten his role as a police officer, was in some other role, and had then confiscated our toolbox. [...] If we think about preventing crimes, we know from research that criminologists could probably predict very early on who might grow up to be a criminal using this kind of probability calculation. But in reality, such early means of influencing are not available to the police. We cannot go to the maternity clinic and threaten with coercive measures and say, "it won't be a good move if this or that happens." Those tricks come from somewhere else. (PP2, Police)
>
> If a police officer thinks that this [what I do] is a prank, it just shows that that police officer hasn't internalized what I do [...] if I had a team leader at this same police station, I wouldn't be able to move around so freely, because I would have to constantly be explaining what I'm doing. And when what I do isn't the deepest core of the police, that supervisor is quick to say, "we don't do that," and "that's not the police's business." I myself would like and hope that the police would also become more of a community influencer. They would take a

> stand on issues. On issues that affect the well-being of the community. And not just always be behind the uniform, saying, "The Police Act says blah, blah, blah" or "but then we'll lose all those tools." (PP23, Police)

In addition to regional differences, the above quotations highlight a strong sense of self-direction that can steer development in a direction that goes beyond the field of police work. Unclear organizational-level definitions and guidance lead to individuals defining their work autonomously, making the action appear fragmented and contradictory when viewed from an organizational level. This lack of direction creates a confusing starting point for the development of action at all levels. This raises questions about boundaries, leadership, and, ultimately, what PP actually is and should be.

In addition to regional differences and an unclear definition and strategy, the distribution of resources produces variation in how work is done. In some places, PP focuses on being in the field (with customers and stakeholders) on projects and development, while in others, long investigation queues consume most of the working time, taking away space from working with target groups (e.g., young people). The ambiguities in resourcing partly stem from the ambiguities in the work's definition:

> If you want to do preventive work, I would leave the preliminary investigation out of it [...] The police are left with a lot of [phenomena] to be ignored. If you want to prevent, then the understanding of [the environment in which you operate] should be deeper. (PP19, Police)

> At its best, preventive work would be not to be here at the computers investigating these crimes, but to be out there in the field seeing young people, working with young people, and stakeholder groups. We would be in active cooperation with schools. (PP8, Police)

Those describing their work as being carried out in the field and on projects see PP as innovative, continuously developing and producing novelty value and social and societal benefit (see Chap. 4). They also experience their own expertise in preventive activities as strong and useful. Thus, the starting point for innovation seems to be the opportunity to do the work that they themselves understand as preventive police work and in which they have developed their competence. A key challenge arises when *preventive police work* is not realized in the way that individuals (and their superiors) see and assume it to be. For example, those doing PP may be used as a resource for *a little bit of everything* because the *plot* has not been defined. In this case, days may be spent on tasks that are not motivating for them to do or develop because they are not at the core of their own competence and their appropriateness is not perceived, leading to a decline in development activity:

> When I look at our work, we have a huge desire to develop, and we are quite enthusiastic, and some damn good ideas come up. But in reality, these kinds of [requirements for preliminary investigations and unfounded work requests] are blocking us, and now that it has been like that all the time, I can see a little fatigue in that [group], that they are already thinking, "Well, what's the point of even trying then?" (PP2, Police)

> Most police officers are highly motivated and do things they consider important; things are handled well. But if we think about preventive action, we are currently conducting purely preliminary investigations. We can use the words "preventive action," but is that the same thing as a criminal investigation? (PP19, Police)

The key challenge in police innovation is therefore how preventive work can be developed if one does not first know what it is and one has no possibilities to do it.

In the *technology organization*, the central discussion around innovation focuses on a fundamental question: *What is innovation?* Participants found it difficult to see innovation as conforming to any single, concise definition:

> The most difficult thing is to understand what innovation is. It might be a small thing—a drop of glue that made the whole product work. Or if we discover a defect, isn't that also an innovation? (TP28, Technology)

Employees actively brought up examples, building a diverse picture in their speech of what innovation can mean in their work. The image of innovation is built as a journey—a continuous process in which learning moments, interim results, solutions, and development steps build over time (see also Chap. 3). It is therefore a continuous, comprehensive, and endless process. In this journey, it can be difficult to see one's own place or role, the meaning of one's activities, and the benefits of one's work:

> The term innovation is tricky, because the world is full of real Leonardo da Vincis and Benjamin Franklins. I can't claim to invent gold every day. Sometimes a little gold is born—but I don't know if it necessarily ends with a product. (TP21, Technology)

If innovation were understood only in terms of big, clear outcomes, breakthroughs, revolutions, or patents, it would become distant and difficult to achieve from the employees' perspective. Since the outputs developed in innovation (e.g., products or new operating models for implementation) are seen as being built from small solutions, uncertainty and unpredictability are part of the process: But what is the wholeness of which these small solutions are the parts? In this situation, awareness of the significance of the work and learning can remain fragile. Uncertainty and unpredictability, which are always somehow embedded in innovation activities, can lead to a lack of perspective, making it difficult to maintain motivation and participation, especially in situations with no immediate benefit. According to participants, meaningfulness should be found in the journey and participation—not in the outputs:

> So [a manager] said, dare to fail. Because success may come from many failures. You kind of beat your head against the wall for so long that if it looks like it's really going to lead nowhere, only then it is worth looking at alternative routes. (TP22, Technology)

> Not everything is new, for example, in products, but the combination is something new or better. […] It has to have an advantage over the previous state. […] I can show photos of our current product [parts] and the older ones, so it hasn't always felt like it was some kind of innovation, but they've changed an awful lot over the years, and I guess it's, I don't know, evolution […] I don't know if innovation has to be, like bigger than evolution. […] I don't think I'm any dumber than some patent cracker, I just think […] a patent is the wrong way to measure innovation. We've talked a lot about how to reward it [innovation], but it's tricky. (TP16, Technology)

Since innovation is seen as a continuous process, it is challenging and inappropriate to set detailed and broad strategic goals that are attached to it from the top level of the organization. Goals are partly constructed during the co-development process, which can make them appear unclear and constantly evolving. This creates tension between the organization's strategic direction and a participatory innovation culture: Top management strives to determine the direction of innovation at the top level, but the implementation of the process remains open and imprecise so that collaboration, staff creativity, and participation do not suffer:

> If you just say, "this is how we're going to do this" and everyone just nods, it'll never develop. (TP20, Technology)

This allows for freedom, employee orientation, and learning, which are important for innovation, but it can lead to frustration and questions about what exactly an employee is doing, what is expected of them, and whether they are doing the right things. Uncertainty is especially pronounced among those who have had no experience with similar development processes, the organization's innovation philosophy, or the management culture:

> It's hard to manage if you come straight from school. [...] There's not a clear enough guiding support network. We've had projects that were supposed to be completed in six months but took three years. (TP21, Technology)

> It's kind of a wonderful thing and a little scary at the same time. It's wonderful that you get to create it yourself, but on the other hand, it's scary that you don't know how to create the right kind. And that you don't know what to create. (TP4, Technology)

The key challenge related to the goals of innovation activities thus culminates in the question of what innovation is.

5.2.1.2 Disappearing Voice of Employee, Limited Participation and Breaking Social Bonds

Since LBI is understood as a journey built through employee initiatives and collective learning within the community (see Chap. 3), its central component is bringing forth individuals' ideas and thoughts and enabling them to influence the process, as well as fostering interaction and a sense of community among different actors. In both the police and technology organizations, a central concern related to innovation activities was tied to these factors: the disappearance of individuals' voices, limited participation as well as the weakening of social bonds and sense of community.

In the *police organization*, in particular, the disappearance of the individual's voice within the layers and culture of the organization repeatedly emerged as a challenge for innovation activities, especially when discussions concerned development at the organizational level. Influencing one's own work was perceived as possible (see also Chap. 2), but stronger involvement of employees' perspectives and experiences in the organization's strategy and overall direction was desired, or it was not visible in practice. The neglect of employees' views in organizational development was seen as problematic because the significance of organizational-level decisions for individual employees and the work carried out in the regions is nevertheless central:

> Now they are building a strategy and a way of working for the coming years without there being a single member of the crew who actually does the work. There are only ministers

> and police inspectors. They may understand the concept, but they don't understand the work we do—what it is, in a way, the grassroots work. Because we have enormous challenges in that everyday work that are not in our hands. We are not able to change the legislation. But someone should have that discussion on our behalf, that "hey, we have challenges here [lists the key challenges in detail]." That should open the discussion about how we could build the kind of legislation that would enable our work to the fullest. Of course, with this legislation we can do it, but admittedly sometimes we are in a bit of a grey area. Because if someone with a degree in law started to interpret exactly what we do, they would not necessarily agree with us. (PP23, Police)

The problem of the definition and the actions guided by it is therefore partly a matter of not listening to the personnel. At best, police officers who do preventive work feel that they are constantly receiving information from the field that would be useful in anticipating major phenomena and preparing the police, but their voices are drowned out at different organizational levels. This causes both frustration and experiences of failure in situations in which, as an individual, one is unable to solve or interrupt major developments that are causing concern or to direct one's own actions toward solving them if one does not receive a mandate from the top. At worst, the end result is passivity, which stifles initiative and efforts for development work:

> There is always room for that [innovation], but unfortunately, development has been for the worse in many things in the past 10 years. Of course, there have been some good things. But for example, those job satisfaction surveys, they are just as empty as we are. They have been answered, but the result has been that from the employee's perspective, the management—or whoever is conducting these—is like, "Why did you answer this survey incorrectly so that we now have bad results?" How much you yourself can influence this organization is minimal. You can significantly influence how your working day looks, how you organize your work, how you perform tasks within the framework of the law. But the big lines, they are just followed. You can influence very little. (PP22, Police)

> Sometimes it's frustrating to know that something [a phenomenon or change] will definitely become a bigger problem [in society], and now is the time to intervene. Decision-makers or some guardians of the coffin don't want to believe us if it's not relevant at that moment. We have to live in the moment. (PP6, Police)

This reflects the hierarchical tradition of the police organization. An employee-oriented culture does not yet widely permeate the organization, although participatory activities are emerging within units and teams carrying out preventive work (see Chaps. 2 and 4). The organizational culture strongly reflects top-down thinking, in which higher-level actors or people perceived as experts because of their positions define the rules and pass on information to those performing the work (i.e., employees) for their implementation.

In the *technology organization*, concerns related to innovation activities that touched upon the participation of different actors and the consideration of their perspectives were more strongly tied to internal interaction and joint action within the community. The data highlight the challenges of building trust and signs of weakening commitment to joint action between individuals or departments:

> It is really important that these people feel that they are part of that [continuous process]. […] Innovation is crucially about being together, physically at the same time, in the same place. Moving away from each other is a real problem if we are no longer so familiar. […]

> Trust is built during the process. And now that we are practically separated, trust is not built in the same way. This is particularly problematic when there are new employees who don't have the opportunity to enter that space. The scarcity of interaction has a negative effect within a few years. Creativity is so strongly tied to it; thoughts remain disconnected. (TP1, Technology)

In the organization's history as a family business in which a smaller number of employees worked physically close to one another, building trust and everyday interaction became possible as if by itself: Familiarity and understanding of other people's ways of working, ideas, and expertise were built 'automatically' during work. Increased remote work, partial dispersion of the organization (locations in different parts of the world and in Finland), and growth are challenging the culture of community and can produce feelings of being outsiders:

> Now, lately, when we've had this growth, it's just that you don't know everyone, so there are inner circles like that here. (TP6, Technology)

Furthermore, remote work and the technology-mediated nature of discussions reduces opportunities for learning through physical artifacts, reduces opportunities for diverse forms of observation, and dampens multi-voiced discussion. This increases fear and experiences of the erosion of trust and, with it, social bonds:

> The environment, a concrete workplace to belong to, no longer appears in the same way. (TP7, Technology)
>
> It [innovating] all starts with craftsmanship: It's different to look at a 3D image on a screen than to see and feel all the layers in a tangible form. Seeing a physical object in the environment helps to perceive scale, shapes, and other aspects in relation to the surroundings. (TP22, Technology)

The narrowing of cooperation and the limitation of interaction are seen as reinforcing the dilemma already present in the organization regarding the transfer of tacit knowledge and the personalization of competence. Sustainable (i.e., long and meaningful) careers, described as an organizational value, are an asset in the development of innovations seen as evolutionary. The long history of individuals enables the development of the organizational and cultural–historical competence required in innovation activities (see Chap. 3):

> That's probably why there are people in product development who have been there for over 30 years, that yes, it is like that, and when there is a lot of knowledge there that is almost impossible to transfer, that it is a bit of a so-called gut feeling that only those who design products have some idea of how things should be done. (TP20, Technology)

The organization has been able to create significant careers, leading to individuals who have accumulated exceptionally deep and diverse expertise. However, as the company grows and changes, there is a natural turnover in personnel, so innovation and its management cannot be left to the responsibility of certain key individuals. Strongly personified expertise, combined with difficulties in sharing it due to declining trust and weakened social bonds, poses a risk for innovation and for the smooth functioning of the organization more broadly:

> [Tells an example of a development project]. That it was in a way dependent on his expertise and organization. [...] That it should have been done in a more organized way in advance [...] That those challenges come from having to take a lot of things into account, and then you can't think that one person can take responsibility for it. (TP15, Technology)

> It would be absolutely terrible if one person's departure then shattered everything that many people have done. In our case, for decades. Then it would show that it wasn't on a terribly strong foundation. (TP5, Technology)

> When [a certain person] left, and that [job] was left to me, I opened the computer and looked at it. Then I just hit delete, and I did it all over again. [...] It's become personal.[...] The development then is.. whether someone can do it if I didn't do it. [..] People learn in such different ways, if you tell them about your own experiences, it's possible that the other person doesn't understand anything about them. (TP20, Technology)

5.2.2 *Pedagogical Strategies for Strengthening Direction and Collaborative Participation*

LBI places significant demands on how organizations guide, support, and structure learning within everyday work. The challenges related to unclear goals, limited participation, and weakening interaction highlight the need for pedagogical approaches that strengthen direction while enabling employees to influence and shape innovation processes. Next, I outline key pedagogical solutions, ranging from clarifying goals and institutionalizing participation to fostering participatory leadership and a culture of interactional co-creation, through which the challenges of innovation activities in both the police and technology organizations can be addressed.

5.2.2.1 Specifying Goals and Institutionalizing Participation

As highlighted above, a central challenge for LBI in both the police and technology organizations concerns goals, their construction and communication, and the resulting direction and guidance for advancing individual- and group-driven innovation activities. From the perspective of innovation pedagogy, a key solution thus lies in strengthening attention to goal-setting and goal clarity. In the police data, this was linked to defining the aims and purpose of preventive work more broadly, while in the technology sector it related to innovation goals and strategy. In addition to clarifying goals, the processes and means for achieving them require both freedom and flexibility but also institutionalized practices and structures.

Police officers who carry out preventive work are in a specialist role requiring specialized and broad competence (see Chap. 3). Since work is proactive in nature, it inherently contains the idea of development: Anticipating crime, especially in a constantly changing society, is continuous innovation, involving continuous reflection on what should be done, at what stage, and by what means. In PP, the pedagogical challenges focus on goals, not only in terms of what is achieved through innovation but also, more broadly, in terms of what PP in general is aimed at and what the work is or should be. Reflecting on the challenge, the pedagogy of police work should focus on creating a unified understanding of what preventive work—with its specific features and competence requirements—is or should be.

Hope of such clearer guidance was found among the officers at the time of the interviews (spring 2023):

> I predict that it will be more broadly, in the police, clarified what the police's role is, first of all. If we talk about preventive activities, for example, the police will probably have that discussion [...] about what the role of the police is, the competence required for preventing crimes, where the boundaries are, and through that a better understanding will be created of where the core task of the police is. [...] And if we are talking about the ever-dwindling resources of the police and their allocation, then I think it is essential that we have that discussion [what we need to do], that if there are so damn few of us, and we have so much work to do. (PP2, Police)

> A new strategy for preventive work will probably be written this year, explaining what these five forms of work include. (PP10, Police)

> Now this next strategy will be such that in each [area] there must be a certain PP structure. We're waiting for it eagerly. I also hope that the Police Board will at the same time define the levels of requirements [what is required in a particular police task]. (PP23, Police)

Despite such hope, the previous strategy referred to became obsolete in 2023. No new strategy or guidance has been published at the time of writing this book in the autumn of 2025, and it is reported that none is under development. Strategic guidance is expected across regional borders and departments, although views on its content (i.e., what the work should be and in which direction the police should develop) vary. In terms of the work of those leading and doing PP (individual police officers and their superiors), and in terms of the development and promotion of its effectiveness, it is essential to have a strategic framework in place that provides guidelines for self-direction in police work.

Similarly, in the *technology sector*, the challenge described emphasized goals and their nature. However, in this context the issue was not ambiguity regarding the boundaries or content of work, but rather the organization's innovation ambition and the so-called "innovation roadmap." This concern was particularly tied to larger technological innovation efforts, yet greater clarity and direction were also called for in relation to more everyday development activities. The goal was seen as being defined by whether, and if so in what form, a shared and collectively understood conception of innovation and its meanings becomes established within the organization. A shared understanding of what innovation means helps actors focus, guiding their actions so that they seek feelings of meaning from small moments of everyday life instead of waiting for big breakthroughs:

> The journey is more important than the discovery itself, because they come so rarely. You have to look for the content in that journey—and often only afterwards do you realize whether you've actually invented something. (TP15, Technology)

Equally, the comprehensibility of values and strategy, as well as their communication and articulation, are emphasized, particularly in terms of the controllability of operations and individuals' (typically free) actions. Understanding organizational values helps employees make daily choices:

> It makes it easier; if this is the company's operating principle, then it is easy to choose, even from the alternatives, to go toward [the principle]. (TP28, Technology)

According to participants, even if the innovation strategy is built *along the way* in a communal and flexible manner, it is good to describe or institutionalize certain recurring processes so that one's own or the team's work and its expectations are better understood:

> We would benefit a lot if we could separate the stages of research, innovation, and preliminary work into their own stages. [...] We need clearer goals—like innovation objectives. We would know what we want to innovate. First, we have to shoot for a while before we hit the target—and even then we should stop to think about what we did right and what we can learn from it. (TP21, Technology)

Examples of such support structures already exist (e.g., institutionalized and documented process descriptions, innovation meetings, and a suggestion box—a concrete way for anyone to submit suggestions for development work). However, strong views (e.g., interim directors pursue their own interests and fuel a toxic atmosphere) are not desired; instead, employees want loose support structures that maintain the ideal of continuous development. These can promote the manageability and clarity of initially vague innovation phases or projects:

> I'm developing this kind of [certain] model process for these [certain] development projects, so that we have a unified template that can be used to draw them up, and then it makes communication easier, so that we know what stage the project is at. (TP19)

Strategic policies and guidelines can also be discussed pedagogically together: What do the strategies mean in the work of different actors? Which areas can each actor influence? What has already been decided? The role of the more experienced, particularly those who put the processes and organizational culture into words, is emphasized here. It is often the practice of management and experienced colleagues to help those for whom such experiences are not familiar or safe to perceive the significance and to accept feelings of uncertainty as part of normal innovation work:

> It's not necessarily enough that you've come from somewhere qualified. The customs and culture of the house—you don't learn them in a short amount of time. You have to go through that process calmly, so that you don't get upset right away during the first project, because they last a long time and are quite different. This is the responsibility of those in our house, as to how it is expressed. For my part, I have tried to express it, if someone is clearly upset, that "it's just because there is such a project that no one can do better, and it's miserable now that you are at the center of this." [...] The beginning of the development work is difficult when people think that we should research, but we can't just research for the sake of research. There should be some product toward which it's going. I think this is a good way of doing things and fruitful, but burdensome for people. I think it's our management's [names people] duty to paint the picture for the creators that this is the stage we are in now. (TP15)

5.2.2.2 Participatory Leadership and a Culture of Interactional co-Creation

Another key challenge of innovation is how individuals can take responsibility for their own learning and development if their voices are not heard and how to co-create together something new if social bonds erode. Based on the evidence, this poses pedagogical challenges related to strengthening an organizational culture based on participatory leadership and co-creation. The proposed pedagogical approach emphasizes the development of practices and structures in such a way that employees' views and expertise are genuinely heard, valued, and integrated into the broader organizational processes of operation and development.

In a *police context*, questions about the participation of employees are largely focused on leadership at different levels: Are the concerns and views of individual officers heard? Can they be utilized in building the big picture and strategy? Although there is much power in doing one's own everyday work, the connection of one's own work and views to the organizational level (and vice versa) is felt to be contradictory or unclear. The guidance, articulation, and co-development that occur through leadership, culture, and structures are still seen as lacking in many places, although in other places, there are plenty of views regarding what is better *compared to the past*. The view is dependent on the position, individual leaders, or the area in which one operates:

> Supervisors have a huge impact. They are innovative and want to develop and move forward. We have made a lot of progress in just a year; we have reached a point where we are trying to keep up with the times. The fact that new generations are coming to the upper management level, and they are then taking the knowledge further up, has changed things so that we are not stuck at the level of the twenty-first century. (PP13, Police)

Although employees feel that "it really depends on the supervisor how ready they are to develop the work and accept those ideas" (PP3, Police), it is understood that the authority of one's immediate superiors in the line organization is not unlimited. Ultimately, the legislation and the parties that guide police operations are so far removed from the individual employee and their everyday concerns that there is a powerful sense of the detachment of one's own work from the strategic level:

> This is a line organization. And if you start from the ground floor to take that message up, you have many broken phones, many floors. Often the message doesn't go up to where you would have hoped it would go, but it gets cut off at some point. That's also a big problem in our organization. (PP22, Police)

Thus, pedagogy is about developing an entire organizational-level culture, which should be built on stronger participatory leadership and co-development.

In the *technology organization,* the decrease in face-to-face interaction seemed a huge concern for co-development, requiring regular joint events and in-office days at the workplace. Physical proximity (e.g., having production and product development in the same environment and face-to-face meetings with colleagues) is seen as important for strengthening social relationships, trust, and cooperation. Sufficient resources and time, especially in the earlier and more exploratory stages of work, are seen as key prerequisites for enabling face-to-face interaction:

> So the meeting and the discussion, that remains in Teams. It's a shame. I mean, really a shame. The laughing together and doing things together and the meals and waiting for everything and the coffees. […] That's what I'm worried about, and how we find time at work for that learning. How we find time to stop, so that we dare to throw ourselves into it and dare to invent something new. (TP7, Technology)

> And then these coincidences; they can be so crucial for the next stage. And they can come anywhere. But often, for example, when you've measured and wondered about something in the lab and then you go to a café, we're talking about something completely different, and suddenly it's "Wait a minute! How does this sound?" (TP1, Technology)

Diverse teams, comprising various actors, perhaps representatives of units, and people with different skills, are described as a good starting point for learning and innovation. Building a *team* that is appropriate, flexible, and changeable from the point of view of co-development of innovation enables the sharing of tacit knowledge and the transfer of organizational and historical understanding and thus multi-perspectival discussion. It thus offers the potential for as much multiple-level evaluation, experimentation, and decision-making as possible, which is the starting point for high-quality innovative outcomes. Working in pairs—walking alongside and growing into the role of the other—is also essential:

> People need to be involved in the work so that it leaves a mark on what has been done today, so that 10 years later they can connect—"Back then, we did it like that; I remember those problems, we didn't know how to solve them then, and today I have new medicines"—so that something new can be found again. (TP15, Technology)

> Fortunately, [anonymized personal information] was then there as one person to whom [the person who left] transferred his own knowledge. That [the departure of another person] must have been one of those significant moments [where it was scary what would happen to the organization]. Because that [person] was such a strong person and such a strong factor. That was one situation. And then of course the other one was [tells about another situation where a key person left]. At that point, people must have also thought about what would happen now. (TP5, Technology)

Although multidisciplinary teams are essential for innovative development, it is important to recognize their operational limitations: Teams should not grow too large, and the direction should not be so loose that the whole project disperses in too many directions and decision-making becomes difficult as a result of compromises:

> Innovation should not be squeezed into a form that works for everyone. We cannot satisfy everyone's needs with one solution, but different solutions are needed. If we try to fulfill everyone's wishes, we are kind of lowering the bar for everyone because we have to make compromises on some things. In a way, innovation is watered down if we try to make it suitable for too many people. (TP21, Technology)

This observation highlights how successful teamwork requires a balance between diversity of voices and focused decision-making. Diverse perspectives enrich the development process, but excessive pursuit of consensus can weaken the impact and clarity of innovations. Therefore, team leadership requires a balance: the ability to enable participation while at the same time maintaining a common direction and goal.

As technology-mediated working and distance learning have become an integral part of working life both in Finland and internationally, it is no longer realistic to resist them or stick to previous operating models. Instead, organizations must be able to adapt their operations in such a way that distributed work and learning are possible, but without losing the value of physical encounters. Regardless of whether work and learning take place online or face to face, one pedagogical goal is to maintain a safe and open atmosphere of interaction. This enables critical discussions and debates that are described as important for innovation. The interviews highlight the organization's strength in promoting open discussion and confidential interaction as well as a shared will to maintain this atmosphere in the future:

> You can always question things, and that's important. It's great to be able to tell the CEO that we should do something different, or that I don't like this solution—and that's okay. You can't innovate if you can't speak freely. (TP16, Technology)

> There needs to be a very open atmosphere where everyone dares to say their ideas out loud. I think we do that quite well. At the same time, it requires a balance: When new employees come in, you need to be able to tell them that something has already been tried and didn't work, but in a way that doesn't discourage new enthusiasm. (TP14, Technology)

> An open atmosphere is precisely what it is often said these days—you learn from mistakes and you have to learn. That is something that needs to be highlighted prominently. (TP30, Technology)

Based on these observations, a safe atmosphere for interaction is not only an organizational cultural strength but also a pedagogical prerequisite for learning and innovation—regardless of whether the work takes place physically in the same space or is digitally distributed.

5.3 Toward Innovation Pedagogy at Work: Lessons Learned

Innovation in organizations is a pedagogical issue when approached from the perspective of employee participation and intentional learning at work. In this chapter, I examined key LBI challenges in police and technology organizations. The results illustrate that the challenges are focused on the understanding and goals of innovation and one's own work, unsupported self-direction, weakening social bonds as well as participation in LBI activities. Next, I contextualize and synthesize these findings.

5.3.1 Summary of Findings by Context

The ambiguity of goals is based on the difficulty of understanding what one's own work as part of an organization is (police) or what innovation means in one's work (technology sector). This can make it difficult to commit to the learning required by innovation activities and lead to experiences of frustration, uncertainty, and meaninglessness (see Mitcheltree, 2021). It can be interpreted also as a problem of perceiving the benefits arising from one's own activities, which in turn affects commitment to learning and development (Lemmetty et al., 2023). Ambiguous goals can create space for self-direction in that the individual is given unlimited autonomy to direct their own activities in the direction they want, which, however, creates contradictions from the organizational perspective. Previous research has shown that excessive self-direction is not always justified in organizational development work, as it differentiates the activities of individuals and creates ambiguity, experiences of being left behind, and, at worst, inappropriate ways of working (Collin et al., 2017a, 2017b; Studemund & Wallington, 2016; Lemmetty, 2020).

The decline in community and inadequate opportunities for participation are manifested in the technology sector as a fear of losing trust as a result of increasing remote work and organizational growth and dispersion, leading to a decrease in the observations (including of physical artifacts) and coincidences required for learning. In the police, there is a limitation on employee participation, especially in higher-level organizational development work and decision-making. This can weaken the sense of belonging and remove opportunities to collectively utilize the experiences of different actors as a learning resource and as the background for innovation activities, which has previously been described as a key factor in the commitment of adult learners (Lemmetty et al., 2023). Next we examine these findings more contextually (see Table 5.1).

The results presented in this chapter from the *police organization* offer new insights, but they are not entirely novel within the field of research on preventive policing. For example, Ellefsen et al. (2023) have stated that perceptions of what PP means in practice vary considerably, despite efforts to define and describe it both within the police organization and in research, and the challenges of PP remain significant: Resources are limited, and the results of the activities are difficult to measure. In the police context, it is typical to assume that hierarchical power structures automatically determine what is learned on the job and how. However, research has found that everyday learning situations in police work do not always correspond to official organizational goals (Wieslander, 2019), and the knowledge learned may even be undesirable from the organization's perspective (Hoel & Christensen, 2020). Based on the results of the EDLI project, it can be stated that without clear guidance, police officers may be diverted from innovation activities in line with organizational goals simply because it is not clear to them what these goals mean in their work. At the same time, when autonomy sometimes appears to be excessive in PP, the possibilities for influencing organizational-level development are limited. Studies have shown that employees' ideas may not be realized if the organization's decision-making structure is strictly hierarchical and does not allow for bottom-up influences (Studemund & Wallington, 2016). In the EDLI project, police officers described this phenomenon as a problem of participation: They felt that their voices were not heard. This experience particularly increased emotional tension and resistance toward management and decisions. In some cases, it even led to rebellious action (see Chap. 2), in which

Table 5.1 Summary of findings: LBI challenges and pedagogical solutions across organizations

Theme	Police Organization	Technology Organization
Unclear goals and goal construction/ Unsuppored self-direction	• Preventive work with sometimes unclear content, purpose, boundaries, objectives • Strong regional variation; fragmentation and contradictions • High self-direction risking drift beyond core policing	• Challenge tied to innovation ambition and ongoing goal construction as part of the implementation process • Innovation as continuous journey; unclear meaning and place of work • Goals vague and shifting due to emergent, incremental processes
Limited participation, disappearing employee voice and erosion of social bonds	• Individual voice lost in layers and culture • Influence limited to own/ team work; no impact on strategy • Strategic decisions detached from everyday realities; frustration and passivity • Gap between everyday work and strategic decisions	• Participation weakened by reduced interaction and collaboration • Remote work, dispersion, growth eroding trust and community • Tacit knowledge and long-term competence harder to transfer • Reduced face-to-face interaction weakening trust and shared understanding • Formation of inner circles; increased feelings of exclusion
Specifying goals and institutionalizing participation	• Need for shared definition of preventive work, aims, competencies • Need for strategic framework to guide self-direction and coherent development	• Need for shared organizational conception of innovation and its meaning • Need to lightly institutionalized processes (staged processes, meetings, suggestion channels) clarifying expectations
Participatory leadership & interactional co-creation	• Need to build culture where employee voice is heard and integrated into strategy • Need for participatory leadership and co-development at all levels • Need to bridge communication gaps and connect everyday work with strategic direction	• Need for renewed opportunities for face-to-face interaction and multidisciplinary teamwork • Safe conversational culture (openness, trust, learning from mistakes) essential • Everyday interaction building trust (informal encounters, shared moments) critical for innovation • Pair work and onboarding structures supporting tacit knowledge transfer

employees took advantage of the power that was within their reach, even if there was no official mandate to do so. Stronger involvement of employees in defining work and setting goals together with high-quality supervisory practices (which police officers largely described as good) would support the self-direction needed both for carrying out the work and for its coherent development.

In the *technology organization's* innovation activities, perceiving innovation as a continuous process and thus as an abstract phenomenon was described as posing a challenge, especially for perceiving the meaning of one's own role and activities, as well as the benefits, as part of the process. The solution was not to change the definition of innovation, but to co-construct a shared, understood, and articulated understanding of it within the organization. In the technology sector, changes in social interaction and bonds, which were particularly affected by the increase in remote work, also appeared to be a challenge. As work increasingly shifts to digital environments, this has been found to challenge the nature of interaction and, with it, the sense of belonging (Bellis et al., 2022; Lemmetty, 2024a). Developing virtual pedagogy to support innovation activities may be important, but technology-sector personnel also described the importance of maintaining physical encounters and an open and safe atmosphere for interaction in both close and remote encounters. In the technology sector, the challenges appeared to be not only negative but also often ambivalent. For example, long careers were seen as a value for innovation evolution, while at the same time being experienced as a challenge from the perspective of personalizing competence. The challenges and the solutions described were thus not seen as reflecting clear needs for change in the organization. Rather, they were viewed as observations regarding what has been paid attention to and what is important to focus on in the future so that an innovative culture can be maintained as the organization and working life in general change.

5.3.2 Concluding and Practical Perspectives

From an innovation pedagogy perspective, the findings highlight that both organizations struggle with the foundational conditions of LBI related to goals, shared understanding, and genuine participation. These challenges could weaken employees' capacity to take initiative, learn collaboratively, and connect everyday insights to broader organizational development. At the same time, both organizations already possess useful and functional pedagogical practices that support innovation activities. Previous studies have shown that EDI is strengthened not only by individuals' creativity, prior work experience, positive orientation toward work (González-González & García-Almeida, 2021) and agency (Haapasaari et al., 2018), but also by managerial support, autonomy, collaboration (Smith, 2017; Ulhoi & Kesting, 2012), a clear vision, and the organization and dissemination of innovation activities (e.g., through documentation) (Voxted, 2018). Based on the accounts of participants in this study as well, it can be observed that pedagogical development aimed at fostering innovation should particularly target the vision (goals) and their communication, the organization of innovation activities, as well as leadership and community building. For instance, in the police organization, the development of a more participatory operating culture was described as already emerging at the team and, in some cases, unit level—especially in relation to immediate supervisory work—although a broader cultural shift toward participatory practices across the organization was still seen as ongoing. Similarly, in the technology organization, existing participatory practices and structures for transferring tacit knowledge were considered valuable, but in the context of a changing working life, their further development was seen as requiring increasingly strong investment.

Based on this chapter, the key building blocks of innovation pedagogy are as follows:

- **goals and a shared understanding**, in the direction of which intentional learning and development processes at work can be guided from a self-directed perspective;
- **collective direction building** (i.e., institutional and cultural practices), through which personnel are involved both in innovation activities and in building the goals underlying them;
- **cooperation and interaction**, including spaces, opportunities, resources, and structures for community learning, constructive discussion, ideation, and experimentation, in which tacit knowledge becomes visible and transferred;
- a **safe atmosphere and support** from superiors, which guide and encourage the utilization of experiences and the co-creation of innovations.

Returning to the illustrative story presented at the beginning of this chapter (Lemmetty, 2024b), we can see that the challenges of innovation activities prominently revolve around questions of freedom, excessive individual-orientation and self-direction on the one hand, and compulsion, inflexible structures, and tight control on the other. Based on the analysis in this chapter, innovation pedagogy is fundamentally about navigating a balance between these extremes, both in the police organization and in the technology sector. This balance is built through a clear understanding of goals and purpose, inclusive practices, and supervisory work and organizational culture that are encouraging, humane, and supportive of individuals' actions.

This study highlighted the areas that should continue to be developed within organizations in the future, but it also provided concrete examples of practices that already function well. These existing strengths offer valuable starting points that can be further expanded and reinforced. Strengthening goal clarity, supporting participatory leadership, and cultivating spaces for interactional co-creation therefore become essential pedagogical tasks for enabling LBI. We know, from the previous literature, that workplace pedagogy starts with an understanding of what learning is (Billett, 2002), how adults learn and what learning is directed toward (intentional learning, Weber, 2016). In a similar way, the construction of innovation pedagogy begins with forming an understanding of what innovation means in each specific organization. Once this meaning is collectively understood and established, it becomes possible to set goals that align with it and to create pedagogical co-development practices that support those goals.

References

Al-Saleem, A. I., & Aldakheel, M. K. (2024). Barriers to workforce-driven innovation in healthcare. *Cureus, 16*(10), Article 72316. https://doi.org/10.7759/cureus.72316

Bäckström, I., & Lindberg, M. (2018). Behavioural implications of employee-driven innovation: A critical discourse analysis. *International Journal of Innovation Management, 22*(7). https://doi.org/10.1142/S1363919618500585

Bellis, P., Trabucchi, D., & Buganza, T. (2022). How do human relationships change in the digital environment after COVID-19 pandemic? The road towards agility. *European Journal of Innovation, 25*(6), 821–849. https://doi.org/10.1108/EJIM-02-2022-0093

Billett, S. (2002). Toward a workplace pedagogy: Guidance, participation, and engagement. *Adult Education Quarterly, 53*(1), 27–43. https://doi.org/10.1177/074171302237202

Billett, S. (2023). Utilising pedagogically rich activities to meet emerging workplace challenges. In H. Bound, A. Edwards, K. Evans, & A. Chia (Eds.), *Workplace learning for changing circumstances* (pp. 93–107). Routledge. https://doi.org/10.4324/9781003227946-19

Collin, K., Herranen, S., & Riivari, E. (2017a). What kinds of aspects frame professional agency and creativity in information technology work*? Business Creativity & the Creative Economy, 3*(1), 88–98. https://doi.org/10.18536/bcce.2017.10.3.1.08

Collin, K., Lemmetty, S., Herranen, S., Paloniemi, S., Auvinen, T., & Riivari, E. (2017b). Professional agency and creativity in information technology work. In M. Goller & S. Paloniemi (Eds.), *Agency at work: Professional and practice-based learning* (pp. 263–282). Springer. https://doi.org/10.1007/978-3-319-60943-0_13

Ellefsen, H. B., Bjørkelo, B., Sunde, I. M., & Fyfe, N. R. (2023). Unpacking preventive policing: Towards a holistic framework. *International Journal of Police Science & Management, 25*(2), 196–207. https://doi.org/10.1177/14613557231163403

Glăveanu, V. P. (2015). Creativity as a sociocultural act. *Journal of Creative Behavior, 49*(3), 165–180. https://doi.org/10.1002/jocb.94

González-González, T., & García-Almeida, D. J. (2021). Frontline employee driven innovation through suggestions in hospitality firms: The role of the employee's creativity, knowledge, and motivation. *International Journal of Hospitality Management, 94*, 102877. https://doi.org/10.1016/j.ijhm.2021.102877

Haapasaari, A., Engestrom, Y., & Kerosuo, H. (2018). From initiatives to employee-driven innovations. *European Journal of Innovation Management, 21*(2), 206–226. https://doi.org/10.1108/EJIM-09-2016-0085

Halttunen, T., Dragin-Jensen, C., Kylänpää, C., & Karkov, A. (2023). Collaborative problem solving: A pedagogy for workplace relevance. *Nordic Journal of Vocational Education and Training, 13*, 45–73. https://doi.org/10.3384/njvet.2242-458X.2313245

Hiltunen, E., & Laitinen, T. (2021). Barriers of employee-driven innovation in a small retail store. In A. K. Dey, V.-V. Piispanen, & S. Mishra (Eds.), *Sustainable entrepreneurship: Innovation and transformation* (pp. 93–103). Bloomsbury India. Retrieved from https://www.bloomsbury.com/uk/sustainable-entrepreneurship-9789354350559/

Hoel, L., & Christensen, E. (2020). In-field training in the police: Learning in an ethical grey area? *Journal of Workplace Learning, 32*(8), 569–581. https://doi.org/10.1108/JWL-04-2020-0060

Holmquist, M., & Johansson, A. (2019). Employee-driven innovation: An intervention using action research. *Technology Innovation Management Review, 9*(5), 44–53.

John-Steiner, V., & Mahn, H. (1996). Sociocultural approaches to learning and development: A Vygotskian framework. *Educational Psychologist, 31*(3–4), 191–206.

Keronen, S., Lemmetty, S., & Collin, K. (2025). Conceptions of the leading of learning in supervisory work: A qualitative study based on a Finnish technology organization and a central hospital. *International Journal of Training and Development*. https://doi.org/10.1111/ijtd.70009

Lemmetty, S. (2020). *"Self-learning is present every day—In fact, it's my job": Self-directed workplace learning in technology-based work*. Doctoral dissertation. University of Jyväskylä.

Lemmetty, S. (2024a). Real-time and long-term challenges of remote learning and innovation: Cases from police and technology organisations. *Vocations and Learning, 17*, 565–587. https://doi.org/10.1007/s12186-024-09354-1

Lemmetty, S. (2024b). Explaining the innovation dichotomy: The contexts, contents, conflicts, and compromises of innovation stories. *Frontiers of Narrative Studies, 10*(1), 126–149. https://doi.org/10.1515/fns-2024-2007

Lemmetty, S., & Glaveanu, V. (In Press). From possibility thinking to employee-driven organizational innovation. Accepted for publication in S. Lemmetty, I. Bäckström & M. Pajuoja (Eds.), *Employee-driven innovation in public and private organizations: How people shape change at work*. Palgrave Macmillan.

Lemmetty, S., Hämäläinen, K., & Collin, K. (2023). Adult learners in police and technology work in Finland: Andragogical features behind learning at work. *Australian Journal of Adult Learning, 63*(3), 398–423.

Lidman, L., Gustavsson, M., & Fogelberg Eriksson, A. (2023). Learning and employee-driven innovation in the public sector: The interplay between employee engagement and organisational conditions. *Journal of Workplace Learning, 35*(9), 86–100. https://doi.org/10.1108/JWL-05-2022-0055

Marsick, V. J. (2009). Toward a unifying framework to support informal learning theory, research and practice. *Journal of Workplace Learning, 21*(4), 265–275. https://doi.org/10.1108/13665620910954184

Marsick, V. J., & Watkins, K. E. (1990). *Informal and incidental learning in the workplace*. Routledge.

Mitcheltree, C. M. (2021). Enhancing innovation speed through trust: A case study on reframing employee defensive routines. *Journal of Innovation and Entrepreneurship, 10*(1), Article 4. https://doi.org/10.1186/s13731-020-00143-3

Moosa, N., & Panurach, P. (2008). Encouraging front-line employees to rise to the innovation challenge. *Strategy & Leadership, 36*(4), 4–9. https://doi.org/10.1108/10878570810888704

Rogoff, B. (1995). Observing sociocultural activity on three planes: Participatory appropriation, guided participation, and apprenticeship. In J. V. Wertsch, P. del Rio, & A. Alvarez (Eds.), *Sociocultural studies of mind* (pp. 139–164). Cambridge University Press.

Smith, R. (2017). Work(er)-driven innovation. *Journal of Workplace Learning, 29*(2), 110–123.

Studemund, A., & Wallington, J. (2016). *The challenges of employee-driven innovation and its relation to decision structures* [Summary]. ENTN39 Master's Corporate Entrepreneurship and Innovation Internship and Degree Project. Lund University. https://www.lu.se/lup/publication/8876172/

Ulhoi & Kesting should be: Smith, P., Ulhøi, J.P. and Kesting, P. (2012), "Mapping key antecedents of employee-driven innovations". *International Journal of Human Resources Development and Management, 12*(3), pp. 224–236, https://doi.org/10.1504/IJHRDM.2012.048629

Voxted, S. (2018). Conditions of implementation of employee-driven innovation. *International Journal of Entrepreneurship and Innovation Management, 22*(4–5), 471–488. https://doi.org/10.1504/IJEIM.2018.092974

Vygotsky, L. S. (1978). Mind in society: The development of higher psychological processes. In M. Cole, V. John-Steiner, S. Scribner, & E. Souberman (Eds.), *Mind in society* (pp. 19–58). Harvard University Press.

Weber, P. C. (2016). Pedagogy and organizational learning. In A. Schröer, M. Göhlich, S. Weber, & H. Pätzold (Eds.), *Organisation und Theorie* (pp. 235–245). Springer. https://doi.org/10.1007/978-3-658-10086-5_22

Wenger, E. (1998). *Communities of practice: Learning, meaning, and identity*. Cambridge University Press. https://doi.org/10.1017/CBO9780511803932

Wieslander, M. (2019). Learning the (hidden) silence policy within the police. *Studies in Continuing Education, 41*(3), 308–325. https://doi.org/10.1080/0158037X.2018.1497592

Chapter 6
Conclusions: Learning-Based Innovation

Abstract This chapter provides a concise synthesis of learning-based innovation (LBI), outlining its definition, core components, and the analytical perspectives it enables. As the concluding chapter, it integrates the new insights and empirical findings generated in the EDLI project. The chapter also examines contextual findings, relating them to earlier research on learning and innovation within the same sectors. Additionally, it presents ideas for future research directions and discusses ethical and practical considerations related to the EDLI project.

Keywords Learning-based innovation · Employee-driven innovation · Police organization · Technology organization · Synthesis · Conclusions

> *I remember once when my dad and I were driving somewhere—I don't remember where. It might have been autumn. And my dad said, "A field is always beautiful." I've been thinking about that ever since. In a way, it's the idea that every phase of the field—each stage—is beautiful, and that none of them could exist without the one before it.*
>
> (Innovation metaphor, technology organization)

The aim of this book was to construct a holistic understanding of learning-based innovation (LBI) by drawing on the theoretical foundations and empirical insights generated within the Employee-Driven Learning and Innovation (EDLI) project underlying this volume. Since the 1990s, researchers have increasingly acknowledged that innovation at work both requires and entails employees' learning, yet empirical research and context-sensitive examinations of this relationship remain relatively limited, especially given the extensive attention that innovation receives across multiple academic fields. This book contributes to closing this gap by providing an analysis of innovation as inherently intertwined with learning, with a particular focus on the contexts of policing and the technology sector. It explores the nature of innovation through employees' lived experiences, perspectives, and accounts, thereby situating innovation within everyday work practices and environments. In this concluding chapter, I provide a synthesis of the key insights of this volume, outlining the perspectives from which innovation can be examined as an employee-driven, continuous,

S. Lemmetty, *Learning-Based Innovation*,
SpringerBriefs in Education, https://doi.org/10.1007/978-3-032-26911-9_6

and shared journey both in the everyday life of organizations and in organizational research, as well as the ways in which learning is connected to these perspectives.

6.1 Innovation as a Shared Journey

> It is fascinating where you start and what you end up with in the end. You can never know that in advance. Along the way you learn so much, apply, learn, apply, and refine. It is interesting to see how the process ultimately unfolds. And when you are working with something unknown, no one can "specify" it by saying, "learn this product, this is what we want." You may have some sense of direction, but the rest is essentially searching, learning, and coincidences. The most valuable part of the journey is the questions. The fact that someone, at some point, asks whether this could be like this or that—whether we have tried this or that. These questions are crucial. (TP1, Technology)

Based on this book, LBI is above all an approach for examining and understanding innovation through the lens of learning through participation. Within this approach, innovation can be conceptualized as a continuous, sociocultural process of continuous learning (see Fig. 6.1) through which *actors*' roles and agency evolve, and competence is shared and developed. Taking the form of various *projects*, it can, over time and through accumulation, generate multiple kinds of *outcomes* and *value*. Moreover, innovation as a continuously developing learning-based phenomenon requires purposeful innovation *pedagogy* to guide and support it.

The book reinforces previous research by showing that workplace learning is one of the fundamental mechanisms underlying innovation in organizational contexts.

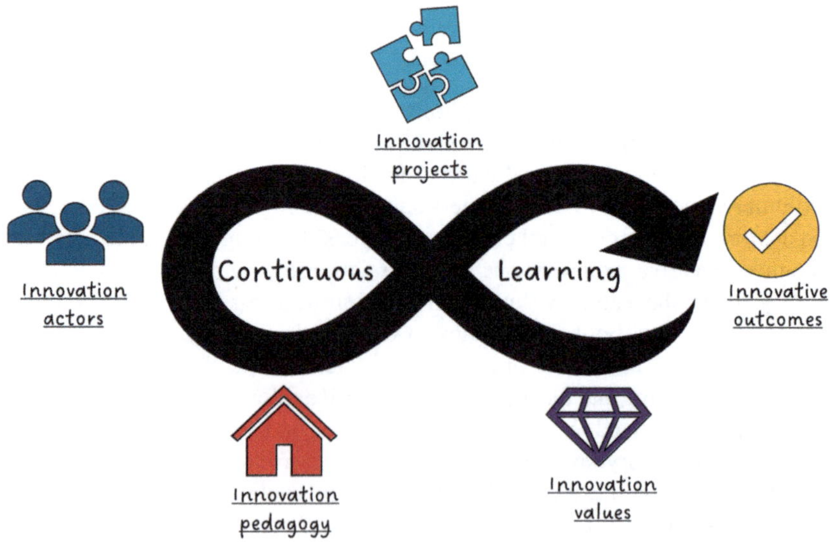

Fig. 6.1 Learning-based innovation

The learning practices of individuals and groups in, for, and through the workplace (Billett, 2014; Smith, 2017) play a central role in the processes whereby new and innovative outcomes are developed in work contexts. Individual learning is integrated into community-wide activities which, through organizational recognition and support, contribute to the creation of something new and valuable for the organization in question (see Chap. 3). Consequently, LBI can be conceptualized as a sociocultural phenomenon in which employee-driven learning and innovation converge into a unified process constructed through interactions among individuals, groups, and organizational environments, along with their material and cultural characteristics. As learning can be understood as both a prerequisite for and a consequence of innovation (see also Høyrup, 2012; Ellström, 2010) it turns innovation into a continuous process, which several participants in the EDLI project described with the words 'flow,' 'evolution,' and 'journey.' Next, I summarize what this innovation journey entails and how it can be examined.

6.1.1 The Journey Continues: Actors, Projects, Outcomes and Values Change through Learning

LBI appears as a journey that unfolds over time and through collective activity. This book offers three main contributions for examining this journey:

- *LBI is constructed through* ***people's*** *competence, learning, and participation.*
- *LBI is manifested as innovative* ***projects****, outcomes, and the values they generate*
- *LBI is supported through innovation* ***pedagogy****, which consists of a shared understanding of innovation, goals that align with it, and co-development practices that promote and construct those goals*

In the following, I reflect on these three perspectives on LBI as well as their meaning in the context of innovation and workplace research.

6.1.1.1 Competence, Learning, and Participation: Constructing the Continuity of Innovation

It has been said that, at the organizational level, an innovation is not truly an innovation until it has been collectively accepted and incorporated into new practices (Lemmetty & Billett, 2023), and that an individual's insight or knowledge alone cannot lead to organizational-level outcomes (Sung & Choi, 2014). In this book, I examined the significance and forms of learning and competence in innovation activities. This perspective (see especially Chap. 3) is central to the book's foundation, as it enables the conceptualization of innovation as a collective, continuous and learning-based process.

Competence emerges as a prerequisite for innovation, as knowledge, skills, and attitudes (see e.g., Mulder, 2014) related to one's own work, the organization, and its background, as well as target groups and clients, form the basis for developing new practices, ideas, and products within the work community. The sharing and integration of competence appear as a learning process in which observing others' work and engaging in dialogue generate a form of collective understanding that serves as the foundation for new developments. Learning new things occurs through experimenting with, testing, and evaluating the evolving innovation itself, producing entirely new insights for participants. These findings reinforce theoretical accounts of learning in innovation as both adaptive and innovative (Ellström & Ellström, 2010; Fenwick, 2003; Høyrup, 2010; Lemmetty & Billett, 2023). The alternation between these forms of learning unfolds through individuals' participation in an innovation process that evolves over time. Thus, competence, learning, and participation together function as mechanisms that ensure the continuity of the innovation process. Descriptions and models of linear innovation processes (Sossa et al., 2019; see also Meissner & Kotsemir, 2016) typically end at the point where the innovation, the final outcome, is completed. However, adopting a learning perspective in the analysis of innovation, as in this volume, highlights how realized innovations continue to evolve and form the basis for subsequent developments. From this perspective, the understanding generated in earlier processes becomes the building material for future ones, with each innovation providing a starting point for the next stages of development (Lemmetty & Billett, 2023).

Participation is a central element from the perspective of the continuity of the previously described innovation and learning process, as it enables the transfer of skills and understanding between people and thus supports individual, group, and organizational learning (Brown & Duguid, 1991; Hasu et al., 2014; Høyrup, 2012). In this book, participation in innovation is seen as intertwined with agency—that is, with individuals' actions and their willingness to engage and influence, but also with the opportunities for participation provided by the surrounding environment (the organization) (Eteläpelto et al., 2013; Glăveanu, 2015). In Chap. 2. I examined how the roles and agency of different actors are constructed in the context of innovation activities. The findings show that *participation in innovation-related activities* provides opportunities for employees to learn, expand their competence, and renegotiate their roles within the organization. Consequently, limited access to such arenas constrains not only opportunities for decision-making and idea generation but also the development of competence and, ultimately, the strengthening of agency. While it is clear that not all employees can be included equally in all phases of organizational innovation, offering differentiated forms of involvement, may create meaningful learning pathways that support the development of innovation agency. Within the employee-driven innovation (EDI) framework, stronger employee participation is recognized as valuable for driving strategic organizational change and innovation (Billett et al., 2023a; Selander & Alasoini, 2023). This research demonstrates that participation is both a manifestation and a generator of agency, highlighting its central role in cultivating learning, competence development, and more inclusive innovation practices. In summary, LBI emerges when competence and learning become embedded in both the innovative outcomes produced within organizations and the communal processes leading to them (Lemmetty & Billett, 2023). In this context, the key aspect of innovation is the participation and knowledge sharing of multiple organizational actors in various phases of the development processes (Billett et al., 2021; Høyrup, 2010; Lemmetty, 2025).

6.1.1.2 Projects, Outcomes, and Value Reflecting the Essence of Innovation

Researchers have described how innovations, when seen as end results, are in reality only glimpses of a continuous process of development (Haapasaari et al., 2018; Smith, 2017). In this book, the continuity of innovation is strongly evident, yet these glimpses can nonetheless be identified and presented as manifestations of innovation. These glimpses are conveyed not only as outputs but also as projects or realizations of the values of different innovations.

This book shows that innovation projects can be examined as distinct entities with clear beginnings, endings, and different kinds of results. These projects can be analyzed in two ways: first, by looking at how employee-driven they are (see Høyrup, 2010), and second, by considering their content and goals (Billett et al., 2023a). According to this book, learning is central to how these projects move forward and become interconnected, whether it occurs at the individual, collective, collaborative, or organizational level. The example from the technology sector (see Chap. 4) illustrates this well. It shows that earlier products, even those that failed commercially, were essential steps toward developing a successful one. In these cases, both individuals and the organization learned from the earlier failures, and this accumulated learning became the foundation for later successful innovations.

Today, the valuation of innovations should more broadly take into account perspectives that extend beyond direct economic or other immediate benefits (see Edwards-Schachter, 2018; Høyrup, 2010). It is worth asking whether an output produced through a communal learning process can be considered an innovation even if it does not generate financial gain, provided that it enhances employees' skills and enables new learning that would not have occurred otherwise. This leads to the broader discussion of how and from what perspectives innovation should be assessed. Innovation research has almost invariably described the outcomes of innovation processes in economic terms, excluding other possible benefits (Høyrup, 2012). The human and social dimensions of innovation have received comparatively little attention, even though EDIs and their related outcomes may equally contribute social, human, or cultural value (Høyrup, 2010).

This study found that the value of innovation can take the form of social benefit, human meaning, or economic advancement. In the context of continuous, learning-based innovation, value creation accumulates over time: an innovation that begins by generating human or social value may, over time, also lead to economic or efficiency-related benefits (see also Lemmetty & Glaveanu, in press). While it is clear that LBI is valuable for organizations, making this value visible is challenging. How do you measure something that only becomes observable after time has passed, when a subjective experience gradually materializes into an objective outcome, as seen in the technology sector? Or how do you measure something that never happened, such as the success of preventative police work, which is demonstrated precisely by the absence of negative events?

6.1.1.3 Innovation as a Sociocultural Learning-Based Phenomenon Demanding Pedagogy

LBI processes are realized in everyday work as part of normal activities, often emerging through collaboration and interaction between actors. This explains why they are closely linked to the constraints, artifacts, interests, processes, work practices, and customers of organizations (Billett et al., 2021; Brandi & Hasse, 2012; Derrick, 2020; Smith, 2017). The findings of this book align with Smith's (2017, p. 4) description of EDI as a socially derived practice of developing new and better ways of doing things through engagement with work. Based on this sociocultural and practice-based definition, innovations are investigated through the interactions between the individual, the environment, and the community and as phenomena embedded in everyday work practices (Billett, 2014; Brandi & Hasse, 2012; Ellström, 2010). Understanding innovation as a sociocultural phenomenon highlights the cultural features of the environment and community that underpin it. Consequently, this book analytically examined both individual actions and the organizational structures and environments that enable, challenge, and guide such actions, while recognizing that organizational structures and practices themselves evolve through individual participation and agency (Giddens, 1984; Lemmetty & Billett, 2023). It is demonstrated that processes and individual actions do not occur in isolation but require both cultural and operational support at the organizational level (Brandi & Hasse, 2012; Holmquist & Johansson, 2019). How innovation is discussed within work communities and how it is supported through organizational culture and practices thus become a crucial pedagogical question.

Workplace pedagogocy (Billett, 2023; Weber, 2016), is examined in this book through the challenges that organizations face in relation to innovation and the solutions that they (could) develop in response. One of this book's contributions is the definition of innovation pedagogy (see Chap. 5). Innovation pedagogy begins by establishing a shared understanding of what innovation means within a particular organization. Once this meaning is collectively understood and agreed upon, it becomes possible to set goals that align with it and to develop pedagogical co-development practices that support and reshape those goals. The findings thus reveal that the foundation of innovation pedagogy lies in understanding what is meant by innovation and, more broadly, the kind of work in which innovation is expected to be practiced, because only after this is it possible to consider how innovation can be practically supported. At the heart of innovation pedagogy lies the balance between guidance and autonomy: sufficient clarity about goals, yet also the freedom to take initiative, contribute to the construction of those goals, and participate in the development of the organization. This balance also requires support from supervisors and colleagues.

6.1.2 *Situating the Findings Within the Organizational Context*

Today, innovation is considered critical for survival in both public and private organizations (Wihlman et al., 2014). Researchers have emphasized the need to study innovation across different organizational contexts to improve the transferability of findings and to develop a more comprehensive understanding of the phenomenon (Derrick, 2020). Extending innovation research to new work contexts and examining it from different perspectives, such as the learning perspective adopted in this study, also open new avenues for understanding innovation, refining its theoretical description, and broadening its definition. Thus, it offers considerable benefits for conceptualizing innovation more comprehensively and, in turn, supporting the practical work that drives it.

6.1.2.1 LBI in Police Organization

The police have long been portrayed as a bureaucratic, hierarchical, and conservative organization (see e.g. Huotari, 2021; Engelmann & Tatnell, 2025). This assumption and perspective have not traditionally encouraged viewing the police as an innovative organization. Over the past 10 years, however, this direction has begun to change. Research (e.g., Filstad & Gottschalk, 2011; Engelmann & Tatnell, 2025; Lemmetty & Collin, 2022) has increasingly portrayed the police as a learning and developing organization, highlighting characteristics that challenge the one-sided image of the police as merely a task-oriented, authoritarian, and conservative institution. For example, Filstad and Gottschalk (2011), have shown that police organization has some features of learning organization, because, in police, collaboration is valued above individual competition, informal communication is more significant than formal communication, and equality and empowerment are seen as more important than authority and hierarchy. According to them, police officers also appear as practical actors for whom safety and honesty are more central values than challenge-seeking or productivity.

This book continues this line of inquiry through four observations: (1) There is open innovation agency in police work at both the individual and team levels, and none of the police officers who participated in the study described their work as merely execution, but rather as work that in some way requires development (see Chap. 2); (2) Police officers possess diverse and specialized competence and they learn alone, together, and with their stakeholders in order to develop and maintain continuous innovation activity (see Chap. 3); (3) Police officers actively initiate and advance social, human, and organizational innovation processes in their everyday work (see Chap. 4), and; (4) They experience freedom and self-direction, as well as encouraging leadership from their immediate supervisors in their learning (see Chap. 5). Thus, the book contributes to portraying the police as an expert organization in which development is strongly embedded in everyday work. At the same time, the study reinforces the understanding that the police organization's strategic development, culture, and institutionalized practices remain partly conservative and hierarchical. Employee-driven practices and the value placed on learning do not appear consistently across the organization, reflecting structural tensions between renewal and traditional ways of working. In addition, police officers' general perception of their organization is that it is not innovative. They describe the organization as 'rigid,' 'slow,' and 'top-down led'. It is also important to note that the participants in this study worked in preventive policing, and they repeatedly emphasized that their work was exceptionally autonomous and innovative compared with other areas of police work. Therefore, broad generalizations about the police organization as a whole cannot be drawn from this study.

A transition toward a learning-oriented and innovative policing culture requires organizational structures that support agency and collective learning capacity (see also Filstad & Gottschalk, 2011). Since police officers learn primarily through practice and interaction with one another (see also Doornbos et al., 2008), the work community plays a key role in supporting innovation and professional development. This is also reflected in the importance of designing work environments that enable innovation and continuous learning; providing structured yet flexible space for development work, fostering a participatory organizational culture (see also Waardenburg et al., 2020), and cultivating an atmosphere that rewards experimentation and collective learning rather than performance-driven displays of competence (see also Hoel & Christensen, 2020). According to this study, strengthening polices' opportunities for influence is essential if the police organization is to develop toward greater innovativeness. This is also important because earlier research shows that influence at work enhances well-being (Annell, 2018), which is a particularly critical concern in policing due to the high demands of the job. At the same time, it is necessary to consider the observation by Janssens et al. (2017) that increased influence can sometimes lead employees to remain within their comfort zone, which in turn may hinder learning. Therefore, participation and influence must be actively supported by the organization.

In this study, also internal communication and collaboration emerged as central elements in police innovation processes. The flow of information within teams, between teams, and in relation to organizational strategy and direction is crucial for innovation and the learning it requires. Earlier studies have similarly shown that strengthening communication, feedback culture, and reflection among members of the police work community supports both general and organizational learning outcomes (Janssens et al., 2017; Schafer, 2009; Smets & Pauwels, 2010). Understanding the organization's strategy and the rationale behind it is also essential for enabling employees to feel genuinely involved in development processes. Research has shown that especially police leadership plays a key role in shaping the organization's future direction (Verfaillie & Vander Beken, 2008) and guiding organizational change (Schafer, 2009). However, effective leadership in policing is often hindered by structural factors (such as the absence of development systems or overly restrictive structures), cultural factors (resistance to change and entrenched police cultures at both macro and local levels), and political factors (Schafer, 2009, 2010). Conservative organizational culture also complicates change efforts (Karp & Stenmark, 2011), even though the autonomy associated with discretionary decision-making appears to support innovation. The responsible use of autonomy requires a sufficient understanding of organizational goals as well as guidance in directing development efforts. In addition to autonomy, police officers need adequate time and space to perform their tasks effectively (Drummond-Smith, 2018).

6.1.2.2 LBI in Technology Organization

Technology organization which participated this study represents small and medium-sized enterprises (SMEs), which are often considered to face greater development challenges than large companies, particularly in terms of learning, adopting new technologies, and updating employee competences. SMEs are often constrained by knowledge gaps, and they also frequently encounter financial limitations when investing in employee training, new tools, or digital technologies (Faiz et al., 2024). For this reason, it is particularly important for SMEs to identify and utilize existing expertise as well as the learning opportunities that emerge in everyday work. This was also evident in the technology company examined in this study. Descriptions of learning as daily, individual, and collective situations, as well as problem-solving and ideation, played a central role in the data, whereas formal (continuing) education was mentioned very little, if at all. The significance of everyday work and the community for innovation through learning was emphasized. This observation aligns with the broader understanding that SMEs' flat organizational structures can lead to more efficient workflows than those in larger firms (Faiz et al., 2024; Short, 2019), and that a small, even family-like community supports everyday learning processes. In addition, SMEs often exhibit lower levels of organizational resistance to change compared to large enterprises, where rigid structures may hinder the adoption of new innovations (Broccardo et al., 2024). This was clearly reflected in the technology organization examined in this study: participation in innovation activities was experienced as motivational and inspiring part of work. Everyday work development appeared also mostly open and accessible to anyone who had the willingness and potential to engage in it.

In technology-sector *expert work*, innovativeness is often supported by the nature of the work itself, which is based on problem-solving, creativity, and continuous learning (Lemmetty, 2020; Scheeres et al., 2010; Collin et al., 2017a, 2017b; Ulrich & Mengiste, 2014). The goal is to develop new, valuable, and usable products and services (Anderson et al., 2014). This likely explains the finding that expert roles, long experience, and broad competence enable some individuals to act as drivers of innovation within the organization, regardless of their formal (managerial) position. Such individuals are able to combine technical, attitudinal, and cultural-historical knowledge in ways that create vision and support the work of others across the organization. This study also supports earlier views (Decius et al., 2021; Saari & Koivunen, 2022) emphasizing that the competence of so-called blue-collar workers is equally essential for organizational learning and innovation, particularly in technology-sector production tasks. Small solutions emerging in production can generate significant individual and organizational benefits as they spread across teams or grow into larger innovation projects (see also Lemmetty & Glaveanu, in press) that enhance the overall efficiency and productivity of the organization.

Low hierarchies and agile practices (Holbeche, 2015), as well as the expectation of self-direction (Lemmetty, 2020), were evident in the target organization. On the one hand, these features appeared to enable participation in innovation activities and the implementation of individuals' creative ideas; on the other hand, they also made it more difficult to guide innovation and establish a clear sense of intentionality. A key question that emerged was how autonomy and thereby innovation can be supported while simultaneously ensuring sufficient direction and strategic development from leadership. In this study, previously identified factors that hinder learning in the technology sector, such as outdated technologies or routine tasks (Vähäsantanen & Eteläpelto, 2018), did not appear as key barriers to innovation activities. Instead, collaboration across different groups (Vähäsantanen & Eteläpelto, 2018), especially in the context of remote work and organizational growth, was feared to decline, potentially weakening collective development efforts.

Thus, remote work and digitalization emerged in the study as potential threats. Participants expressed concerns about the erosion of community and interaction, and about the consequent decline in innovation in the technology sector. Similar observations have been reported in earlier research (Bellis et al., 2022). Therefore, this study highlights the importance of actively strengthening community through clear interaction practices, shared encounters, and collaborative structures to ensure that innovation and knowledge sharing do not weaken in distributed work environments.

6.1.2.3 Practical Conclusions

If we return for a moment to the reflections presented in the introduction (Chap. 1) about what constitutes an innovation and, on the other hand, what makes an organization innovative, we also arrive at the practical relevance of this book and the phenomena it explores. Why does it matter whether employees understand what is meant by innovation? Is it problematic if employees feel that their organization is not innovative?

Based on this study and the arguments presented in this book, I argue that when employees do not know what innovation means, when no shared understanding exists within the organization, one's own work does not appear innovative, and opportunities for innovation arising from everyday tasks go unnoticed. As a result, innovations are not developed, motivation to innovate may be lacking, and the potential for innovation remains unrecognized. This leads to innovation being perceived as distant and unrelated to one's own work. If innovation is nevertheless expected, as it is in almost every field of contemporary working life, viewing innovation as something detached from one's own role can create uncertainty, pressure, and feelings of inadequacy, ultimately diminishing initiative. It becomes problematic if employees start to see the organization as incapable of developing or only changing when absolutely necessary. Such perceptions can erode enthusiasm, hamper efforts toward change and initiative, and push skilled experts, who would have valuable contributions to make, into a mode where they merely perform tasks and begin resisting any change. Consequently, when one's own role and its significance are not understood as part of the wider whole, or when genuine opportunities to participate do not exist, cynicism and frustration may develop. These not only hinder the development of work itself but can also become challenges to overall well-being at work.

The depiction of LBI in this book can help organizational actors identify and understand ongoing learning processes in everyday development and problem-solving work. It invites reflection on the cultural–historical context of the organization and the types of innovation that may emerge relative to these contexts through collaborative learning processes. Furthermore, the findings highlight the importance of both individual competence and team-level diversity in innovation, as well as the mechanisms whereby knowledge and skills are transformed into innovation. To support LBI in practice, organizations should foster employees' agency, willingness, and opportunities to participate in innovation, while creating conditions that enable collective learning processes. Understanding the value of innovation not only in terms of direct economic benefits but also as human, social, and cumulative helps enrich organizational innovation activities and positions them more broadly within everyday work, including the roles of employees beyond product developers and specialists. Similarly, competence should be understood not only as technical skills but also as tacit knowledge embedded in products, practices, and ideas grounded in experience and organizational history. Facilitating continuous LBI requires attention to the pedagogical characteristics of workplaces and the deliberate management of learning processes, which individuals can then autonomously develop further in a safe cultural environment, guided toward desired goals.

6.1.3 Future Research Needs and Ethical Considerations

This book examines the different stages and characteristics of the innovation process from a learning perspective. The collected data include numerous descriptions and examples of the long innovation and development processes in which participants have been involved. Nevertheless, this research has not fully achieved a longitudinal perspective over an extended period, as the monitoring framework of the underlying project covered only the short-term follow-up of a few specific development processes. To understand more fully, potentially across organizational boundaries, the evolutionary nature of innovation and the communal and networked learning processes it entails and to evaluate the value and outputs of different innovation processes, I align with other scholars in emphasizing that studies should focus on the longitudinal innovation processes and acts (Anderson et al., 2014; Haapasaari et al., 2018; Smith, 2017) through which new practices emerge and become routine (Derrick, 2020).

The results of this study show that innovation in both the police and the technology organization does not take place solely within organizational boundaries. In the technology sector, the customer perspective is emphasized, whereas in the police context, also multi-professional collaboration and stakeholder involvement are central. Consequently, innovations often emerge in situations where actors cross organizational boundaries and connect with broader professional networks. In this study, however, the focus was placed on internal organizational actors and their roles in the innovation process. Although the importance of external partners is significant in both contexts, the study did not extend to examining the structures of external networks or the innovations that occur within them. This scope allowed for a focus on employee-driven innovation activity and on how individuals and teams create knowledge, practices, and new solutions within their own organization. In the future, it will nevertheless be important to examine wider networks, communities, and ecosystems in order to develop a more comprehensive understanding of the systemic and collaborative nature of innovation. In particular, understanding open, systemic, and complex innovations requires an approach that considers the diversity of participants' skills, experiences, and backgrounds. Such diversity is a key precondition for responsible innovation, whose social and functional sustainability, and thus its value, rests on the multiplicity of perspectives and the meaningful inclusion of participants in the development process.

In relation especially to responsible and ethically sustainable innovations and innovation processes, research on LBI it should also be examined from more critical perspectives. Innovations are generally treated positively, whereas in reality, they can have destructive or harmful consequences for both individuals and organizations. Similarly, continuous learning can produce unintended outcomes, such as the propagation of misleading practices or negative attitudes toward work, which may impose stress on individuals and the work community and undermine the well-being of both (Lemmetty, 2020). Therefore, innovation and learning should not be approached as inherently good or bad; instead, their nature should be assessed based on specific features and consequences (Kampylis & Valtanen, 2010). Critical research into the impacts of innovation and learning is important for understanding their effects not only on organizational capacity but also on other actors and potentially entire societies (see Kampylis & Valtanen, 2010).

The research behind this book was conducted in the Finnish context, and its results are particularly transferable to other Nordic working environments. In the future, it will be important to extend the examination of LBI more broadly to different countries and work cultures, including comparative analyses of how various forms and dimensions of LBI emerge across diverse settings. Taken together, all these considerations call for future LBI research that is critical, multi-perspectival, sociocultural, and longitudinal in design.

This volume addresses *ethical perspectives* in several ways. In the EDLI project underlying this book, research permission to study police work was obtained from the National Police Board of Finland prior to commencing the study. This approval enabled the researchers to approach individual police departments and recruit participants. Participation was entirely voluntary, and all participants were free to decide whether or not to take part. Participant anonymity was safeguarded throughout both the research process and the reporting of results. Because police research requires particular attention to preventing the disclosure of confidential organizational information (e.g., technical or tactical methods), this manuscript, including the empirical excerpts selected for publication, was reviewed by two senior police representatives who served as project contacts. No changes to the manuscript were required following this review. In the technology organization, the results were presented in a joint briefing and discussed with the contact persons, also from the perspective of reliability.

The *ethical dimensions* of this study can be examined through the principles of qualitative research ethics outlined by Levitt et al. (2017), focusing on four core areas: trustworthiness, methodological integrity, fidelity, and utility. From the perspective of trustworthiness, the central question concerns how convincingly the study captures the phenomenon under investigation (Levitt et al., 2017). To ensure the accurate representation of the focal phenomenon—LBI—the researcher engaged deeply with prior literature on learning and innovation (see Lemmetty & Billett, 2023), creating a comprehensive theoretical grounding for the empirical work. This theoretical foundation informed the design of the data collection and the development of the interview protocol. In the interviews, participants were provided with a preliminary definition of innovation as used in this study (see Chap. 1), ensuring that their accounts and examples referred specifically to innovation-related activities.

Methodological integrity (Levitt et al., 2017) emerges from the interaction of fidelity and utility. Fidelity relates to the accurate and credible representation of the phenomenon, researchers' reflexive awareness of their own interpretive influence, and the adequacy and groundedness of the data. In this book, fidelity is demonstrated by presenting direct empirical excerpts to support observations and findings, enabling readers to assess the validity of the researcher's interpretations. All analytical perspectives are anchored in existing research and theory, which are introduced in the individual chapters of this volume. As the project's researcher and the author of this volume, it is possible that my prior experiences conducting research in these contexts, the police and the technology organization, may have shaped the interpretations, particularly through the formation of preconceptions. However, self-awareness regarding these assumptions and of my own role in the research process has been central throughout the project. This reflexive orientation enabled the continual questioning, reviewing, and reassessing of the interpretations. The strong grounding of the findings in the data, combined with the clarity and richness of the dataset, further strengthens the research's credibility and the justification of its conclusions.

Regarding my own role, it is important to note that before the research began, I already had some prior understanding of both sites: I was familiar with preventive police work through my earlier research projects, and I knew the technology organization through previous collaboration with them. I did not personally know the participants, but I did have some advance knowledge about their work and its conditions. However, I had not previously conducted innovation research in either organization. I was aware of the possible influence that my assumptions and prior knowledge could have on the research process. At the same time, this starting point compelled me—more than usual, in my view, to ensure the accuracy of my interpretations through careful analysis procedures, thoughtful research design, and the writing of this study. I see that my earlier understanding of the contexts turned out to be a strength rather than a limitation, as it allowed me to grasp the basic features and dynamics of the fields and focus more deeply on the aspects relevant to innovation activities. A strong theoretical framework and familiarity with previous research literature were also essential for supporting the conclusions and interpretations.

Regarding utility, the key considerations concern the contextualization of results and the study's contributions, namely, how effectively the findings address the research aims (Levitt et al., 2017). Although the findings are described firmly in relation to their specific contexts, the book also presents broader, transferable insights. The results are linked to wider discussions within working-life and organizational studies. However, as this was based on the qualitative research, the results cannot be reliably generalized to all work contexts; therefore, no definitive conclusions can be drawn about what innovation in working life universally means or should mean and what factors influence, challenge, or guide it in different organizations. Nevertheless, the framework developed here for examining LBI, along with its constituent elements, provides a relevant approach for understanding and investigating innovation as a continuous, human-centered process in contexts beyond policing and the technology sector. The substantial qualitative dataset, combined with the thorough literature review conducted alongside the empirical work, gives rise to an analytical framework and general descriptions that can be applied not only within the studied contexts but also more broadly, even though the specific nuances of the observations are strongly context-dependent. The findings thus contribute to the research's central objective of constructing an account of LBI.

6.2 Closing Remarks

In the introductory chapter of this book (see Chap. 1), two speech bubbles were presented alongside two intriguing questions: *Why is the very concept of innovation challenging for a top expert whose job is to develop innovations in technology sector?* and *Is it true that the police are as un-innovative as the quotation from the police officer might initially suggest?* We are accustomed to thinking about innovations as almost mythical, world-changing forces, great achievements accomplished by a few geniuses, occurring far from everyday work and ordinary people. Early innovation research has also emphasized this view. For this reason, experts in the technology sector, and police officers even more so, do not necessarily perceive their work or their organization as innovative: the prevailing image of innovation creates too radical a comparison point for their everyday work and development efforts.

In the technology sector, understanding what counts as an innovation is difficult precisely because innovation is a continuum—something gradually built over time through small everyday improvements, through individual and collective learning. In such a continuum, one's own role may fade into the background and become invisible both to the individual and to the organization more broadly. As one participant from the technology sector described, the essential thing is to "find meaning in the journey itself." Regarding the second question, whether the police are truly entirely uninnovative, the answer is twofold. Based on the findings of this book, police work is not uninnovative; on the contrary, in preventive policing the work is characterized by continuous development. Police officers are allowed and able to innovate. At the same time, however, strong power hierarchies, difficulties in participation, and ambiguity surrounding work boundaries and goals create barriers to innovative activity. Still, the potential to develop into an innovative organization by fostering a culture that supports employee participation and learning is significant, even though dismantling the rules, legal foundations, clear structures, or even the hierarchies, of police work would not be appropriate given the nature of the work and the organization.

Research into EDI has evolved considerably over the last 10 years and contributed useful concepts for the purpose. Leading researchers on learning and innovation (e.g., Billett et al., 2021; Brandi & Hasse, 2012; Derrick, 2020; Ellström, 2010; Høyrup, 2010, 2012; Smith, 2017) have engaged in critical and constructive debate on how learning should be seen as an integral part of innovation processes. They have also located wide scientific and research gaps in the research on (employee-driven) innovations, especially regarding their versatility and their longitudinal and contextual aspects. I feel privileged to have had the opportunity to contribute to and continue these openings and discussions. This book links to a modern understanding of innovation as a continuous process of change, in which novelty and value take on different forms and meanings over time and across cultural–historical contexts (Kerosuo et al., 2010; Lemmetty & Billett, 2023; Martins & Terblanche, 2003; Rehn & Vachhani, 2006). It creates the story of innovation as a journey, not a single invention or a discrete outcome, but a continuous process through which individuals, projects, and organizations evolve by learning.

> All the events and actions along the journey are meaningful. They are what shape the path, leaving behind something every time: learning. (TP 4, Technology)

As Schumpeter (1934) already has noted, innovation does not always entail something entirely new; it may just as well consist of a novel combination or application of existing knowledge, an improvement on what already exists, or a fresh perspective on the familiar. In this sense, the present volume can itself be regarded as a form of innovation. While it is not wholly unique in its starting points, perspectives, or findings, it brings together learning-based approaches on innovation in a distinctive way. First, it integrates perspectives on agency and roles, learning and competence, as well as projects, values, and pedagogy. Second, it draws on two markedly different empirical contexts and grounds its analyses in rich, contextually embedded data. The volume emphasizes the continuity of innovation as a phenomenon that is fundamentally constructed through learning, and it offers a framework for examining this process through the lenses of actors, diverse projects, outputs, values, challenges, and forms of support.

During the week I was finalizing this book, I asked my 10-year-old son about his thoughts on learning. I asked him whether he thought adults learn as well. He replied as follows:

> "Umm… I think learning never really stops in life. Well, maybe it could, if you did all the work in the world. But even then, there wouldn't be enough time in your whole life. You'd need a thousand million motherboards in your head to fit it all."

As my son said, we can never reach a final endpoint in learning. Likewise, we can never reach a final endpoint in innovation, as it transcends the boundaries of individual actors, projects, and outputs, creating value whose meanings are experienced and interpreted differently by different people with different backgrounds, at different times and contexts, and for different purposes. Thus, it is something that happens in the present, grounded in the past but oriented toward the future.

References

Anderson, N., Potočnik, K., & Zhou, J. (2014). Innovation and creativity in organizations: A state-of-the-science review, prospective commentary, and guiding framework. *Journal of Management, 40*(5), 1297–1333. https://doi.org/10.1177/0149206314527128

Annell, S., Lindfors, P., Kecklund, G., & Sverke, M. (2018). Sustainable recruitment: Individual characteristics and psychosocial working conditions among Swedish police officers. *Nordic Journal of Working Life Studies, 8*(4), 3–24.

Bellis, P., Trabucchi, D., & Buganza, T. (2022). How do human relationships change in the digital environment after COVID-19 pandemic? The road towards agility. *European Journal of Innovation, 25*(6), 821–849. https://doi.org/10.1108/EJIM-02-2022-0093

Billett, S. (2014). Mimesis: Learning through everyday activities and interactions at work. *Human Resource Development Review, 3*(4), 462–482. https://doi.org/10.1177/1534484314548275

Billett, S. (2023). Utilising pedagogically rich activities to meet emerging workplace challenges. In H. Bound, A. Edwards, K. Evans, & A. Chia (Eds.), *Workplace learning for changing circumstances* (pp. 93–107). Routledge. https://doi.org/10.4324/9781003227946-19

Billett, S., Tan, J., Chan, C., Chong, W. H., & Keat, J. S. C. (2023a). Employee-driven innovations: Zones of initiation, enactment and learning. In W. O. Lee, P. Brown, A. L. Goodwin, & A. Green (Eds.), *International handbook on education development in Asia-Pacific*. Springer. https://doi.org/10.1007/978-981-16-2327-1_67-1

Billett, S., Yang, S., Chia, A., Tai, J. F., Lee, M., & Alhadad, S. (2021). Remaking and transforming cultural practices: Exploring the co-occurrence of work, learning, innovation. In S. Lemmetty, K. Collin, V. P. Glăveanu, & P. Forsman (Eds.), *Creativity and learning: Context, processes and support* (pp. 219–244). Palgrave Macmillan.

Brandi, U., & Hasse, C. (2012). Employee-driven innovation and practice-based learning in organizational cultures. In S. Høyrup, M. Bonnafous-Boucher, C. Hasse, M. Lotz, & K. Møller (Eds.), *Employee-driven innovation: A new approach* (pp. 127–148). Palgrave Macmillan.

Brown, J.S., & Duguid, P. (1991). Organisational learning and communities of practice: Toward a unified view of working, learning and innovation. *Organisation Science 2*(1), 40–57.

Broccardo, L., Tenucci, A., Agarwal, R., & Alshibani, S. M. (2024). Steering digitalization and management control maturity in small and medium enterprises (SMEs). *Technological Forecasting and Social Change, 204*, 123446. https://doi.org/10.1016/j.techfore.2024.123446

Collin, K., Herranen, S., & Riivari, E. (2017a). What kinds of aspects frame professional agency and creativity in information technology work? *Business Creativity & the Creative Economy, 3*(1), 88–98. https://doi.org/10.18536/bcce.2017.10.3.1.08

Collin, K., Lemmetty, S., Herranen, S., Paloniemi, S., Auvinen, T., & Riivari, E. (2017b). Professional agency and creativity in information technology work. In M. Goller & S. Paloniemi (Eds.), *Agency at work: Professional and practice-based learning* (pp. 263–282). Springer. https://doi.org/10.1007/978-3-319-60943-0_13

Decius, J., Knappstein, M., Schaper, N., & Seifert, A. (2021). Investigating the multidimensionality of informal learning: Validation of a short measure for white-collar workers. *Human Resource Development Quarterly, 34*(1), 45–74. https://doi.org/10.1002/hrdq.21461

Derrick, J. (2020). "Tacit pedagogy" and "entanglement": Practice-based learning and innovation. *Journal of Workplace Learning, 32*(4), 273–284. https://doi.org/10.1108/JWL-07-2019-0094

Doornbos, A. J., Simons, R., & Denessen, E. (2008). Relations between characteristics of workplace practices and types of informal work-related learning: A survey study among Dutch police. *Human Resource Development Quarterly, 19*(2), 129–151. https://doi.org/10.1002/hrdq.1231

Drummond-Smith, I. (2018). "Yes, sir": Leadership and blind obedience in hierarchical organisations. *International Journal of Emergency Services, 7*(1), 24–31. https://doi.org/10.1108/IJES-04-2017-0016

Edwards-Schachter, M. (2018). The nature and variety of innovation. *International Journal of Innovation Studies, 2*(2), 1–15. https://doi.org/10.1016/j.ijis.2018.08.004

Ellström, P.-E. (2010). Practice-based innovation: A learning perspective. *Journal of Workplace Learning, 22*(1/2), 27–40. https://doi.org/10.1108/13665621011012834

Engelmann, L., & Tatnell, A. A. T. (2025). Blending the 'craft' and 'science' of policing: Challenges and opportunities for police as professional learning organizations. *Policing: A Journal of Policy and Practice, 19*. https://doi.org/10.1093/police/paaf036

Eteläpelto, A., Vähäsantanen, K., Hökkä, P., & Paloniemi, S. (2013). What is agency? Conceptualizing professional agency at work. *Educational Research Review, 10*, 45–65. https://doi.org/10.1016/j.edurev.2013.05.001

Faiz, F., Le, V., & Masli, E. K. (2024). Determinants of digital technology adoption in innovative SMEs. *Journal of Innovation & Knowledge.*

Fenwick, T. (2003). Innovation: Examining workplace learning in new enterprises. *Journal of Workplace Learning, 15*(3), 123–132. https://doi.org/10.1108/13665620310468469

Filstad, C., & Gottschalk, P. (2011). Becoming a learning organization: The espoused values of police managers from two Norwegian districts. *The Learning Organization, 18*, 486–500. https://doi.org/10.1108/09696471111171321

Giddens, A. (1984). *The constitution of society: Outline of the theory of structuration.* University of California Press.

Glăveanu, V. P. (2015). Creativity as a sociocultural act. *Journal of Creative Behavior, 49*(3), 165–180. https://doi.org/10.1002/jocb.94

Haapasaari, A., Engestrom, Y., & Kerosuo, H. (2018). From initiatives to employee-driven innovations. *European Journal of Innovation Management, 21*(2), 206–226. https://doi.org/10.1108/EJIM-09-2016-0085

Hasu, M., Honkaniemi, L., Saari, E., Mattelmäki, T., & Koponen, L. (2014). Learning employee-driven innovating: Towards sustained practice through multi-method evaluation. *Journal of Workplace Learning, 26*(5), 310–330. https://doi.org/10.1108/JWL-10-2013-0079

Hoel, L., & Christensen, E. (2020). In-field training in the police: Learning in an ethical grey area? *Journal of Workplace Learning, 32*(8), 569–581. https://doi.org/10.1108/JWL-04-2020-0060

Holbeche, L. (2015). *The agile organization: How to build an innovative, sustainable and resilient business*. Kogan Page.

Holmquist, M., & Johansson, A. (2019). Employee-driven innovation: An intervention using action research. *Technology Innovation Management Review, 9*(5), 44–53.

Høyrup, S. (2010). Employee-driven innovation and workplace learning: Basic concepts, approaches and themes. *Transfer: European Review of Labour and Research, 16*(2), 143–154. https://doi.org/10.1177/1024258910364102

Høyrup, S. (2012). Employee-driven innovation: A new phenomenon, concept and mode of innovation. In S. Høyrup, M. Bonnafous-Boucher, C. Hasse, M. Lotz, & K. Møller (Eds.), *Employee-driven innovation* (pp. 3–33). Palgrave Macmillan.

Huotari, T. (2021). *Innovaatio ja innovatiivisuus poliisitoimessa: esseitä historiasta, teoriasta ja filosofiasta* [Innovations and innovativeness in the police and policing: Essays on history, theory, and philosophy]. Police University College.

Janssens, L., Smet, K., Onghena, P., & Kyndt, E. (2017). The relationship between learning conditions in the workplace and informal learning outcomes: A study among police inspectors. *International Journal of Training and Development, 21*(2), 92–112. https://doi.org/10.1111/ijtd.12095

Karp, S., & Stenmark, H. (2011). Learning to be a police officer: Tradition and change in the training and professional lives of police officers. *Police Practice & Research, 12*(1), 4–15. https://doi.org/10.1080/15614263.2010.497653

Kampylis, P.G. & Valtanen, J. (2010). Redefining creativity–analyzing definitions, collocations and consequences. *Journal of Creative Behaviour, 44*(3), 191–214.

Kerosuo, H., Kajamaa, A., & Engeström, Y. (2010). Promoting innovation and learning through change laboratory: An example from Finnish health care. *Central European Journal of Public Policy, 4*(1), 110–131. Retrieved from https://doaj.org/article/9ea8e1c1aee64b6dbe573ec4a6bee528

Lemmetty, S. (2020). *"Self-learning is present every day—In fact, it's my job": Self-directed workplace learning in technology-based work*. Doctoral dissertation. University of Jyväskylä.

Lemmetty, S. (2025). "Failure is future success": Expanding knowledge through learning practices in a continuous innovation process. *Innovation*. https://doi.org/10.1080/14479338.2025.2573102.

Lemmetty, S., & Billett, S. (2023). Employee-driven learning and innovation (EDLI) as a phenomenon of continuous learning at work. *Journal of Workplace Learning, 35*(9), 162–176. https://doi.org/10.1108/JWL-12-2022-0175

Lemmetty, S., & Collin, K. (2022). Co-occurrence of sociocultural elements and self-direction in learning situations: A police organization case study. *Adult Learning, 34*(4), 220–229. https://doi.org/10.1177/10451595221094072

Lemmetty, S., & Glaveanu, V. (In Press). From possibility thinking to employee-driven organizational innovation. Accepted for publication in S. Lemmetty, I. Bäckström & M. Pajuoja (Eds.), *Employee-driven innovation in public and private organizations: How people shape change at work*. Palgrave Macmillan.

Levitt, H. M., Motulsky, S. L., Wertz, F. J., Morrow, S. L., & Ponterotto, J. G. (2017). Recommendations for designing and reviewing qualitative research in psychology: Promoting methodological integrity. *Qualitative Psychology, 4*(1), 2–22. https://doi.org/10.1037/qup0000082

Martins, E. C., & Terblanche, F. (2003). Building organisational culture that stimulates creativity and innovation. *European Journal of Innovation Management, 6*(1), 64–74. https://doi.org/10.1108/14601060310456337

Meissner, D., & Kotsemir, M. (2016). Conceptualizing the innovation process towards the "active innovation paradigm": Trends and outlook. *Journal of Innovation Entrepreneurship, 5*(14). https://doi.org/10.1186/s13731-016-0042-z

Mulder, M. (2014). Conceptions of professional competence. In I. S. Billett, C. Harteis, & H. Gruber (Eds.), *International handbook of research in professional and practice-based learning* (pp. 107–137). Springer. https://doi.org/10.1007/978-94-017-8902-8_5

Rehn, A., & Vachhani, S. (2006). Innovation and the post-original: On moral stances and reproduction. *Creativity and Innovation Management, 15*(3), 310–322. https://doi.org/10.1111/j.1467-8691.2006.00390

Saari, T., & Koivunen, T. (2022). Tacit knowledge in blue-collar work: How workers use it to fulfil their side of the psychological contract. *International Journal of Organizational Analysis, 30*(7), 173–183. https://doi.org/10.1108/IJOA-09-2021-2972

Schafer, J. A. (2009). Developing effective leadership in policing: Perils, pitfalls, and paths forward. *Policing: An International Journal of Police Strategies & Management, 32*(2), 238–260. https://doi.org/10.1108/13639510910958163

Schafer, J. A. (2010). Effective leaders and leadership in policing: Traits, assessment, development, and expansion. *Policing: An International Journal of Police Strategies & Management, 33*(4), 644–663. https://doi.org/10.1108/13639511011085060

Scheeres, H., Solomon, N., Boud, D., & Rooney, D. (2010). When is it OK to learn at work? The learning work of organizational practices. *Journal of Workplace Learning, 22*(1/2), 13–26. https://doi.org/10.1108/13665621011012825

Schumpeter, J. A. (1934). *The theory of economic development*. Harvard University Press.

Selander & Alasoini should be 2023: Selander, K., & Alasoini, T. (2023). Digitaalinen kehittyneisyys, verkostot ja henkilöstön osallistuminen yritysten innovaatioaktiivisuuden avaintekijöinä [Digital maturity, networks, and employee participation as key factors in firms' innovation activity]. Työterveyslaitos.

Short, H. (2019). Learning in SMEs. *Human Resource Development International, 22*(5), 413–419. https://doi.org/10.1080/13678868.2019.1658368

Smets, L. & Pauwels, C. (2010). The feasibility and practicability of police training In vestigative interviewers' perceptions towards coaching. *Policing: An International Journal of Police Strategies & Management, 33*(4), s. 664–680. https://doi.org/10.1108/13639511011085079

Smith, R. (2017). Work(er)-driven innovation. *Journal of Workplace Learning, 29*(2), 110–123.

Sossa, J., Rebolledob, J., Manuel, J., Hincapiéc, M., & Zartad, R. (2019). Innovation management models: A literature review. *International Journal of Innovation, Creativity, and Change, 10*(6), 175–194.

Sung, S. Y., & Choi, J. N. (2014). Do organizations spend wisely on employees? Effects of training and development investments on learning and innovation in organizations. *Journal of Organizational Behavior, 35*, 393–412. https://doi.org/10.1002/job.1897

Ulrich, F., & Mengiste, S. A. (2014). The challenges of creativity in software organizations. In B. Bergvall-Kåreborn & P. A. Nielsen (Eds.), *Creating value for all through ITB* (pp. 16–34). Springer.

Vähäsantanen, K., & Eteläpelto, A. (2018). Professional agency and learning in the work of software professionals. In C. Harteis (Ed.), *Machines – change – work: An educational view on the digitalization of work* (pp. 161–179). Springer.

Verfaillie, K., & Vander Beken, T. (2008). Proactive policing and the assessment of organised crime. *Policing: An International Journal, 31*(4), 534–552. https://doi.org/10.1108/13639510810910564

Waardenburg, M., Groenleer, M., de Jong, J., & Keijser, B. (2020). Paradoxes of collaborative governance: Investigating the real-life dynamics of multi-agency collaborations using a quasi-experimental action-research approach. *Public Management Review, 22*(3), 386–407. https://doi.org/10.1080/14719037.2019.1599056

Weber, P. C. (2016). Pedagogy and organizational learning. In A. Schröer, M. Göhlich, S. Weber, & H. Pätzold (Eds.), *Organisation und Theorie* (pp. 235–245). Springer. https://doi.org/10.1007/978-3-658-10086-5_22

Wihlman, T., Hoppe, M., Sandström, U., & Sandmark, H. (2014). Employee-driven innovation in welfare services. *Nordic Journal of Working Life Studies, 4*(2), 159–180. https://doi.org/10.19154/njwls.v4i2.3869

GPSR Compliance

The European Union's (EU) General Product Safety Regulation (GPSR) is a set of rules that requires consumer products to be safe and our obligations to ensure this.

If you have any concerns about our products, you can contact us on ProductSafety@springernature.com

In case Publisher is established outside the EU, the EU authorized representative is:

Springer Nature Customer Service Center GmbH
Europaplatz 3
69115 Heidelberg, Germany

Batch number: 10321585

Printed by Printforce, the Netherlands